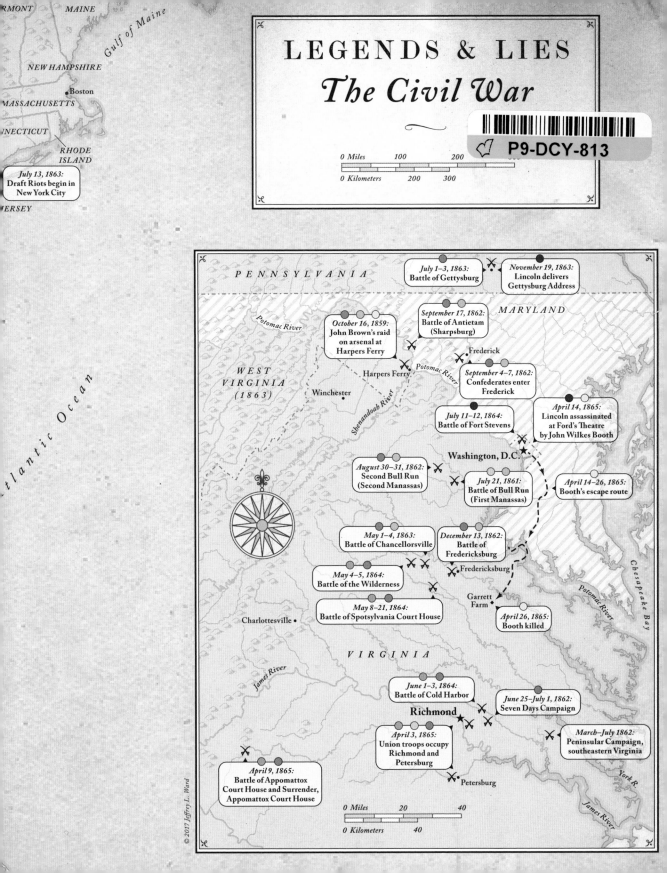

# LEGENDS & LIES
## *The Civil War*

0 Miles 100 200

0 Kilometers 200 300

**P9-DCY-813**

*July 13, 1863:*
Draft Riots begin in
New York City

PENNSYLVANIA

*July 1–3, 1863:*
Battle of Gettysburg

*November 19, 1863:*
Lincoln delivers
Gettysburg Address

MARYLAND

Potomac River

*October 16, 1859:*
John Brown's raid
on arsenal at
Harpers Ferry

*September 17, 1862:*
Battle of Antietam
(Sharpsburg)

Frederick

WEST
VIRGINIA
(1863)

Harpers Ferry

*September 4–7, 1862:*
Confederates enter
Frederick

Winchester

Potomac River

Shenandoah River

*July 11–12, 1864:*
Battle of Fort Stevens

*April 14, 1865:*
Lincoln assassinated
at Ford's Theatre
by John Wilkes Booth

Atlantic Ocean

Washington, D.C.

*August 30–31, 1862:*
Second Bull Run
(Second Manassas)

*July 21, 1861:*
Battle of Bull Run
(First Manassas)

*April 14–26, 1865:*
Booth's escape route

*May 1–4, 1863:*
Battle of Chancellorsville

*December 13, 1862:*
Battle of
Fredericksburg

Chesapeake Bay

*May 4–5, 1864:*
Battle of the Wilderness

Fredericksburg

Potomac River

*May 8–21, 1864:*
Battle of Spotsylvania Court House

Garrett
Farm

*April 26, 1865:*
Booth killed

Charlottesville

VIRGINIA

James River

*June 1–3, 1864:*
Battle of Cold Harbor

*June 25–July 1, 1862:*
Seven Days Campaign

Richmond

*March–July 1862:*
Peninsular Campaign,
southeastern Virginia

*April 3, 1865:*
Union troops occupy
Richmond and
Petersburg

York R.

*April 9, 1865:*
Battle of Appomattox
Court House and Surrender,
Appomattox Court House

Petersburg

James River

© 2017 Jeffrey L. Ward

0 Miles 20 40

0 Kilometers 40

# BILL O'REILLY'S

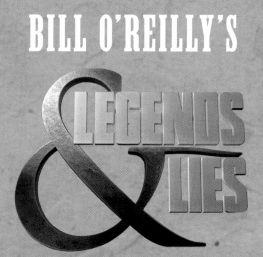

# BILL O'REILLY'S

# LEGENDS & LIES

# The CIVIL WAR

WRITTEN BY DAVID FISHER

Henry Holt and Company
New York

Henry Holt and Company
*Publishers since 1866*
175 Fifth Avenue
New York, New York 10010
www.henryholt.com

Henry Holt® and ® are registered trademarks of Macmillan Publishing Group, LLC.

Distributed in Canada by Raincoast Book Distribution Limited

Library of Congress Cataloging-in-Publication Data is available upon request.

ISBN: 978-1-250-10984-2

Our books may be purchased in bulk for promotional, educational, or business use. Please
contact your local bookseller or the Macmillan Corporate and Premium Sales Department at
(800) 221-7945, extension 5442, or by e-mail at MacmillanSpecialMarkets@macmillan.com.

First Edition 2017

*Designed by Nancy Singer*
*Endpaper map by Jeffrey L. Ward*
*Photo research by Liz Seramur of Selected Shots Photo Research, Inc.*
*with assistance from Nancy Singer*

Printed in the United States of America

10 9 8 7 6 5 4 3 2 1

# CONTENTS

# INTRODUCTION

If you are a history buff like me, you like to learn new things. The Civil War has been written about so many times, it's hard to even contemplate what has not been said. Yet legends and lies persist about the War between the States. Myths were created, and today some remain intact, even though the truth is out there.

This big book lays it all out. What really happened, and what is fiction. That's the beauty of the *Legends and Lies* concept.

David Fisher, who composed the words you will soon read, is a master at painting a vivid historical picture. And then, of course, there are the real pictures—spread throughout the book. We want you not only to understand the history, but to experience it visually. Take a good look at John Brown's face in chapter 1. Study his stern countenance. This was a man who was possessed to end slavery, who would stop at nothing. Brown's story is unique and compelling, a fascinating way to begin this book.

As you may know, the Civil War was perhaps the most important conflict in our nation's history, because we would not have a country as we know it today if the South had prevailed. And the Confederate forces almost did win—led by the brilliant commander Robert E. Lee. You will soon get to know Lee and his Union counterpart, Ulysses S. Grant. Very different men fighting for causes that, at times, weighed on them with extraordinary ferocity.

The brutal intensity of the fighting is staggering. Most of the combatants were boys or men just out of their teens. If wounded, they could expect little help. If captured—well, the ordeal was hellish. The South, in particular, could barely feed its own army, much less Northern prisoners. But amid all the chaos, heroes emerged. On both sides. We will tell you about them. The villains, too.

And then there were the slaves, human beings bought and sold. Even though some believe the Civil War was primarily about the rights of individual states to determine their societies, the true emotional nature of this war was freedom for black people. Again, study the face of Frederick Douglass on page 112. This was an African-American who attained freedom but could not rest until his brethren did the same. What a compelling human being, Frederick Douglass. You will get to know him well in these pages.

You will also learn about the bravery of Abraham Lincoln, who aged dramatically during the war. His empathy for the suffering soldiers and slaves is what sets him apart from most politicians. Lincoln is a towering figure, perhaps our best president. You will see how he himself suffered over the years knowing that victory was not assured.

In fact, we spend a good amount of time on the battle that saved Lincoln and the Union: Gettysburg. That incredible fight remains the most important battle ever fought on American soil. And to the very end, the outcome was in doubt. The reader of this book will experience that battle as it was actually fought—not romanticized or sanitized. We will take you to southern Pennsylvania for a reading experience you will not soon forget.

The relevance today of *Legends and Lies* will unfold before your eyes. We are living in a time of conflict; terrorists overseas want to kill us, politics at home can be vicious. We are a divided nation, as the presidential election of 2016 demonstrated. Sometimes, emotions between citizens run high, and there have even been violent political protests. And when we see these on television, it might be wise to think back to the 1860s—when the country fractured and Americans killed one another, sometimes in savage displays.

That kind of thing will never happen again, but for the aware American, it is important to understand why it did happen once upon a time. The War between the States shaped attitudes for decades, and, to this day there are reverberations from the carnage. The Black Lives Matter movement, for example, bases its call for social justice on slavery and the massive abuse it caused. As for freemen, millions of Americans on both sides had their families shattered by death during the bloodiest war in American history.

So, there is much to know about the Civil War, and you are about to absorb many things. No longer will the conflict be a fable or a movie. Reading *Legends and Lies* will provide you with the factual picture of an American tragedy that led to triumphs decades later. The true nature of freedom was defined during the Civil War, and all of us carry that freedom today as we live life in America.

David Fisher and I are proud of this book and very glad you have chosen to read it.

Bill O'Reilly
FEBRUARY 2017
NEW YORK CITY

**February 8**
creation of the Confederate
States of America

**February 18**
Jefferson Davis is
appointed president of
Confederate States

**February 6**
U. S. Grant
captures
Fort Henry

The *Dred Scott* Decision

**1857**

**March 4**
Lincoln is inaugurated

**February 16**
Grant captures Fort
Donelson

**1862**
**September 4–7**
Confederates
enter Frederick,
Maryland; Barbara
Fritchie legend
begins

**April 12**
War begins with
the shelling
of Fort Sumter

John Brown's raid
on Harpers Ferry
results in him
being hanged

**February 22**
Jefferson Davis is
inaugurated as
president of
Confederate States

**1859**

**May 24**
Union troops cross
the Potomac;
Colonel Elmer Ellsworth
is killed in Alexandria

**April 6–7**
Battle of Shiloh

**September 7**
Lee crosses
the Potomac
and threatens
Washington

Frederick Douglass
escapes to
Massachusetts

**1838**

**1862**

**1861**

**1858**
Lincoln-Douglas
Debates

**1861**
**May 25**
Lincoln suspends
habeas corpus

**1862**
**September 17**
Battle of
Antietam

**1846**
The Mexican-American
War

**1860**
**November 6**
Abraham
Lincoln
elected

**July 21**
First
Bull Run/Manassas
begins;
"Stonewall"
Jackson
nicknamed

**1862**
**June 25–July 1**
Seven Days'
Campaign

**December 13**
Battle of
Fredericksburg

**December 20**
South Carolina
becomes the first
state to secede

**August 28–30**
Second Bull Run/
Second Manassas

**September
12–15**
Robert E. Lee
directs first offensive, is beaten
at Cheat Mountain, Virginia

**January 31**

Congress passes the 13th Amendment, freeing the slaves

**February 17**

Submarine *Hunley* sinks the *Housatonic*

**1863**
**July 1–3**

Battle of Gettysburg

**January 1**

Lincoln signs the Emancipation Proclamation

**February 1**

Sherman leaves Savannah to march through the Carolinas

**1865**
**April 9**

Battle of Appomattox and surrender at Appomattox Court House

**March 8**

Mosby's Rangers kidnap General Stoughton

**July 4**

Vicksburg surrenders

**February 28–March 3**

Kilpatrick's unsuccessful raid on Richmond and plot to assassinate Davis

**1864**
**July 11–12**

Battle of Fort Stevens (attack on Washington, DC)

**July 13**

Draft riots in New York

**May 4–5**

Battle of the Wilderness

**March 4**

Lincoln inaugurated for his second term

**April 14**

Lincoln is assassinated at Ford's Theatre by John Wilkes Booth

**1863**

**September 1**

Sherman takes Atlanta

**1865**

**July 18**

Attack on Fort Wagner by 54th Massachusetts; Shaw is killed

**1864**

**November 8**

Lincoln reelected

**1864**
**November 16**

Sherman begins his march to the sea

**1865**
**May 10**

Jefferson Davis is arrested

**1863**
**September 19–20**

Battle of Chickamauga

**1863**

**April 2**

Bread riots in Richmond

**1864**
**May 7**

Sherman begins his march through the South

**December 10**

Sherman occupies Savannah

**May 26**

Last Confederate soldiers agree to surrender

**April 30–May 6**

Battle of Chancellorsville; Jackson is shot and dies of pneumonia on May 10

**November 19**

Lincoln delivers the Gettysburg Address

**1865**
**April 1**

Battle of Five Forks

**May 8–21**

Battle of Spotsylvania Court House, Virginia

**November 23–25**

Battle of Chattanooga

**April 3–4**

Union troops take Petersburg and Richmond

**May 18**

Siege of Vicksburg begins

**June 1–3**

Battle of Cold Harbor

# ONE

# A GRAVE BEGINNING

## John Brown Stirs America's Passions

On Sunday, October 16, 1859, John Brown and his band of twenty-one men came out of the dark night to change American history. "The terror of all Missouri," as the *New York Times* had called the fifty-nine-year-old abolitionist, was known nationally as a leader of the antislavery movement—and a zealot who had murdered at least five pro-slavery men in cold blood. His stated purpose that night was to seize the federal armory and its thousands of weapons in the quiet town of Harpers Ferry, Virginia, expecting it to be the spark that ignited a rebellion of slaves in the region. In fact, he would start a war that would inflame the entire nation.

While history records that the Civil War began early in the morning of April 12, 1861, when Confederate troops began shelling Union-occupied Fort Sumter in Charleston, South Carolina's, harbor, many historians believe war became inevitable the night of John Brown's raid. Today Brown is remembered mostly for the verse "John Brown's body lies a-moldering in the grave . . . his soul is marching on," but his daring

When abolitionist John Brown was hanged for his attempt to ignite a slave rebellion, Ralph Waldo Emerson wrote that his execution would make "the gallows as glorious as the cross."

raid at Harpers Ferry put the nation on the path that would lead to the bloodiest war in American history.

Decades earlier the founding fathers had successfully managed to weave together the thirteen colonies into a nation without resolving the momentous debate over slavery. Since an English ship, the *White Lion*, sailing under a Dutch flag in 1619, had traded the first twenty enslaved Africans to the Jamestown colonists in exchange for food and supplies, Americans had wrestled with the moral and economic implications of treating human beings as property. The agrarian South, with its tobacco economy, relied on slave labor far more than the industrialized North. In 1780, Pennsylvania became the first state to begin banning slavery, passing a law that moved exceedingly slowly toward emancipation. After long and bitter debates that threatened to tear apart the newly won country, the delegates attending the 1787 Constitutional Convention passed the Three-Fifths Compromise, which counted slaves as three-fifths of a person when determining a state's representation in Congress but gave those slaves no rights. Slaves were property to be bought, sold, and worked until they died—and all of their children were born into slavery.

With schoolteacher Eli Whitney's 1793 invention of the cotton gin, the so-called engine that could rapidly clean seeds from raw cotton, cotton replaced tobacco as the South's most profitable crop—and required even more slaves to pick it. America's 1790 census recorded almost seven hundred thousand slaves, a number that increased by more than half a million in the next two decades. By 1850 it was estimated there were more than three million slaves in the United States, and one in four Southerners owned slaves.

While New England's textile industry had once depended on slave labor, the Northern states had mostly abolished slavery by 1804—although in some cases the statutes remained legally in force. In 1808 Congress outlawed the importation of slaves from Africa, but the domestic slave trade, the exchange of existing slaves and their families, continued to flourish in the South.

The Missouri Compromise, passed in 1820, arranged a tenuous peace between pro- and antislavery interests, by dividing the twenty-two states equally into slave and free states. But while Northern politicians continued to speak out publicly and mostly ineffectually against slavery, others began taking covert action. The abolitionist movement created the Underground Railroad, a vast network of way stations consisting of hiding places in caves and in cellars, beneath church floors and in barn lofts, through which "conductors" guided escaping slaves trying desperately to make their way north to freedom. Among these conductors and stationmasters were legendary figures such as Harriet Tubman, an escaped slave who risked

In 2020 Harriet Tubman, an escaped slave who led hundreds of others to freedom on the Underground Railroad, will become the first woman since Martha Washington to appear on American currency when she replaces slaveholder Andrew Jackson on the $20 bill.

her life leading hundreds of others to freedom, as well as common folk such as the parents of teenager James Butler "Wild Bill" Hickok, whose small farm in Homer, Illinois, served as a way station. The penalties for working on this railroad were severe; the Fugitive Slave Act of 1850 made it a federal crime to assist escaping slaves and included large fines and possible imprisonment for offenders.

England peacefully abolished slavery throughout its empire in 1833, but this "peculiar institution," as Southerners referred to it, remained the foundation of the Southern agricultural economy. The issue threatened to rip the country apart; Ralph Waldo Emerson spoke for most Northerners when he said, "I think we must get rid of slavery, or we must get rid of freedom."

In 1851, a Connecticut woman named Harriet Beecher Stowe began writing a serial for the antislavery magazine the *National Era*, in which she "painted a word picture of slavery" based loosely on actual stories. A year later her more-than-forty-installment series was published as the two-volume book *Uncle Tom's Cabin; or, Life Among the Lowly*. Its portrayal of the brutal realities of American slavery shocked the world. The book became a best seller in the United States, Europe, and Asia, eventually being translated into sixty languages; stage plays based on the story—Tom shows—were immensely popular. By the end of the century *Uncle Tom's Cabin* had sold more copies than any book other than the Bible, and it is credited with forcing many Americans to face the true horrors of the slave trade. "I wrote what I did," she explained, ". . . because as a Christian I felt the dishonor to Christianity—because as a lover of my country, I trembled at the coming day of wrath."

Public consciousness had been raised, but still the nation was divided. When Congress passed the Kansas-Nebraska Act in 1854, which allowed residents of those territories to vote to decide whether they would enter the Union as slave states or free states, real fighting finally broke out. The bill, sponsored by Illinois senator Stephen Douglas, was an attempt at compromise. Instead, it further split Congress between the antislavery North and pro-slavery South, and caused the demise of the once-powerful Whig Party, which in turn led to the formation of the new and strongly antislavery Republican Party. And it ignited the long-lasting guerrilla war that journalist Horace Greeley named, sadly, Bleeding Kansas.

Pro-slavery gunslingers, known as Border Ruffians or bushwhackers, raced into the Kansas territory from Missouri, where they were met by the equally violent abolitionist Jayhawkers. What has on occasion been called the first battle of the Civil War took place on May 21, 1856, when as many as eight hundred men rode into the newly formed antislavery town of Lawrence, Kansas, terrified the residents, and destroyed several buildings—although the only fatality was the result of an accident, when a building collapsed.

For half a century politicians had been able to find ways to compromise about slavery, but they were running out of solutions. In May 1856, angry words became violent deeds in Congress when pro-slavery congressman Preston Brooks from South Carolina viciously attacked Massachusetts abolitionist senator Charles Sumner, smashing him on his head and shoulders with his cane, stopping only when the cane broke into pieces. It took Sumner three years to recover from his injuries—while Brooks became a hero in the South and received new canes from his admirers.

Abolitionists found their own hero three days later in Osawatomie, Kansas. John Brown was the Bible-quoting father of twenty children who had moved to Kansas to fight to end slavery. The son of strict Calvinists, he grew up among mostly Native American families in

This 1860 lithograph portrays five significant events in the violent life of John Brown. The figure in the bottom center appears to be the spirit of America in mourning. ☞

# OLD JOHN BROWN'S CAREER
## ILLUSTRATED.

THE TRAITORS DOOM

RECEIVING MONEY AND SHARPS RIFLES TO GO AND DO HIS KANSAS WORK

DOING HIS KANSAS WORK MURDERING DOYLE AND HIS TWO SON'S.

STILL DOING HIS KANSAS WORK DRAGGING WILSON FROM THE SICK BED OF HIS WIFE.

COMMENCING HIS VIRGINIA WORK. ATTEMTING TO GATHER RECRUITS.

Presented to the yearly subscribers of the
Philadelphia Weekly (All over the Land)
by E. S. Dean Publisher & Proprietor 337 Chesnut St Philadelphia — Pa.

western Ohio. When he was twelve years old, he watched helplessly as a young slave boy was beaten and forced to sleep in the cold wearing only rags, an experience that he later wrote transformed him into "a most determined Abolitionist." He helped escaping slaves flee north to Canada, promoted black education, and insisted that his two black employees sit by him in his Congregational church—for which he was expelled. At an antislavery meeting when he was thirty-seven years old he stated, "Here, before God, in the presence of these witnesses, from this time, I consecrate my life to the destruction of slavery!"

He later befriended Frederick Douglass, the best-known black man in America, who himself had escaped from slavery in Maryland to become a legendary defender of human rights and who described Brown as "in sympathy a black man . . . and as deeply interested in our cause, as though his own soul had been pierced with the iron of slavery."

When Brown learned of the sacking of Lawrence, Kansas, and the attack on Senator Sumner, he vowed to retaliate, telling his followers that it was their sacred duty to "strike terror in the hearts of the pro-slavery people." On the night of May 24, Brown's seven-

Frederick Douglass, photographed at age sixty-one, escaped slavery to become a leader of the abolitionist movement and one of the most celebrated men in America. "No man," he wrote, "can put a chain about the ankle of his fellow man without at last finding the other end fastened about his own neck."

man raiding party, including four of his sons, attacked pro-slavery settlers near Pottawatomie Creek, Kansas. Carrying rifles, knives, and swords, the Pottawatomie Rifles, as Brown called his militia, dragged victims out of their homes and hacked them to death, killing five men in what would become known as the Pottawatomie Massacre. As a member of that raiding party later dispassionately recalled, "The old man Doyle and two sons were called out and marched some distance from the house. . . . Old John Brown drew his revolver and shot the old man Doyle in the forehead, and [his] two youngest sons immediately fell upon the younger Doyles with their short two-edged swords." Brown was indicted for murder but was able to evade capture—and almost instantly became a revered figure in the abolitionist movement.

The Supreme Court further inflamed the already fervent abolitionists with its decision in the 1857 *Dred Scott v. Sandford* case. Scott was a slave who had lived for a time with his owner in the free state of Illinois and the territory of Minnesota—and when his owner died and he became the possession of the widow, he sued for his freedom. Ironically, a substantial portion of his legal fees was paid by the sons of his original owner, one of them an antislavery Missouri congressman named Henry Taylor Blow. After a Missouri state court ruled that Scott was still legally bound because he had not sued for his freedom while living in a nonslave state, his case slowly made its way to the Supreme Court.

Several similar cases decided at the state level had freed the petitioning slaves, establishing the doctrine of "once free, forever free." But five of the nine Supreme Court justices hearing the *Dred Scott* case came from slave-owning families. The eleven-year legal battle was concluded in March 1857, when Chief Justice Roger Taney issued what scholars often consider the single worst verdict in Supreme Court history, ruling that an African-American could never be a citizen and therefore Scott had no standing to sue for his freedom in a federal court, and, more important, that the federal government had no right to regulate slavery in any territory acquired after the signing of the Constitution. Slaves were property, Taney wrote in the majority opinion. "They had for more than a century before been regarded as beings of an inferior order, and altogether unfit to associate with the white race, either in social or political relations; and so far inferior, that they had no rights which the white man was bound to respect." The court went even farther than that, declaring that slave owners were protected by the Fifth Amendment guarantee that citizens could not be deprived of their property "without due process of the law." As a result, the court found that the Missouri Compromise was unconstitutional and slavery could not legally be prohibited anywhere in the federal territories.

Perhaps fittingly, ten weeks after the decision was issued, Congressman Henry Blow purchased Scott's freedom, as well as that of his wife and two daughters, for $750. Dred Scott

Chief Justice of the Supreme Court Roger Taney,
as photographed by Mathew Brady.

found work as a porter in a Saint Louis hotel but lived as a free man for only nine months, dying of tuberculosis in 1858 at age sixty-three.

Rather than settling the issue, as many had hoped it would, the *Dred Scott* decision propelled the nation into a crisis. The clever compromises of the past that had held the Union together tenuously no longer were possible. Fifteen months after the decision, former Illinois congressman Abraham Lincoln delivered one of his greatest speeches to the state Republican convention in Springfield, Illinois, warning that with this ruling, the court had taken away from states the right of self-determination and that eventually slavery could be imposed upon the entire nation. "A house divided against itself cannot stand," he said. "I believe this government cannot endure, permanently, half slave and half free. I do not expect the Union to be dissolved—I do not expect the house to fall—but I do expect it will cease to be divided. It will become all one thing, or all the other."

When the slave Dred Scott sued for his freedom because he had lived in slave-free areas, Supreme Court Chief Justice Roger Taney (photographed at left by Mathew Brady) wrote in his 1857 decision that blacks had no constitutional rights and could be "bought and sold and treated as an ordinary article of merchandise and traffic." *Frank Leslie's Illustrated Newspaper* was published weekly and was one of the most popular publications in the country. Featuring the Scott family on its cover demonstrated the significance of this decision.

The seven debates in 1858 between Republican Abraham Lincoln and his rival for an
Illinois Senate seat, Democrat Stephen Douglas, riveted the nation. Lincoln, seen here
speaking in September in Charleston, Illinois, believed the issues they discussed were
so important that they would continue to be debated long after "these poor tongues
of Judge Douglas and myself shall be silent."

Those words marked the beginning of Lincoln's campaign for the Senate against two-
term Democratic incumbent Stephen Douglas. Throughout the fall of 1858 Lincoln and
Douglas met in seven historic debates that riveted the nation and set the stage for the
presidential election two years later, when they would meet again. Their positions on slavery
actually were much more different than is commonly accepted. "The Little Giant," as the
five-foot-four Stephen A. Douglas was known, was a towering political figure who strongly
supported the doctrine of popular sovereignty, the belief that voters in each state and territory

should decide for themselves contentious issues such as slavery. Although personally he was opposed to the institution, he argued that majority rule was the essence of democracy and the very foundation on which this nation had been founded. "If there is any one principle dearer and more sacred than all others in free governments," he proclaimed, "it is that which asserts the exclusive right of a free people to form and adopt their own fundamental law, and to manage and regulate their own internal affairs and domestic institutions." For that reason, he argued against President James Buchanan's efforts to strong-arm Kansas into the Union as a slave state—a political position that resulted in his gaining supporters from the opposition Republicans in Congress.

Lincoln was not yet the Great Emancipator he was to become. While he believed slavery was morally wrong and a violation of the constitutional declaration that "all men are created equal," he was not an abolitionist. He argued that slavery should be prohibited in new states and territories, but he did not advocate outlawing it where it existed. In fact, as he said during the fourth debate, "I will say then that I am not, nor ever have been, in favor of bringing about in any way the social and political equality of the white and black races." Basically, he believed free black men and women should have the right to work and be paid a fair wage, move without restriction in society, and make their own decisions. He did not support giving freed slaves the right to vote, serve on juries, hold political office, or marry whites. In fact, for a time he supported colonization, suggesting that slaves be freed and sent to the African nation of Liberia. Given the strife that existed between the races, he said in 1862, it would be "better for us both, therefore, to be separated."

Interest in the hours-long debates was so intense that many newspapers printed the entire texts. Although Douglas won the Senate election, Lincoln gained the national recognition and support that would result in his becoming the Republican Party's presidential candidate in 1860.

All those fancy words and highfalutin ideas had little impact on fightin' men like John Brown. While Lincoln and Douglas were busy speechifying and Stowe was writing her books and plays, Brown was taking action. He intended to start an uprising that would lead to the end of slavery. He proved his capabilities in the winter of 1858, when he liberated twelve slaves from two farms in Verona, Missouri, and led them on a hazardous eighty-two-day, thousand-mile journey to freedom in Canada.

That raid settled most doubts about Brown. As abolitionist Gerrit Smith said, "I was once doubtful in my own mind as to Captain Brown's course. I now approve of it heartily." Brown secured the intellectual and financial backing of many Northern abolitionists, among them Henry David Thoreau, Ralph Waldo Emerson, and a group of businessmen, ministers, and teachers known as the Secret Six—all of whom purportedly did not know his precise plan, which was to raid the federal arsenal at Harpers Ferry, Virginia, believing that this would initiate an uprising of slaves throughout the South. Among the people with whom he shared his dream was his friend Frederick Douglass. Brown had stayed in Douglass's Rochester, New York, home, where he had drafted a provisional constitution for Virginia that he intended to put in place after the successful uprising.

Weeks before the raid Douglass met secretly with Brown in a stone quarry in Chambersburg, Pennsylvania, to try to dissuade him. Harpers Ferry was bordered by rivers and mountains, he warned; it was "a perfect steel trap" and he worried that Brown would not get out of there alive.

But Brown would not be deterred, telling Douglass, "I want you for a special purpose. When I strike, the bees will begin to swarm, and I want you to help hive them." Apparently he intended to remain in Harpers Ferry only long enough to collect sufficient weapons. Then he would retreat into a stronghold deep in the Allegheny Mountains, where he would build his army and launch guerrilla raids on plantations.

John Brown's dream that his raid might convince slaves to throw off their chains and fight for their freedom was not completely irrational. Less than three decades earlier in Southampton County, Virginia, a thirty-one-year-old literate slave named Nat Turner had led a murderous uprising of an estimated seventy enslaved and freed blacks. Turner, who believed he was ordained to "slay my enemies with their own weapons," began with six followers, but that number grew rapidly as he cut a bloody trail through the countryside, freeing slaves and killing almost every white man, woman, and child they encountered. By the time the rebellion was put down, as many as seventy whites had been murdered. Rumors spread rapidly that the rebellion was widespread, that "armies" of slaves were marching, indiscriminately killing whites with axes, shovels, and other farm tools. Retaliation was swift and brutal; soldiers and terrified white citizens randomly attacked and killed blacks. No one knows how many people died as a result of the uprising, certainly hundreds of both slaves and free blacks were killed by soldiers and mobs—many of them having no connection to the rebellion. Although the insurrection was quelled in only two days, Turner successfully eluded capture for two months. When apprehended, he was sentenced quickly and hanged, and his corpse was skinned and ripped apart, then burned to leave no trace of him to be martyred. Several of his followers were decapitated and their heads were mounted on stakes as a warning to any slaves who might follow their course.

Nat Turner's rebellion forever changed the relationship between slaves and their owners. It is doubtful that slave owners, overseers, or most Southern whites ever again felt completely safe with their slaves. Harsh laws were passed as a result in some states, making it illegal to teach slaves to read or to allow them to preach, carry a gun, hunt, or own livestock.

John Brown also had learned important lessons from Nat Turner's failure—and spent years planning the details of his attack. In addition to Frederick Douglass, he received considerable assistance from the remarkable Harriet Tubman. "General Tubman," as Brown called her, was more militant than Douglass. After escaping from a plantation in Maryland in 1849 by following the North Star into free Pennsylvania, she returned to the South nineteen times to conduct slaves to freedom on the Underground Railroad. If one of her passengers faltered or threatened to go back, she was known to take out a pistol and warn, "Dead Negroes tell no tales. You'll be free or die." Her daring missions made her famous—she became known as "the Moses of her people"—and provoked plantation owners to offer a $40,000 bounty for her capture. Tubman supposedly helped Brown plan his mission by raising funds, recruiting men, and providing intelligence about the railroad in Virginia. According to legend, while Douglass refused to participate in the actual raid, Harriet Tubman did intend to go with John Brown—but illness made it impossible and saved her life.

On that Sunday night in 1859, John Brown led a group of sixteen white men, four free black men, and one fugitive slave, armed mostly with new Sharps breech-loading rifles, across the Potomac River into Virginia. United in their hatred of slavery, they had joined Brown's "provisional army" for a variety of personal reasons. Former slave Dangerfield Newby, for example, hoped the raid would allow him to rescue his wife from slavery. Aaron Stevens was a man on the run; after he'd been sentenced to death for mutiny and assaulting an officer while serving in the 1st United States Dragoons, President Franklin Pierce commuted his sentence to three years of hard labor. Stevens had escaped from Fort Leavenworth, changed his name, and became a colonel in the Kansas militia—and then he met John Brown.

Moving quickly on a cold, dark, rainy night, the raiders cut the telegraph lines and seized the bridges leading into Harpers Ferry, isolating the small town. The few night watchmen offered no resistance as the raiding party captured the armory, the arsenal, and Hall's Rifle Works, a privately owned rifle manufacturing factory, then fanned out into the countryside. They began going from house to house rounding up hostages, among them Colonel Lewis Washington, the great-grandnephew of President George Washington, and other prominent citizens. Slave owner John Allstadt testified later that he was awakened in his bed by armed men warning him, "Get up quick or we will burn you up." Slaves were freed and offered pikes, but most of them resisted, having little understanding of what was happening and fearful of the consequences of betraying their owners. Eventually as many as sixty townspeople were taken hostage.

Ironically, the first casualty was Hayward Shepherd, a freed black man working as a porter and assistant station manager for the B&O Railroad. At one thirty that morning Shepherd had met the express from Wheeling, which Brown had detained for five hours before permitting it to continue to Baltimore, then walked to the Potomac River railroad bridge. When confronted there by two of Brown's men he turned and ran—and was shot in the back. He managed to stumble back to the railroad office and died later that day. The town honored him as a black man who had refused to join Brown's effort to destroy slavery, but his

The engine and guardhouse in which John Brown's raiders barricaded themselves was later celebrated as John Brown's Fort, seen here in this late-1880s photo. During the war Union troops often broke off pieces of brick and wood as souvenirs, while Confederate troops cursed as they passed.

actions that day—why did he turn and run?—have long been debated without any resolution.

Brown's men could have taken hundreds of weapons and lots of ammunition and fled into the foothills, but they hesitated, perhaps hoping that slaves in the area would rise up and race to join them—and before they could escape, the townspeople organized a defense and surrounded the armory. Many of them believed their greatest fear was being realized: slaves were rising up to kill them. They knew this uprising had to be crushed before it gained strength—whatever the toll. They fought back and forced the remnants of Brown's army

John Brown's raid terrified many Southerners, who feared it signaled the beginning of a slave uprising. *The Richmond Enquirer* wrote that it had "advanced the cause of disunion more than any other event . . . since the formation of [our] government." Depicted here by British artist Henry Marriott Paget, it became worldwide news.

to take cover with about ten hostages inside the arsenal's fire-engine house, a small brick building with reinforced oak doors that later became known as John Brown's Fort.

Brown and his men were trapped. Hoping he might trade his hostages for safe passage out of town, he sent out his son Watson Brown and another man carrying a white flag to negotiate terms. But passions were too strong; the men of Harpers Ferry weren't simply putting down an attack, they were defending their way of life. Both men were shot within a few steps. Oliver Brown helped his brother get back inside—and he, too, was mortally wounded. In fighting that raged throughout the day, several more of Brown's men, as well as three citizens, including Harpers Ferry mayor Fontaine Beckham, were killed. The standoff had begun.

When the B&O express reached Baltimore with news of the raid, a company of marines under the command of Lieutenant Colonel Robert E. Lee was dispatched to Harpers Ferry. By the time they arrived, Brown had been holed up with his hostages without any provisions for a full day. After securing the area, Lee ordered Lieutenant James Ewell Brown ("Jeb") Stuart to offer Brown surrender terms. When Brown refused, Lee's men stormed the armory. Lieutenant Israel Green and his men smashed through the door of the armory and rushed inside. As Green later remembered, John Brown had just fired his weapon. "I brought my saber down with all my strength upon his head. . . . He fell senseless on his side, then rolled over on his back. . . . Instinctively I gave him a saber thrust in the left breast. The sword I carried was a light uniform weapon and either not having a point or striking something hard in Brown's accouterment's, did not penetrate. The blade bent double."

When questioned after his capture, Brown warned that the raid was only a beginning: "I claim to be here . . . to aid those suffering great wrong. I wish to say, furthermore, that you had better—all you people at the South—prepare yourselves for a settlement of that question that must come up for settlement sooner than you are prepared for it. . . . You may dispose of me very easily. I am nearly disposed of now; but this question is still to be settled—this negro question I mean; the end of that is not yet." Later in the questioning he said, "'Whom the gods would destroy they first made mad,' and you are mad."

Exaggerated rumors about the raid spread rapidly; supposedly as many as seven hundred slaves had rebelled and were at large. Terrified that another Nat Turner was stalking whites, towns throughout Virginia and North Carolina called out their militias to protect their white citizens. The *Charleston Mercury* reported, "Three of the whites are said to have escaped with four hundred negros." In reality, ten of Brown's men were either killed in the fire-engine house or died later of their wounds—Dangerfield Newby had been the first to die, his throat cut

James Ewell Brown ("Jeb") Stuart, who
was to gain fame as a brave and innovative
Confederate cavalry general during the war,
negotiated surrender terms with John Brown
at Harpers Ferry and, when negotiations
failed, gave the signal to attack.

from ear to ear by a six-inch spike. Perhaps in retaliation, Newby's widow and their children
were "sold south" to Louisiana. Five members of the raiding party managed to escape, but the
rest of them, including John Brown, were captured. Brown and his men were transported to
Charleston and turned over to civil authorities for trial. One marine died in the attack.

By objective standards the raid was a failure. Colonel Robert E. Lee, who was lauded for
his decisive leadership at Harpers Ferry, wrote that Brown "acknowledges that he has been
disappointed in his expectations of aid from the black as well as white population, both in
the Southern and Northern States. The blacks whom he forced from their homes in this
neighborhood, as far as I could learn, gave him no voluntary assistance. . . . The result proves
that the plan was the attempt of a fanatic or madman, which could only end in failure; and
its temporary success was owing to the panic and confusion he succeeded in creating by
magnifying his numbers."

Brown's raid rallied the abolitionist forces across the growing nation. At a different
time, an insurrection against the federal government might have been put down quickly
with little fanfare. But not at this time, and not in this place. Even with the rudimentary
communications of the era, the raid quickly became a major turning point in the seemingly
inevitable march toward civil war. John Brown almost instantly became one of the most

admired—and despised—men in the country. As the *Raleigh Register* wrote in 1859, "The affair at Harper's Ferry marks a new and most important era in our country's history. It will bring to an immediate solution the question as to whether the Union can be preserved, and the right of the South to hold property in slaves be maintained. This is the issue to be tried now. The trial can no longer be deferred. The issue has been forced upon the South, and let the result be what it may, her skirts will be clear of all responsibility." There was no longer any possibility of compromise.

John Brown and his men were indicted on Virginia state charges of treason, inciting slaves to rebel, and murder. His trial began within a week. His supporters and defense attorneys urged him to plead insanity, which might lighten the penalties, but he rejected that path, telling them, "If I am insane, of course I should know more than all the rest of the world. But I do not think so."

Virginia's governor, Henry Wise, who had questioned Brown in prison, wrote, "They are themselves mistaken who take him to be a madman. He is a man of clear head, of courage, fortitude and simple ingenuousness."

Six hundred people—among them numerous reporters from Northern newspapers—crowded into the courtroom, snapping open peanuts and chestnuts throughout the trial. While Brown complained that he was not being permitted time to wage a tolerable defense, he was clearly resigned to the outcome. Upon being sentenced to hang Brown rose from the cot on which he had spent most of the trial and made a speech that Ralph Waldo Emerson would later describe as equal to the Gettysburg Address in its power. "I am yet too young to understand that God is any respecter of persons," he said. "I believe that to have interfered, as I have done . . . in behalf of His despised poor, was not wrong, but right. Now, if it is deemed necessary that I should forfeit my life for the furtherance of the ends of justice, and mingle my blood further with the blood of my children and with the blood of millions in this slave country whose rights are disregarded by wicked, cruel, and unjust enactments, I submit; so let it be done!"

Southerners believed it was proper that Brown pay with his own life for the death and destruction he had brought to Harpers Ferry—as well as threatening their legal rights to own slaves. Abolitionists fought for him; Emerson proclaimed in a lecture he gave in Boston six days after the sentencing: "That new saint, than whom none purer or more brave was ever led by love of men into conflict and death,—the new saint awaiting his martyrdom, and who, if he shall suffer, will make the gallows glorious like the cross." Henry David Thoreau wrote in "A Plea for Captain John Brown" that he was "a man of rare common sense and directness of speech, as of action . . . a man of ideas and principles. . . . Not yielding to a whim or transient impulse, but carrying out the purpose of a life." Thoreau then quoted pro-slavery Ohio congressman Clement Vallandigham, who described the raid as "among the best planned and executed conspiracies that ever failed."

On December 1, Mary Day Brown was permitted a visit with her husband. A gallows was set up in Charles Town. Cadets from the Virginia Military Institute, under the command of Thomas Jackson—later to become known as "Stonewall" Jackson—guarded the site. Among the spectators watching with what he later described as "unlimited, undeniable contempt" for the "traitor and terrorizer" was a volunteer in the Virginia militia named John Wilkes Booth.

It was later reported that Brown's body "jerked and quivered" for five minutes after the trapdoor had opened, snapping his spinal cord. Thomas Jackson's aide, Major J. T. L. Preston, shouted out while his body was still convulsing, "So perish all such enemies of Virginia! All such enemies of the Union! All such foes of the human race!" In the North it was a day of mourning. Church bells tolled and commemorative services were held. Citizens of Albany, New York, fired a one-hundred-gun salute. Black-owned businesses were closed for the day. And any hope of peaceful resistance to slavery was essentially abandoned. An article by Frederick Douglass appearing in William Lloyd Garrison's abolitionist magazine the *Liberator* concluded, "Moral considerations have long since been exhausted upon slaveholders. It is in vain to reason with them. One might as well hunt bears with ethics and political economy for weapons, as to seek to 'pluck the spoiled out of the hand of the oppressor' by mere force of moral law. Slavery is a system of brute force. It shields itself behind *might*, rather than right. It must be met with its own weapons."

And on that morning Henry Wadsworth Longfellow wrote in his personal journal, "This will be a great day in our history; the date of a new Revolution. . . . Even now as I write, they are leading old John Brown to execution in Virginia for attempting to rescue slaves! This is sowing the wind to reap the whirlwind, which will come soon."

In addition to Brown, six members of his provisional army were hanged. Southerners rejoiced but were wary of the consequences. Many of them believed Brown represented what they began to refer to as "the Black Republican Party" of the North and started worrying that a Republican victory in the coming presidential elections of 1860 would initiate an effort to legislate the end of slavery. In Congress, Senator Jefferson Davis verbally attacked William Seward, the leading candidate for the Republican nomination, declaring, "We have been invaded, and that invasion, and the facts connected with it, show Mr. Seward to be a traitor, and deserving of the gallows." For the first time, Southerners began discussing the possibility and the ramifications of secession.

The *Charleston Mercury* echoed the fears of Southerners when it warned that the Harpers Ferry raid "fully establishes the fact that there are at the North men ready to engage in adventures upon the peace and security of the southern people, however heinously and recklessly. . . . It is a warning profoundly symptomatic of the future of the Union with our sectional enemies."

It had become obvious, as plantation owner Edmund Ruffin wrote, that the presidential election of 1860 would determine "whether these southern states are to remain free, or to be politically enslaved."

New York senator William Seward was the leading candidate for the Republican nomination, but members of his own party believed his radical stance against slavery made him unelectable. No man was more despised throughout the South than "the Black Republican" Seward. Even many Northerners believed his election would lead to the end of the Union, perhaps even a civil war. They began searching for a more conciliatory candidate who could hold the country together.

Although not yet officially a candidate for the presidency, in February 1860 Abraham Lincoln had been invited to New York to address the Young Men's Republican Union at the

After losing a bitterly contested fight for the 1860 Republican nomination for the presidency, New York senator William Seward accepted Lincoln's offer to become secretary of state. Supposedly his Auburn home had been a stop on the Underground Railroad, and among the escaping slaves he assisted was Harriet Tubman, but many historians doubt that story.

Cooper Union. He used the opportunity to artfully weave a moderate path that could placate both the North and the South—emphasizing that John Brown's actions did not represent the Republican Party. While he accepted that slavery was legal throughout the South, he strongly believed the practice should not be extended to new states or territories. Citing the words of the founding fathers, he told the packed hall,

> Mr. Jefferson did not mean to say, nor do I, that the power of emancipation is in the Federal Government. He spoke of Virginia; and, as to the power of emancipation, I speak of the slaveholding States only. The Federal Government, however, as we insist, has the power of restraining the extension of the institution—the power to insure that a slave insurrection shall never occur on any American soil which is now free from slavery.
>
> John Brown's effort was peculiar. . . . In fact, it was so absurd that the slaves, with all their ignorance, saw plainly enough it could not succeed. . . .
>
> And how much would it avail you, if you could, by the use of John Brown, Helper's Book, and the like, break up the Republican organization? Human action can be modified to some extent, but human nature cannot be changed. There is a judgment and a feeling against slavery in this nation, which cast at least a million and a half of votes. You cannot destroy that judgment and feeling—that sentiment—by breaking up the political organization which rallies around it. . . .
>
> But you will break up the Union rather than submit to a denial of your Constitutional rights.
>
> That has a somewhat reckless sound; but it would be palliated, if not fully justified, were we proposing, by the mere force of numbers, to deprive you of some right, plainly written down in the Constitution. But we are proposing no such thing.

Lincoln's Cooper Union speech thrilled Republicans, instantly making him a strong challenger for the presidential nomination. As one member of the audience later reported, "When Lincoln rose to speak, I was greatly disappointed. He was tall, tall,—oh, how tall! and so angular and awkward that I had, for an instant, a feeling of pity for so ungainly a man." But once he began speaking, "his face lighted up as with an inward fire; the whole man was transfigured. I forgot his clothes, his personal appearance, and his individual peculiarities.

This photograph was taken in late February 1861, just after Lincoln arrived in Washington for his inauguration. Lincoln was noted for his unusually large hands, as seen here.

Presently, forgetting myself, I was on my feet like the rest, yelling like a wild Indian, cheering this wonderful man." Abraham Lincoln had taken his first step into history.

As Lincoln liked to tell people, he was a simple and humble man, born in a one-room log cabin on the Kentucky frontier in 1809. He was mostly self-educated, with less than a year of formal schooling. After growing up in Indiana, he moved with his family to New Salem, Illinois, when he was twenty-one. A strong, athletic, but quiet young man, Abe Lincoln served as a captain in the Illinois militia during the Black Hawk War. He was twenty-three years old when he entered elective politics, running for the Illinois General Assembly. During that campaign he demonstrated the easy, amiable, and approachable style that years later would make him so popular—although without any financial support, he failed to win a seat in the assembly. But even in those formative years he clearly had the ultimate political gift— he didn't seem to be a politician. "Honest Abe," as he became known for his unquestioned integrity, was the proverbial "man of the people."

After working as a shopkeeper—and falling deeply into debt, then as the postmaster of New Salem and a surveyor, he decided to study law. In 1834, he ran as a Whig for the state legislature from Sangamon County—and won the first of his four terms in state government. Two years later he was admitted to the bar and moved to Springfield.

It was in Springfield in 1839 that he met Mary Todd, the daughter of a wealthy Kentucky slave owner, and after a somewhat rocky courtship they married in 1842. By then he had established his reputation as an able lawyer. In 1849, he argued and lost a case concerning the statute of limitations and liability in front of the United States Supreme Court. He developed a legal philosophy that would later become the foundation of his presidency. He wrote: "Discourage litigation. Persuade your neighbors to compromise whenever you can. Point out to them how the nominal winner is often the real loser—in fees, expenses, and waste of time. As a peacemaker the lawyer has a superior opportunity of being a good man."

During his career as a lawyer, he defended several men accused of murder. In an 1858 case he won an acquittal for his client by showing that the moon was at a low angle the night of the killing, discrediting an eyewitness who claimed to have seen the murder in the moonlight.

In 1846, pledging to serve only a single term, he was elected to the House of Representatives—the only federal election he would win before running for the presidency. During his failed 1855 campaign for the Senate he emphasized that he was not an abolitionist but rather was against the extension of slavery into new states or territories. That moderate stance on slavery was among the reasons he was essential in the formation of the new Republican Party and received the nomination as the Republican candidate in the 1860 election.

His Democratic opponent, once again, was Stephen A. Douglas, whom he had faced off against in the now legendary debates only two years earlier. But the pro-slavery Southern Democrats, known as Fire-Eaters, rejected Douglas's popular sovereignty doctrine and held their own convention, nominating Vice President John C. Breckinridge. Conservative Whigs, desperate to prevent secession over slavery, joined a number of Southern Democrats to form the Constitutional Union Party and nominated Tennessee's John Bell for president.

While Lincoln followed established tradition and did not personally campaign, Douglas traveled throughout the nation, pointing out that "people saw candidates in the flesh less often than they saw a perfect rainbow," while preaching against abolition in the North and against secession in the South. But it was hopeless; Edmund Ruffin, a leader of the Fire-Eaters, made it clear what was at stake. "If the southern states and people can be brought together," he thundered, ". . . I trust that by next November, and the election of an abolitionist, some one or more of the southern states will promptly secede." He reinforced that point by purchasing several of the pikes carried by John Brown's men during the Harpers Ferry raid and sending one to the governor of each slaveholding state—and to these razor-sharp spears he had affixed a label reading SAMPLE OF THE FAVORS DESIGNED FOR US BY OUR NORTHERN BRETHREN.

Abraham Lincoln was elected the sixteenth president of the United States solely by the free-soil states in the North and the West, winning all of the Northern states, while Breckinridge won all of the Southern states. Although there was an extraordinary turnout of 81.2 percent of eligible voters, the second-highest in history, Lincoln received only 39.8 percent of the vote, second only to John Quincy Adams as the lowest winning percentage of the popular vote. But it proved sufficient to provide a landslide majority in the electoral college.

Within days of the election, South Carolina, Georgia, and Mississippi called their legislatures into special session to vote on withdrawing from the Union. When some Republicans urged Lincoln to consider some form of compromise, he refused, telling them he did not want to make it "appear as if I repented for the crime of having been elected, and was anxious to apologize and beg forgiveness." Slavery would not be permitted in new states or territories, he wrote to Republicans. "On that point hold firm, as with a chain of steel."

South Carolina seceded on December 20, calling on the other Southern states to form a "great slaveholding confederacy, stretching its arms over a territory larger than any power in Europe possesses." Within the next several weeks, Mississippi, Florida, Alabama, Georgia, Louisiana, and Texas followed. The nation was being ripped apart. In his inaugural address

The Lincoln-Douglas debates received national attention. There was no direct vote for senators in 1858, so no one actually cast a vote for Lincoln or Douglas. Votes were cast for the Illinois legislature, and the majority of those votes were Republican; but the apportionment plan of the legislature gave the power to select the senator to Democratic legislators.

on March 4, Lincoln made one last, futile attempt to appeal for unity, telling Southerners, "I have no purpose, directly or indirectly, to interfere with the institution of slavery in the States where it exists. I believe I have no lawful right to do so, and I have no inclination to do so." But he also warned them of what was to come: "no State upon its own mere motion can lawfully get out of the Union. . . . In *your* hands, my dissatisfied fellow-countrymen, and not in 'mine,' is the momentous issue of civil war. . . . You can have no conflict without being yourselves the aggressors. . . . We are not enemies, but friends. We must not be enemies."

But it was far too late. On February 18, meeting in Montgomery, Alabama, the Confederate Convention selected West Point graduate and Mississippi senator Jefferson Davis as president of the Confederate States of America. Davis left no doubt about his intentions when he told delegates that "the time for compromise has now passed," and under his leadership the South would "make all who oppose her smell Southern powder and feel Southern steel."

His vice president, former Georgia congressman Alexander Stephens, spoke for the

South when he said, "Slavery . . . is his [the Negro's] natural and normal condition. This, our new government, is the first, in the history of the world, based upon this great physical, philosophical, and moral truth."

By the time Davis and Stephens assumed office, Confederate military operations had already begun. Militia in the seceding states had seized almost all the federal mints, depots, forts, and arsenals within their territory without a single shot being fired. The loyalty of American troops and federal government officials was being tested, and each individual had to make the momentous personal decision about their allegiance. Among the very few federal fortifications that remained under Union control was Fort Sumter, which was located on a two-and-a-half-acre man-made island in the center of Charleston Harbor.

With tensions boiling following Lincoln's election, President James Buchanan ordered Major Robert Anderson to take command of the federal troops stationed in Charleston's Fort Moultrie. Anderson's appointment may well have been a gesture to the South; born in Kentucky, he was a pro-slavery former slave owner. He was a thirty-five-year army veteran, and had supposedly enlisted and discharged a young Abraham Lincoln during the Black Hawk War. But when he had to make his fateful decision about whether or not to join the secessionists, he remained faithful to the Union. Without orders, under the cover of night on December 26, he ordered his two companies of the 1st US Artillery Regiment to abandon vulnerable Fort Moultrie and occupy the far more defensible Fort Sumter.

The Confederacy was outraged, and government officials demanded that Anderson's troops return to Fort Moultrie. Jefferson Davis reportedly offered to pay the expenses for transporting the entire garrison. Anderson refused, insisting that his only objective was to protect his men, stating firmly, "I cannot and will not go back," then defiantly raised a large thirty-three-star US flag clearly visible in Charleston. Anderson's loyalty and courage made him the North's first hero of the coming war. President Buchanan responded by secretly ordering a merchant vessel, the *Star of the West*, carrying two hundred troops, to reinforce Fort Sumter.

Sumter's brick walls were fifty feet high and in many places five feet thick. But the reality was that it could not be held for any length of time. Surrounded by Confederate artillery, it lacked sufficient ammunition or supplies to survive a siege. News got out about Buchanan's attempt to reinforce the fort by sea. As the *Star of the West* came into sight early on the morning of January 9, 1861, Southern batteries opened fire—arguably the first shots of the Civil War. Anderson debated returning fire. One of his aides, Captain Abner Doubleday, who later would gain renown as the man who invented baseball, urged him to respond. Anderson hesitated, fearful of starting a war, and the ship turned around and sailed out of range.

Before becoming president of the Confederacy, Jefferson Davis had served the United States as a soldier in the Mexican-American War, a senator from Mississippi, and secretary of war under President Franklin Pierce.

Lincoln, newly inaugurated as president, considered a proposal to order the fort evacuated if Virginia agreed to remain in the Union, but that plan was never realized. The standoff continued into April, infuriating Southerners and thrilling Northerners. Six thousand Confederate troops, commanded by General Pierre Gustave Toutant Beauregard, who ironically had been an artillery student of Anderson's at West Point in the 1840s, were dug in around the harbor. By that time Anderson and his eighty-four artillerymen—including the regimental band—were running out of rations. As he admitted to Confederate officers, "If you do not batter us to pieces, we shall be starved out in a few days."

The nation waited. A fort that few people outside Charleston even knew existed, a fort that had little military value, had become the potential flash point to begin the Civil War.

Secretary of State William Seward, perhaps anxious to avoid starting the war over an indefensible position, secretly sent word to Confederate leaders that Lincoln soon would evacuate the fort. Lincoln, however, determined that if war was to come it would be started by the South, instead decided to send vitally needed supplies—but no reinforcements—to

The Civil War began in Charleston Harbor on the morning of April 12, 1861,
with the shelling of Fort Sumter. On April 14, Confederate general P. G. T. Beauregard
reported, "before sunset the flag of the Confederate States floated over the
ramparts of Fort Sumter."

Anderson. On April 6, he announced that Union ships carrying those provisions had sailed, adding that "no effort to throw in men, arms, or ammunition" would be made unless the Confederates prevented the ships from landing.

Jefferson Davis would not permit the fort to be resupplied. On April 11, General Beauregard sent former senator James Chesnut and Captain Stephen Lee to deliver his ultimatum: time was up. Anderson had one day to surrender or the attack would begin. As Chesnut and Lee left the fort after delivering the message, Anderson shook their hands and said solemnly, "If we never meet in this world again, God grant that we may meet in the next."

That night Chesnut's wife, Mary, wrote in her diary, which years later would become a best seller titled *A Dairy from Dixie*, "I did not pretend to go to sleep. How can I? If Anderson does not accept terms—at four—the orders are—he shall be fired upon. I count four—Saint Michael chimes. I begin to hope. At half-past four, the heaving booming of a cannon.

"I sprang out of bed. And on my knees—prostrate—I prayed as I never prayed before."

There is considerable speculation about who actually fired the first shot from Fort Johnson, a ten-inch mortar shell that trailed flame visible from the rooftops of Charleston. Supposedly Captain George S. James of the South Carolina Artillery offered the honor of pulling the lanyard to fire the signal cannon to Fire-Eating Virginia congressman Roger Pryor, but he declined, explaining, "I cannot fire the first gun of the war." According to legend, Edmund Ruffin stepped forward and fired the cannon. But historians believe that Captain James gave the order to fire and the lanyard actually was pulled by Lieutenant Henry S. Farley.

Almost instantly forty-three Confederate cannons began a relentless barrage. Captain Stephen Lee remembered that the first shot "burst immediately over the fort, apparently about one hundred feet above. The firing of the mortar woke the echoes from every nook and corner of the harbor, and in this the dead hour of the night, before dawn, that shot was a sound of alarm that brought every soldier in the harbor to his feet." Many Charleston residents watched the bombardment from their balconies, offering toasts to the brave soldiers defending their honor and culture.

In a headline calling it "A Splendid Pyrotechnic Display," the *Charleston Mercury* reported that "at the break of day, amidst the bursting of bombs, and the roaring of ordnance, and before thousands of spectators, whose homes, and liberties, and lives were at stake, was enacted this first great scene in the opening drama of what, it is presumed, will be a most momentous military act."

In the North the *New York Herald* wrote, "Civil war has at last begun. A terrible fight is at this moment going on between Fort Sumter and the fortifications by which it is

When he surrendered Fort Sumter,
Union major Robert Anderson took its
thirty-three-star US flag with him.
Almost precisely four years later he
returned and proudly raised that same
flag over the fort.

surrounded. . . . Troops are pouring into the town by hundreds, but are held in reserve for the present, the force already on the island being ample. People are also arriving every moment on horseback, and by every other conveyance. Within an area of fifty miles, where the thunder of the artillery can be heard, the scene is magnificently terrible."

Lacking sufficient cannons or ammunition, Anderson held his fire until seven a.m., when he ordered Captain Doubleday to begin firing the fort's heavy siege guns. "In aiming the first gun fired against the rebellion I had no feeling of self-reproach," Doubleday remembered. ". . . The United States was called upon not only to defend its sovereignty, but its right to exist as a nation." Fort Sumter's heavier cannons were in exposed positions on the ramparts and Anderson chose not to risk the lives of his men by manning those emplacements in what clearly was a futile effort. But one brave sergeant, John Carmody, raced onto the ramparts and single-handedly fired the loaded weapons. His courage was celebrated by Sergeant James Chester, who described it as "Carmody against the Confederate States."

Throughout the next day Anderson's men tried to fight back. Lacking supplies, they cut up their clothing and sheets and sewed them into gunpowder bags. At nightfall came a storm that raged into the next morning, making the defenders even more miserable.

The bombardment lasted thirty-six hours, setting the wooden barracks and gunpowder magazine on fire. As Doubleday later wrote, "It seemed impossible to escape suffocation. The roaring and crackling of the flames, the dense masses of whirling smoke, the bursting of the enemy's shells, and our own which were exploding in the burning rooms, the crashing of the shot, and the sound of masonry falling in every direction made the fort a pandemonium." Only the fact that the wind suddenly changed direction enabled the garrison to survive. As the fire reached the gunpowder stores, Anderson ordered his men to throw the barrels of powder into the Atlantic Ocean.

On the afternoon of April 13, Anderson surrendered. He informed Secretary of War Simon Cameron by telegram, "The quarters were entirely burned . . . the magazine surrounded by flames . . . four barrels and three cartridges of powder only being available, and no provisions remaining but pork, I accepted terms of evacuation."

General Beauregard accepted the surrender honorably, allowing Anderson's men to fire a fifty-gun salute to the American flag as it was lowered. Incredibly, there had been no Union fatalities during the barrage, but during this surrender ceremony a cannon exploded, and Private Daniel Hough became the only soldier to die in this battle. A week later a second federal soldier, Edward Galloway, one of five men wounded in the bombardment, would succumb to his wounds.

Northerners were shocked by the defeat. Poet Walt Whitman remembered that news "ran through the Land, is if by electric wires."

Anderson and his men were given safe passage to the North, where they were greeted as heroes. A week after the surrender an estimated one hundred thousand New Yorkers squeezed into Union Square Park to cheer Anderson and the flag he had rescued at Fort Sumter. It was the largest assembly of people in American history. Days later Anderson was promoted to brigadier general and sent on a morale-raising tour to help recruit volunteers; he eventually was given command of the Department of Kentucky.

Among the few who welcomed the war was Frederick Douglass, who wrote, "God be praised! . . . war has come at last! . . . The government is aroused, the dead North is alive, and its divided people united. . . . Drums are beating, men are enlisting, companies forming, regiments marching, banners are flying."

It had been only eighteen months since John Brown and his men had lit the fuse that finally exploded over Fort Sumter. The more than half century of compromise was done and, as Lincoln would later say at Gettysburg, the bloody struggle to determine if this nation, "or any nation so conceived, and so dedicated, can long endure," had begun.

Being chosen to carry your unit's flag was the most cherished and deadly honor for a Civil War soldier. The flags they carried were the beloved symbols of pride, patriotism, and loyalty, to be protected no matter the cost. Capturing the enemy's battle flag was considered a tremendous achievement, while losing your own flag was a humiliating disgrace. Unarmed flag bearers led their units into combat and became a primary target. When they fell, others raced to grab the flag before it could touch the ground. Even though bearing the flag was often a death sentence there was never a shortage of volunteers. At Antietam, for example, First Texas lost eight flag bearers—as did the northern 69th New York Volunteer Infantry. At Gettysburg one North Carolina unit lost fourteen men who carried their flag. Several flag bearers eventually were awarded Medals of Honor.

The value placed on flags is seen in the many mentions in Civil War songs. In "The Battle Cry of Freedom," Union troops promised

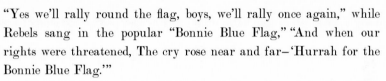

"Yes we'll rally round the flag, boys, we'll rally once again," while Rebels sang in the popular "Bonnie Blue Flag," "And when our rights were threatened, The cry rose near and far—'Hurrah for the Bonnie Blue Flag.'"

There were numerous flags representing the national armies, state militias, and individual units. While the red, white, and blue Stars and Stripes remained the Union banner throughout the war, the Confederacy had three different flags. The original "stars and bars," which bore a great resemblance to the United States flag, was replaced after two years of war by a flag bearing a small blue cross in its upper left corner containing white stars against a red background, with a great white field. The flag mistakenly considered the Confederate flag, a blue cross containing white stars stretching from corner to corner against a red background, actually was the Army of Northern Virginia battle flag.

Flags of the 124th Reg't N. Y. Vols.,

PRESENTED BY

THE LADIES OF ORANGE, MARCH, 1864.

ITS BATTLES:

Manassas Gap, Wilderness, Po River, Spottsylvania, North Anna, Cold Harbor, Petersburgh, Deep Bottom, Strawberry Plains, Boydton Road, Hatchers' Run, 25th of March, Sailors' Creek.

FOR SALE AT REMILLARD'S,

82 Water St., and at the Newburgh Bookstores.

# TWO

# The South
# RISES

## The Union Is Ripped Asunder

A moonless night was an escaping slave's best weapon. On the evening of May 23, three slaves rowed a stolen skiff across the James River from Virginia's Norfolk County to Union-held Fort Monroe. When challenged by a guard, they identified themselves and asked for asylum. Ironically, this was the same spot where the *White Lion* had landed its cargo of twenty slaves almost 250 years earlier.

Frank Baker, Shepard Mallory, and James Townsend were field slaves leased by their owners to the Confederate army and were under the command of Colonel Charles Mallory. They had been put to work building an artillery emplacement in the harbor and made their escape when they learned they were to be sent to the Carolinas to work on fortifications. They were escorted through the gates of Fort Monroe into a new and uncertain world. The laws on which the country had been founded no longer applied and no one yet knew what would replace them.

⌐ As the war began, no one anticipated its bloody consequences; many people viewed it as little more than a fight between Presidents Lincoln and Davis.

Soon after their escape they were questioned by Major General Benjamin Franklin Butler, who had taken command of Fort Monroe only one day earlier. In civilian life Butler had been a successful Massachusetts lawyer and Democratic state legislator, respected for his thorough understanding of the law and his ability to weave creative legal paths around it. The three slaves told him they had been working on Confederate gun emplacements that were far from completion. At any previous time in American history, Butler would had been legally obligated to return these fugitive slaves to their owners. But one day earlier Virginia had voted to secede from the Union. That was the loophole Butler needed.

Within hours, Confederate major John Baytop Cary, carrying a flag of truce, arrived at the fort to demand that Butler return the escaped slaves. Butler refused, pointing out that Virginia had declared its separation from the Union and therefore was no longer entitled to any benefit of American law. Additionally, he continued, the law allowed an army to seize any enemy property being used for military purposes. As slaves were considered property and these men were being used to build fortifications, they were technically contraband of war. "You say you have seceded," said Butler, "so you cannot consistently claim them. I shall hold these Negroes as contraband of war, since they are engaged in the construction of your battery

Fort Monroe commander Benjamin Franklin Butler employed a clever legal strategy to save escaped slaves by designating them as war contraband, a status eventually claimed by tens of thousands of fleeing black men, women, and children.

and are claimed as your property." It was a clever and novel interpretation of the law—but representative of the way the world was about to suddenly and drastically change forever.

Butler's decision had greater implications. This new word, "contraband," spread rapidly among Virginia slaves. Two days later eight more slaves arrived at the fort claiming to be contraband. The next day forty-seven more men, women, and even babies asked for asylum—as enemy contraband.

Lincoln did not initially support Butler's decision, pointing out that the federal government refused to recognize the Confederacy as a separate nation, and therefore that federal laws still applied in South Carolina. But within a few days the story had spread throughout the nation, forcing the president to decide, as the *Chicago Tribune* asked in a headline, "What's to Be Done with the Blacks?" Lincoln's postmaster general replied for the cabinet, informing Butler that "the business you are sent upon . . . is war, not emancipation," but he gave him no

THE (FORT) MONROE DOCTRINE.

Butler's decision created a complex dilemma: The Confederates were insisting that the laws they had rejected one day earlier still had to be respected, while Northerners, who refused to recognize the legality of secession, claimed those laws no longer applied because the state had seceded.

orders how to proceed. Each day more human "contraband" arrived at "Fort Freedom," as Fort Monroe was called. When it was suggested to Butler that he accept only those slaves able and willing to work, he responded, courageously, "If I take the able-bodied only, the young must die. If I take the mother, must I not take the child?"

Legally the slaves were not free, they were military contraband—but in fact they were free. Within weeks escaped slaves were showing up everywhere Union soldiers camped, claiming contraband status. Many of them were put to work and paid a small salary. By mid-1862 it was estimated that more than ten thousand former slaves were living in contraband camps, a number that continued to grow by thousands throughout the war—depriving the

On a landing in this building, which could be seen from the White House, Lincoln's young friend Elmer Ellsworth became the first Union officer killed in defense of the nation.

Confederacy of desperately needed laborers. In a world turning upside down, Butler's simple humane act at the very beginning of the war made a significant difference as it unfolded.

On the day Fort Sumter was captured, the United States Army consisted of about sixteen thousand officers and men, the majority of them posted in company-sized detachments west of the Mississippi. President Lincoln responded to the Confederate attack by tasking the Northern states with supplying seventy-five thousand men from their state militias to suppress the rebellion. Each state was given a quota to fill. There was some debate among Lincoln's advisers concerning the number of troops to be activated; a month earlier sixty thousand Southerners had responded to Jefferson Davis's call for volunteers. Stephen Douglas urged Lincoln to mobilize two hundred thousand men, telling him, "You do not know the dishonest purposes of those men [the Southern leaders] as well as I do."

But Lincoln still did not grasp the depth of Southern determination. He believed this war could be ended quickly with few casualties. By federal law these seventy-five thousand militiamen could be enlisted for only ninety days—or less if the war could quickly be resolved. Many Southerners also misjudged the scope of the conflict, claiming, "A lady's thimble will hold all the blood that will be shed."

Patriotism soared throughout both the North and South. The Confederate states raised the flag of their new nation, the Stars and Bars, while the Stars and Stripes flew from almost every building and home in the North. Individuals and institutions were forced to make a momentous decision about their loyalty. Families and businesses were ripped apart. Friendships ended. Rumors raced across the country. The laws, the customs, the everyday routines of life no longer applied. The United States had come apart.

The Virginia legislature, which only two weeks earlier had voted not to secede, reconvened the day after Lincoln's call to arms and reversed that decision, voting to join the Confederacy. The commander of the federal arsenal at Harpers Ferry, acknowledging that his men could not defend the position, abandoned the site of John Brown's raid after destroying the arsenal and setting the weapons-making facilities on fire. Only the Potomac River separated the Union capital, Washington, DC, from enemy territory. It actually was possible to look through a spyglass from a White House balcony and see the Confederate flag flying proudly over the Marshall House Hotel, only six and a half miles away in Alexandria.

By the end of May, Arkansas, North Carolina, and Tennessee had joined the rebellion. While many citizens of slave states like Missouri, Kentucky, and Maryland sympathized with the Confederacy, those states remained in the Union but supplied soldiers to both armies. The divided loyalties erupted into violence on April 19.

Fearful that Southern troops might march on Washington, which essentially was defenseless, Northern governors rushed their militias to defend the capital. The 6th Massachusetts Regiment arrived in Baltimore by rail midmorning and immediately began transferring to the B&O line that would take them the last forty miles into Washington. The mile distance between the two stations was usually completed by uncoupling the passenger cars from the arriving train, which would then be pulled by horses across "Mob town," as the city was once known, and hooked up to the waiting locomotive. The first seven companies made the short trip without serious injuries, but throughout the morning a mob of secessionists and street gangs with names like the Blood Tubs and Plug Uglies gathered and began taunting the soldiers of the four remaining companies. As one soldier recalled, "They . . . threw at the car bricks, pieces of iron and coal, and . . . the vilest epithets they could invent for us." They blocked the railroad track with an anchor and built barricades to prevent the remaining soldiers from getting to Washington. The last four companies were forced to abandon the cars and march through the streets while being pelted with paving stones and rocks. A soldier was struck in the face and fell. George W. Booth, who eventually would fight for the Confederacy, remembered that the soldier "dropped his musket, which was immediately seized by a citizen, who raised it to his shoulder and fired into the column. The rear files faced about and delivered a volley into the crowd, who responded with pistol shots, stones, clubs, and other missiles. A perfect fusillade was kept up between the troops and the enraged mob." By the time they fought their way to Camden Station, four soldiers had been killed and thirty-six wounded. Many historians consider these men the first casualties of the Civil War. At least a dozen civilians were also killed, with scores more wounded in what became known as the Pratt Street riot.

Secessionists saw this as another victory and promised more bloodshed if Union troops tried to pass through the city again. To prevent that violence, Baltimore's mayor and marshal ordered the railroad bridges burned, cutting all access by rail to the North.

When the 6th Massachusetts reached Washington, the wounded were taken to a makeshift hospital that had been set up in the Capitol Building, which was being

The rapidly occurring events of 1861 were illustrated in periodicals and lithographs. *The Massacre at Baltimore* appeared only weeks after the event. The satirical cartoon below from about the same time depicts two-headed Baltimore, whose allegiance was questioned, pulling at Uncle Sam's coattails while the Confederacy is destroyed. ☞

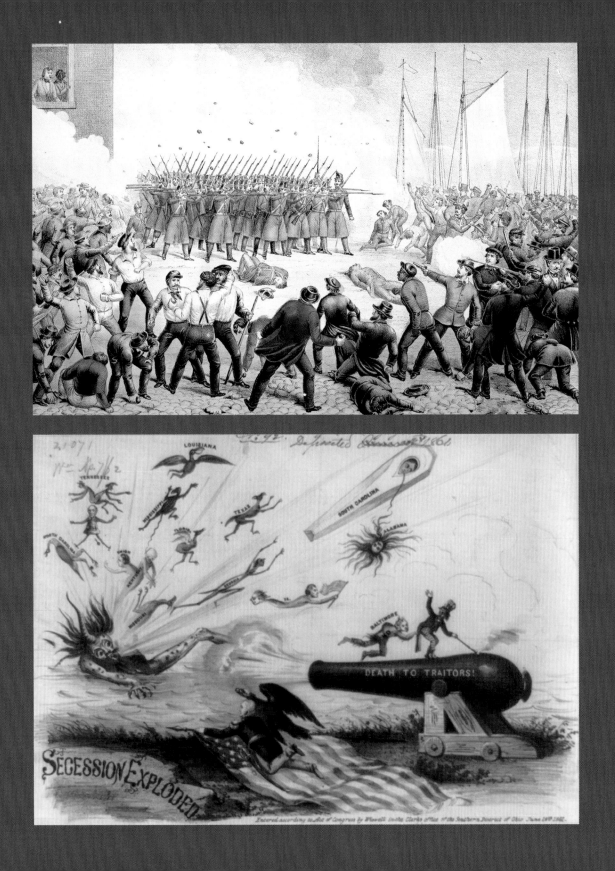

reconstructed and did not yet have its dome. Among those civilians who rushed to offer assistance was the first female recording clerk at the US Patent Office, a woman named Clara Barton. She was stunned to discover that the army was completely unprepared to care for its wounded. She began collecting medicine, food, clean clothing, blankets, and other supplies from her friends in Washington, eventually reaching out to people in New York, New Jersey, and Massachusetts, creating a supply network that would save countless lives throughout the war and later expand to become the American Red Cross.

Washington was isolated, separated from the loyal Northern states by Maryland. The rail lines were closed. Telegraph lines had been cut. Lincoln's only means of communication was by courier. In the city, residents began preparing for a siege. Confederate loyalists left the city and traveled south. General Winfield Scott, commander of the United States Army, acknowledged that the city "is now partially besieged, threatened and in danger of being attacked on all sides in a day or two or three."

In response to this threat, on May 23 Lincoln took the extraordinary step of suspending the constitutional guarantee of habeas corpus along the military rail line between Philadelphia and Baltimore, permitting Scott's troops to detain or arrest any person without providing them full legal protections. They did not even have the fundamental right to be informed of the charges against them or brought before a judge. Eventually that suspension was extended to include the entire Union. It was far better to do that, Lincoln said, than "let the government itself go to pieces." The president claimed the Constitution gave him the right to do so "in cases of rebellion or invasion." When a Confederate sympathizer named John Merryman was arrested for raising troops for the rebels but not charged with a crime, his attorney appealed to the chief justice of the Supreme Court, Roger Taney. Taney eventually supported Merryman's right to know the nature of his crime, finding that only Congress could suspend constitutional rights. Lincoln simply ignored the ruling. In a chilling reminder of what the thirteen colonies had rebelled against during the American Revolution, at least two thousand "political prisoners" were taken into custody and held without trial simply for actions or comments someone believed to be disloyal to the Union. This included Baltimore's mayor and chief of police as well as thirty members of Maryland's legislature. When Baltimore newspaper editor Frank Key Howard, the grandson of Francis Scott Key, wrote editorials critical of Lincoln, he, too, was arrested and held without charges for fourteen months in Fort McHenry—the same place his grandfather had described in "The Star-Spangled Banner" nearly a half century earlier. After being released, Howard wrote a book about his detention—and two men who published it were arrested.

Whether constitutional or not, Lincoln's action worked; the rail line was protected and

Union troops poured into Washington. They set up camp on the White House lawn, in the East Room, and even inside the Capitol Building. Washington was saved. Additional troops were landed in Annapolis, Maryland's state capital, and occupied Baltimore. The state legislature was called into special session and voted strongly against secession. While officially Maryland remained neutral throughout the war, in fact it was Union territory.

Meanwhile, Virginia's legislature had voted to join the rebellion. When voters ratified that decision on May 23, Lincoln ordered eleven regiments into northern Virginia. The march into Alexandria was led by the 11th New York Volunteer Infantry Regiment, the "Fire Zouaves," under the command of twenty-four-year-old colonel Elmer Ephraim Ellsworth, a close personal protégé of President Lincoln's.

Elmer Ellsworth had studied law in Chicago before joining Lincoln's Springfield law firm as a clerk in 1860. While in Chicago he had joined the local militia. He had long admired the Zouaves, hard-fighting French colonial troops who dressed in brightly colored jackets and baggy red pantaloons, and he soon organized his own drill team, which toured throughout the North.

The young clerk won Lincoln's respect and admiration with his calm manner, intelligence, and fortitude. Ellsworth joined his campaign staff and after the victory moved with Lincoln to Washington, working with the new president in the White House—and befriending the Lincolns' young sons, Tad and Willie.

In May 1861, Lincoln followed up his call for short-term state militias with an order to recruit 42,000 volunteers for three-year terms. Ellsworth enlisted his militia regiment, which consisted mostly of street-toughened volunteer firemen, as the 11th New York Volunteers. He and his regiment were ferried across the Potomac in the early morning hours of May 24 and took control of Alexandria's port, telegraph office, and rail stations. As they moved through the town, Ellsworth caught sight of the massive fourteen-by-twenty-four-foot Confederate flag flying from the Marshall House Hotel roof that Lincoln had seen waving from the White House balcony. Undoubtedly Ellsworth considered this a fine war trophy to hand to his mentor. Accompanied by a journalist and two of his men, Corporal Francis Brownell and Lieutenant H. J. Hinser, he climbed through a trapdoor onto the roof and personally cut down the wool flag. As the four men descended, they encountered the hotel's owner, James William Jackson, who in fact was a captain in a Confederate artillery company in Alexandria. Jackson had taken great pride in the fact that his flag could be seen from the White House, and he did not intend to take this insult without retribution. With a double-barreled shotgun in his hands, he waited on a landing of the steps.

## MURDER OF COL. ELLSWORTH OF THE FIRE ZOUAVES,

AND THE DEATH OF JACKSON, HIS ASSASSIN, BY THE HAND OF FRANK BROWNELL, AT ALEXANDRIA, VIRGINIA., MAY 24, 1861

Published and For Sale at Magee's Stationery Store, 316 Chestnut Street, Philadelphia

Ellsworth's killing roused passions throughout the North. In the month following his death, more than two hundred thousand men volunteered to fight. Lincoln's secretary John Hay promised, "They have sworn, with the grim earnestness that never trifles, to have a life for every hair of the dead colonel's head. But even that will not repay."

Ellsworth was folding his flag when he looked up and saw Jackson. He had no idea who he was but told him, "Here is my trophy."

"And here is mine," Jackson responded, leveling his shotgun. Private Brownell lunged at him, but Jackson fired both chambers. Buckshot ripped into Ellsworth's chest, killing him. Brownell fired a split second later, and as the *New York Times* reported, "The ball struck

Jackson on the bridge of the nose, and crashed through his skull, killing him instantly. As he fell Brownell followed his shot by a thrust of his bayonet which went through Jackson's body."

Elmer Ellsworth was the first Union officer to die in combat, making President Lincoln one of the very first Americans to suffer the extraordinary personal pain of losing someone close in battle. Ellsworth's body lay in state in the East Room of the White House. The bereaved Lincoln called him "the greatest little man I ever met," adding, "So much of promised usefulness to one's country, and of bright hopes for one's self and friends, have rarely been so suddenly dashed, as in his fall."

Ellsworth's death galvanized the North. Songs were written about him and "Remember Ellsworth" became a patriotic slogan and was said to have caused thousands of men to enlist. New York's 44th Volunteer Infantry Regiment took the nicknames "Ellsworth Avengers" and "The People's Ellsworth Regiment."

Years later Private Brownell was awarded the Congressional Medal of Honor, the first soldier in that war to earn it. Jackson was honored by the Confederacy as the "First Martyr to the Cause of Southern Independence," noting he had been "killed while defending his property and personal rights."

Ellsworth's death ratcheted up demands on Lincoln to put down the rebellion quickly and harshly. Newspapers demanded that the Union army march on Richmond, believing that capturing the Confederate capital would end the war. But the US Army's senior general, Winfield Scott, urged a more tempered response. Lincoln had already imposed a naval blockade on the Southern coast, preventing supplies from reaching those ports by ship. "Old Fuss and Feathers," as Scott was known, proposed sending as many as eighty thousand troops down the entire length of the Mississippi River to the Gulf of Mexico, capturing all the points along the way, followed by an occupying force to cut the South in half, while at the same time massing Union troops along the entire northern border. The South would be trapped in an economic stranglehold, unable to either ship or receive goods and supplies, and forced to surrender.

Scott's "Anaconda Plan," as newspapers called it, comparing it to the deadly snake that slowly squeezed its victims to death, was widely unpopular. Northerners wanted this war ended quickly by a bold and overwhelming force, and Lincoln believed one massive stroke would scatter the rebels. The war cry "Forward to Richmond" was as much a demand as a patriotic

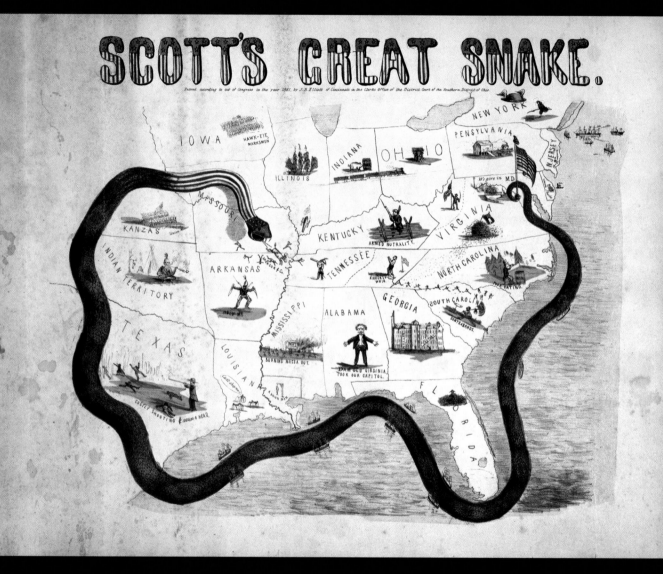

At the beginning of the war army general in chief Winfield Scott, wary of sending untrained armies of green recruits directly into battle against the Confederacy, proposed cutting off Confederate supply lines, as an anaconda slowly squeezes its victims, but impatience and rising bitterness made that impossible.

slogan. The president ordered General Irvin McDowell to take command of the motley collection of militia and raw volunteers and launch that offensive.

The road to Richmond ran right through Manassas Junction, the railroad hub twenty-five miles from Washington that connected Beauregard's Confederate Army of the Potomac with Major General Joe Johnston's Confederate Army of the Shenandoah. But to reach the junction McDowell's troops would have to cross a tributary of the Potomac known as Bull Run. Beauregard's twenty thousand men were camped on its banks, waiting for Lincoln to make his intentions known. Beauregard, still basking in his victory at Fort Sumter, wrote, "If I could only get the enemy to attack me . . . I would stake my reputation on the handsomest victory that could be hoped for."

Confederate president Jefferson Davis had considerably fewer options than Lincoln. Substantially outmanned and outgunned, the Confederacy would be forced to defend its territory. The problem was figuring out where Lincoln would mount his offensive. Davis's senior military adviser, General Robert E. Lee, believed Lincoln would march on Richmond, a city woefully unprepared to resist a determined attack. He needed to delay the Union army to provide sufficient time for the city to be fortified. But to accomplish that, he had to know which route they would follow.

McDowell had never commanded an army in battle and was respected far more for his logistical expertise than his strategic brilliance. He also was a realist, warning Lincoln that his army was untrained, untested, and often unruly. Lincoln reassured him, "You are green, it is true, but they are green also; you are all green alike." Historians generally fail to point out that Lincoln was as inexperienced in the art of warfare as most of his officers and was clearly influenced more by political necessities than military realities. He had been inaugurated only a few months earlier and since then had dealt with an unending series of crises. He had no long-term strategy, just a fervent hope that by capturing the Confederate capital the rebellion could be ended quickly and with as little bloodshed as possible.

McDowell agreed to march on Manassas but was adamant that Joe Johnston's nine-thousand-man Shenandoah army be prevented from reinforcing Beauregard. Union general Robert Patterson was ordered to move south from Maryland to engage Johnston.

At that time, it was difficult to know where a person's loyalties lay. Among the leading socialites in Washington was the merry widow Rose O'Neal Greenhow. The forty-seven-year-old mother of four daughters had long been connected closely to the government's power brokers, among them the bachelor president James Buchanan, senators, judges, business and administration executives—and military officers. Little happened in the capital that she did not know about. But what very few people knew about her was that she had given her allegiance to the Confederacy, joining an elaborate spy ring operating in Washington. She had been recruited by a former Union quartermaster, Confederate captain Thomas Jordan, who taught her a twenty-six-cipher code. While no one knows precisely how Rose Greenhow obtained her information, she admitted, "I employed every capacity with which God has endowed me, and the result was far more successful than my hopes could have flattered me to expect."

Among those men on whom she lavished her reputedly remarkable charms was Massachusetts senator Henry Wilson, the powerful chairman of the Military Affairs Committee. Presumably it was from Wilson that she learned that McDowell was about to march on Manassas. She concealed her coded warning in the hair bun of a young accomplice named Betty Duvall, who delivered it to General Beauregard near Bull Run. Several days later she sent a second message informing Beauregard that, as he remembered, "The enemy—55,000 strong, I believe—would positively commence that day his advance from Arlington Heights and Alexandria on to Manassas [near Bull Run], via Fairfax Courthouse and Centerville." Based on this intelligence President Davis ordered General Johnston to move immediately to reinforce Beauregard by rail. Patterson believed he had arrived in time to prevent Johnston from reinforcing Beauregard; in fact he sent a telegram announcing, "I have succeeded, in accordance with the wishes of the General-in-Chief, in keeping General Johnston's force at Winchester." But in reality Johnston's army had slipped away and was racing to Manassas by rail, by wagon, and on foot.

Rose Greenhow's warnings proved invaluable. After the battle Greenhow received a telegram reading, "Our President and our General direct me to thank you." Within months, though, her deception was uncovered by Allan Pinkerton, head of Union intelligence gathering. After several months in the Old Capitol Prison she was banished to the South. Eventually she spent two years in Europe raising funds for the Confederacy. She was granted an audience with Queen Victoria and was briefly engaged to an earl. She sailed home on a blockage-runner, which was spotted and chased by a Union ship near Wilmington, North Carolina. Against the captain's advice she boarded a lifeboat and attempted to row to shore. The lifeboat capsized in foul weather and the $2,000 in gold coins she had sewn into her undergarments and hidden in a pouch dragged her under. Her body was discovered on the banks of the Cape Fear River the next day.

As McDowell's thirty thousand men leisurely marched south, with soldiers stepping out of the ranks to pick berries, drink water, enjoy a patch of shade, or eat their rations,

Both sides used women to spy on the enemy. Harriet Tubman
returned often to the South to gain intelligence from slaves. And
early in the war Washington, DC, socialite Rose O'Neal Greenhow
used her feminine wiles to charm information out of Union leaders.
Her warning prepared Confederate troops at Bull Run for battle.

Beauregard's smaller force dug in along eight miles of Bull Run, guarding the bridges and
fords. McDowell's men took two days to finally get there. Meanwhile, spectators rushed to the
area, anxious to witness what many believed would be the climactic battle of the insurrection.
After the Union troops had thoroughly thrashed the rebels, they would occupy Richmond;
this battle would allow the Confederacy to surrender with honor—and rejoin the Union.

McDowell's battle plan was sound. While his main force would make a frontal assault,
several divisions would attack the Confederate flank and move behind them, catching them

President Lincoln flanked by the head of General McClellan's intelligence
service, Allan Pinkerton, and Major General John A. McClernand
at Antietam in 1862.

in a vise and cutting off their escape route to Richmond. His problem was that his officers were far too inexperienced to coordinate their movements and his men were barely able to follow orders. But the same was true for the Confederate army. Beauregard modeled his plan on Napoleon's brilliant tactics at Austerlitz, but success required a flanking maneuver far too complex for his army to execute.

On the morning of July 21, as politicians from Washington settled in near the battlefield to witness the great Union victory while enjoying food and drink, McDowell attacked. But to everyone's surprise, carefully planned strategies would make little difference in the outcome of this battle. The Battle of Bull Run was going to be the first great test of men and wills. It was to be the day the Civil War truly began.

Within minutes the innocent confidence on both sides had disappeared, replaced first by shock, then fear, and eventually horror and heroism. What Lincoln's ninety-day soldiers and the proud sons of the South had initially seen mostly as a brief adventure, a means of earning some needed money, demonstrating regional pride, or simply a taste of glory, dissolved almost instantly into a desperate attempt at survival. There was little communication between commanders, so any attempt at maintaining order failed; some soldiers deserted their posts and ran. Troops were dressed in an array of clothing representing their militias and designed more for parading than fighting—some Union troops were wearing gray and some rebel troops were in blue. Others were wearing their civilian work and farm clothes, making it difficult to determine friend from enemy. The fighting was so fierce that it is believed that General Beauregard had four horses shot out from under him during the battle. As *Boston Journal* reporter Charles Coffin wrote, "Men fall. . . . They are bleeding, torn, and mangled. . . . The trees are splintered, crushed, and broken, as if smitten by thunderbolts. . . . It is a new, strange, unanticipated experience to the soldiers of both armies, far different from what they thought it would be."

In the early fighting McDowell's numerical superiority allowed him to push the rebels back, and the Confederate troops began retreating toward Manassas Junction. Among the first heroes to emerge that day was Major Chatham Roberdeau Wheat, the commander of a flamboyant Confederate battalion called the Louisiana Tigers. Wheat's Tigers sustained a ferocious attack from the 2nd Rhode Island, but rather than retreating, Wheat's Tigers, wearing red shirts and carrying bowie knives, took the offensive, swarming down Matthews Hill and charging into the Union ranks. Roberdeau was shot in the lung and appeared to be dying; instead he said clearly, "I don't feel like dying today" and survived his wound. The Tigers' gallant stand had temporarily halted the Union advance—providing the time desperately needed for Joe Johnston's reinforcements to reach the battlefield.

Jefferson Davis had arrived at the battlefield in the early afternoon and was told, "Our line was broken, all was confusion, the army routed, and the battle lost." Union troops had successfully crossed Bull Run and were ready to advance on Manassas Junction. McDowell, too, believed, "The day is ours."

For the spectators it had begun as a glorious show. William Howard Russell reported in the London *Times*, "A lady with an opera glass . . . was quite beside herself when an unusually heavy discharge roused the current of her blood—'That was splendid. Oh my! Is not that first rate? I guess we will be in Richmond this time tomorrow.'"

The disorganized rebels retreated to a hill topped by the home of widow Judith Henry. They were relieved to join a brigade of five Virginia regiments commanded by a former Virginia Military Institute professor of natural and experimental philosophy and instructor of artillery, General Thomas Jonathan Jackson. Amid all the confusion and bloodshed, Jackson's well-trained and disciplined troops stood firm and composed, relentlessly firing their thirteen light cannons. He had cleverly placed them on the crest of the hill—and as they fired, their recoil drove them down the slope, where they could be reloaded safe from enemy fire. Confederate general Barnard Bee, trying desperately to rally his men, pointed to Jackson and shouted, "There is Jackson standing behind you like a stone wall! Let us determine to die here, and we will conquer. Rally behind the Virginians."

The first scratches of names that eventually would be deeply etched into American history were made that day—beginning with "Stonewall" Jackson. Jackson's Virginians had stood fast and stopped the Union attack—while suffering the largest number of casualties of any Confederate unit. During the battle Jackson had calmly raised his left hand high into the air—and his middle finger was hit by a bullet or piece of shrapnel. Although the wound was serious enough for doctors to recommend amputation—which he refused—he wrapped a handkerchief around it and continued fighting.

While most historians believe Bee admired Jackson's stand, others believe his words were meant as criticism, implying that Jackson's men had stood in place—like a stone wall—rather than rushing into the battle to support Bee's beleaguered troops. Bee died that afternoon before he might clarify his remarks.

Whatever the truth, no one would doubt Jackson's military leadership or personal courage. Just as General Beauregard was ready to accept defeat, admitting, "At this moment, I must confess my heart failed me," seventeen hundred of Joe Johnston's reinforcements reached the battlefield and a counterattack was launched. Union artillery, which had been brought up to Henry House Hill, was attacked by the 33rd Virginia, whose blue uniforms confused Union troops long enough to allow them to overrun the position. Jackson's emboldened troops rushed forward and captured several more artillery pieces.

McDowell ordered more Union regiments into the fight for Henry House Hill, but Jackson pressed his attack, ordering his troops: "Reserve your fire until they come within fifty yards! Then fire and give them the bayonet! And when you charge, yell like furies!" They did as ordered, instantly creating the famed Confederate battle cry known as the Rebel Yell. No one knows

General Irvin McDowell, seen here leaving his headquarters at Robert E. Lee's abandoned home in Arlington. McDowell's prewar experience was limited to staff work, and his poor leadership contributed to the Union defeat at the First Battle of Bull Run. He eventually became so unpopular that after a horse fell on him, one of his men wrote, "I heard someone propose three cheers for the horse."

precisely what the Rebel Yell sounded like—there probably were several different screams. It has been described as everything from a Native American war whoop to the shrill scream of a banshee, meant as much to transform an attacker's fear into courage as to terrorize the enemy.

With this great cry Jackson's men charged the center of the Union lines, while Johnston's reinforcements launched an attack on McDowell's depleted right flank. The Union line collapsed, and very quickly a strategic withdrawal turned into a panicked retreat that spread throughout the entire army and soon became a total rout.

Thousands of soldiers dropped their weapons and ran. McDowell's army had fallen apart. Union troops fled back across Bull Run, overrunning stunned spectators who also turned and ran for their lives. The roads back to Washington became clogged with dispirited troops, ambulances, horses, and carriages. Union general Ambrose Burnside described the scene: "For three miles . . . army wagons, sutler's teams, and private carriages, choked the passage. . . . [Wounded] horses, many of them in death-agony, galloped at random forward. . . . Wounded men, lying along the banks . . . appealed with raised hands to those who rode . . . but few regarded such petitions."

Late in the day Lincoln read a dispatch from a captain that stated, "General McDowell's army in full retreat through Centerville. The day is lost. Save Washington and the remnants of this army." Not until noon the following day did it become clear that the Confederates were not marching on the city.

Jefferson Davis had considered ordering Johnston to pursue and punish the federal troops, and perhaps chase them to the capital, but his army had also suffered grievous losses and was not capable of sustaining an offensive. But on that day it didn't matter: the Confederacy had won an astonishing victory. With it came a newfound confidence both in their ability to defeat a larger army and in the righteousness of their cause.

Northern arrogance also was shattered. The belief that this would be a brief and relatively bloodless war ended at Bull Run. McDowell lost 2,896 men killed, captured, or wounded, in addition to thousands of horses and a vast store of weapons; the Confederates suffered 1,982 casualties.

Although after an investigation the US Congress's Joint Committee on the Conduct of the War concluded that it was General Patterson's inability to detain Joe Johnston's forces in the Shenandoah that led to the defeat, McDowell received the blame. While Lincoln told him,

As this hand-drawn *Skeleton Map of Battlefield of Bull Run Virginia* illustrates, a lack of intelligence and poor communications made planning strategy very difficult. Battles turned on instantaneous and improvised decisions. ☞

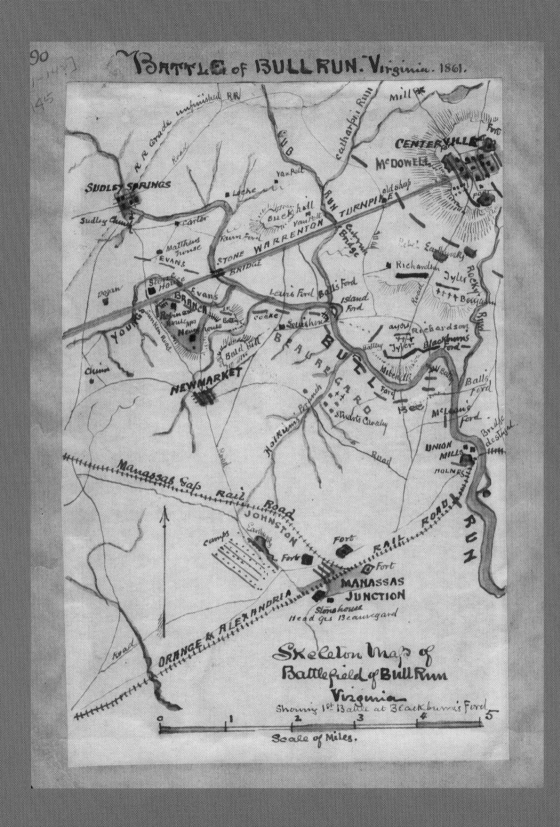

"I have not lost a particle of confidence in you," he replaced McDowell as commander of the dispirited Army of the Potomac with thirty-five-year-old general George McClellan. The very popular McClellan promptly set about building an army. New volunteers were enlisted for three years. The industrial North went to work turning out the necessities of war. "Little Mac," as the troops called him, had become greatly respected by his troops for keeping them well supplied and properly trained, and never committing them to battle without thorough preparation. His commitment to drilling and training, then more drilling and training, brought a sense of professionalism to his troops. But, relying on dubious intelligence, McClellan overestimated the number of Confederate troops. By then Congress had authorized the army to accept an additional five hundred thousand volunteers—and for the first time Lincoln considered enlisting free black men as well as escaped slaves. He finally decided against taking this controversial action, concerned that it might push border states like Missouri into the Confederacy.

Jefferson Davis also had to make command decisions. Rather than praising General

Johnston, who had been the most senior Union officer to resign his commission and join the Confederacy, Davis was critical of him for failing to pursue McDowell's retreating army. Johnston received a promotion but was furious that he did not get more credit for the victory at Bull Run and that several officers who had ranked below him in the prewar US Army now outranked him. President Davis, he complained, "seeks to tarnish my fair fame as a soldier and a man." The result was a bitterness between Davis and Johnston that was never healed. Beauregard also had difficulties with Davis, quarreling publicly about strategy and even suggesting that it was Davis's interference that had prevented his troops from pursuing McDowell all the way to Washington. While Johnston retained command of the Confederate army in northern Virginia, Beauregard was sent to the Mississippi to assist Confederate forces there, and the

Photographer Mathew Brady received permission from Lincoln to document the war—at his own expense. "A spirit in my feet said 'Go,' and I went," he said. This 1861 picture shows General George McClellan and his generals of division.

suddenly famous Stonewall Jackson was promoted to major general and dispatched to defend the Shenandoah Valley.

The Union was beginning to accept that the Confederacy was far stronger and more determined than initially believed. Congress authorized the army to accept an additional fifty thousand volunteers.

During this period both sides made attempts to standardize uniforms. While in history the North and the South are often referred to as the Blue and the Gray, even after the First Battle of Bull Run uniform colors and designs were mostly haphazard. Uniforms were usually made of wool, issued in only four sizes, and rarely washed, to prevent them from shrinking—although some poorly manufactured Union dress was made of a material called shoddy, while Confederates were known to use a cotton-wool mixture that became known as jean. Federal troops had traditionally been dressed in blue, while Confederate gray supposedly was based on West Point uniforms. In fact, soldiers on both sides wore whatever clothing was readily available. Some Confederate states provided smart, regulation uniforms, while others let their volunteers fend for themselves. By the end of the war, rather than the gray of legend, many Confederate troops were reduced to wearing coats and pants dyed a mousy color called butternut.

Northern regiments had greater resources and were more consistently clothed in their familiar blue uniforms, although that did not prevent some units from wearing flamboyant variations. Debonair George A. Custer, for example, who first gained recognition for retaining his composure and providing cover for the Union at Bull Run, later became known for his tailored blue uniform heavily trimmed in gold.

The Confederate flag—the red, white, and blue Stars and Bars—had also caused considerable confusion at Bull Run, as it too easily was mistaken for the US Stars and Stripes. It was even blamed for one Confederate artillery unit firing on another. To prevent that from happening again, General Beauregard requested a distinctly different battle flag be designed. When the first states seceded, Southern politician William Porcher Miles had proposed a red flag with a blue cross containing white stars for the new Confederacy. Although originally rejected—some members of the selection committee thought it looked too much like "a pair of suspenders"—it fit perfectly Beauregard's request for "a war flag to be used only on the field of battle." The original flag was sewn by a beautiful young Southern patriot from Baltimore named Hetty Carr Cary. Miles introduced his battle flag with the hope that the South, "under its untarnished folds . . . find . . . everlasting immunity from an atrocious despotism." While throughout the rest of the war there were several different versions of the flags, Miles's "Southern Cross" eventually became commonly recognized and accepted as the Confederate flag.

For one or both of us the time is come,
If Slavery is fit to live, let Freedom fall.

TRIAL BY BATTLE.

Oh, ho, if that's the case come on, Old Link
And down with him who first cries — Hold!
*Let's have a drink.*

Historians argue that there were several causes of the war. But as this hand-colored lithograph published during the first year of the war illustrates, it really was fought over slavery. Without slaves, the cotton-based Southern economy couldn't survive.

Following the stunning outcome at Bull Run, both the North and South paused to adjust to the new situation. While the growing armies were trained and equipped, there was little fighting in the east. As months passed Lincoln continued to praise McClellan in public—and when seventy-five-year-old Winfield Scott retired, Lincoln named McClellan general-in-chief of the Union army—but privately Lincoln became anxious about McClellan's lack of initiative. At one point in early 1862 he said in frustration, "If General McClellan isn't going to use his army, I'd like to borrow it for a time."

But McClellan refused to be pressured to take action until he believed his army was fully prepared, writing to his wife, "I can't tell you how disgusted I am becoming with these wretched politicians—they are a most despicable set of men. . . . The President is nothing more than a well-meaning baboon."

While McClellan dawdled in Virginia, in the west General Ulysses Grant finally gave the north the victory it had been demanding. Born Hiram Ulysses Grant in Ohio in 1822, his name had been jumbled when he enrolled at West Point and he became Ulysses Simpson Grant—after his mother's family, the Simpsons. He had been ordered by General Henry W. Halleck to hold Memphis and western Tennessee. "Old Brains," as Halleck was known, preferred to consolidate his victories and defend as much territory as possible rather than continuing to press the enemy. But this proved too tame for the audacious Grant.

As both presidents Lincoln and Davis were very aware, the British government was watching events closely, debating whether or not to recognize the Confederacy. A conclusive rebel victory in either the east or west might have resulted in England officially recognizing the American South as an independent nation. Other European countries quite probably would have followed the lure of cheap cotton, convincing them to provide support for the southern cause—which would have been a disaster for the Union. Conversely, wrote Lincoln's minister to Great Britain, Charles Francis Adams, "I feel that one clear victory at home might perhaps save us a foreign war."

The first test would come in the west. Two generally parallel rivers created a military highway into the Confederate west; the Cumberland River flowed to Nashville and the Tennessee provided a water route to northern Mississippi and Alabama. Just over the Kentucky border the Confederates had constructed two forts to prevent the Union from gaining access to those natural highways—Fort Henry on the Tennessee River and, just twelve miles away, Fort Donelson, guarding the Cumberland. Grant had previously requested permission from Halleck to attack Fort Henry, planning to march his fifteen thousand troops behind a flotilla of nine ironclad gunboats, "and I had not uttered many sentences before I was cut short as if my plan was preposterous."

When the greatly outnumbered Confederate general Albert Sidney Johnston launched an offensive to occupy Kentucky, hoping to gain by gumption and cunning what he lacked in men and resources, Halleck responded by ordering Grant to put his plan into action.

Grant captured Fort Henry in a fight lasting only two hours. The fort had been poorly constructed at water level, and the combination of rising spring tides and a relentless pounding from the gunboats made defending it impossible. The nation had finally found a general who

George Peter Alexander Healy gained fame for his oil portraits of famous Americans, like this flattering portrayal of U. S. Grant. When in the field Grant generally preferred the utilitarian dress of a Union soldier.

One of the first stirring Union victories of the war was the February 1862 capture
of Fort Henry in an attack led by ironclad gunboats that lasted only two hours
before the Confederates surrendered. Steam-powered ironclads changed naval warfare
forever; most of the world's navies still relied on wooden warships, and ironclads could
ram wooden ships and survive most artillery shells. To meet the threat, submarines
and submerged explosives called torpedoes were developed.

loved to fight. Grant immediately marched on Fort Donelson. To protect Nashville, Johnston reinforced the fort with an additional seventeen thousand troops. The Confederates were ready for this fight; firing from a higher position, the fort's artillery successfully disabled the gunboats. As the commander of the ironclad USS *Carondelet* remembered, "Our decks were so slippery with the blood of the brave men who had fallen, that we could hardly stand on them until we covered them with sand." Another shot from the fort "beheaded two seamen and cut another in two, sending blood and brains over the captain, officers, and men who were standing near them."

But worn down after three days, the Confederate garrison attempted to break out and make it to Nashville. They almost succeeded; Grant was away from the battlefield when they made their break at five o'clock in the morning and successfully took control of the road to Nashville. By the time Grant returned his flank was collapsing, but here he built his legend. Galloping into his lines, he shouted to his demoralized men, "The enemy is trying to escape and he must not be permitted to do so!" His confidence spread through the ranks and his army stiffened, turning back the attempt to escape. The road was recaptured, forcing the Confederates to return to the fort.

Like so many men fighting against each other in this war, Grant and the Confederate commander, Simon Bolivar Buckner, had once served together. In fact, after the Mexican-American War, when Grant was penniless in New York, Buckner had assisted him. But when

Before secession, the dashing Confederate general Simon Bolivar Buckner had served with Grant in Mexico and in civilian life provided him with help when he was in need. But when Buckner, in command of Fort Donelson, asked Grant for terms, he was offered nothing other than unconditional surrender.

Buckner asked for surrender terms Grant responded, "No terms except an unconditional and immediate surrender can be accepted. I propose to move immediately upon your works."

"Unconditional Surrender" Grant, as the suddenly enamored public nicknamed him, wired Halleck that he had captured "12,000 to 15,000 prisoners, . . . 20,000 stands of arms, 48 pieces of artillery, 17 heavy guns, from 2,000 to 4,000 horses, and large quantities of commissary stores." He also had captured the imagination of the American public and, more important, the attention of President Lincoln.

"The blow was most disastrous and almost without remedy," A. S. Johnston wrote to Davis. As a result Nashville was evacuated and Johnston withdrew most of his troops from Tennessee. And in England, those politicians urging public support for the Confederacy were quieted. The threat of European intervention was ended, a devastating blow to the Confederacy.

Lincoln had only a very few days to savor this victory. While the armies were battling at Fort Donelson, inside the White House Lincoln's two young sons, Willie and Tad, were

fighting for their own lives, both of them struck with "bilious fever." The president and Mary Todd Lincoln had four sons. Their second son, Edward Baker Lincoln, was not yet four years old when he died in 1850 of pulmonary tuberculosis. The public image of the Lincolns and their sons living happily in the White House seemed to delight the nation. Mary Todd Lincoln was the first woman to be referred to as the First Lady, although she was not especially popular. Among the first things she did after Lincoln took office was begin renovating the dilapidated White House, trying to bring new style and elegance to the presidential residence by replacing ripped and stained carpeting, cleaning tobacco-stained floors and woodwork, and getting rid of rats. The cost was far greater than the congressional appropriation, which looked unseemly to a nation at war. But Mary Lincoln had to fight demons far worse than public opinion.

Four days after the surrender in the west, eleven-year-old Willie Lincoln died of what

While the Union victory at Fort Donelson in February 1862 did not captivate the public like the massive battles in the east, it provided a huge morale boost to the staggered North, cost the Confederacy the manufacturing capacity of the upper South, and served to elevate the obscure U. S. Grant to national prominence.

later was believed to be typhoid fever. The Lincolns were devastated. "My poor boy," the president said. "He was too good for this earth. God has called him home. I know he is much better off in Heaven, but then we loved him so! It is hard—hard—to have him die!" He did not return to his office for several days, but the death of a second son was particularly hard on Mary Lincoln. She began showing the first signs of derangement, although it would be many years before her oldest son, Robert, had her institutionalized.

In her grief Mary Lincoln eventually turned to spiritualists, believing it might be possible to make contact with her beloved son in the afterlife. While attending a circle, or a séance, at the Georgetown home of a well-known Washington medium, Cranstoun Laurie, she met twenty-one-year-old Henrietta "Nettie" Colburn, a medium with whom she very quickly became close, even arranging for her a position as a clerk in the Department of Agriculture. Eventually Mary Lincoln was hosting séances in the Red Parlor of the White House. Although the president may have wandered into at least one of these circles, giving rise to stories that he, too, was a believer in the supernatural, most historians agree he tolerated these visits to help his wife deal with her growing depression.

Lincoln's own despair was channeled into frustration at McClellan's lack of progress; rumors spread in Washington that McClellan secretly sympathized with the South on the issue of slavery and lacked the will to push for an all-out victory. McClellan was outraged and during a meeting with Lincoln told him, "In a manner perhaps not altogether decorous . . . I could permit no one to couple the word treason with my name." Finally, in March, Lincoln relieved McClellan of overall command of the Union armies, instead placing him in charge of the federal army around Washington, which became known as the Army of the Potomac. McClellan, who was so convinced of his own superiority that he was sometimes contemptuous of the president, accepted his demotion, promising to "work just as cheerfully as ever before, and . . . no consideration of self will in any manner interfere with the discharge of my public duties." Lincoln obviously accepted that—then ordered him to move on Richmond.

As the War of the Rebellion, the Great Rebellion, or the War for Southern Independence, as it was known at various times in the different regions of the country, reached the end of its first year, any semblance of the original innocence and confidence was long gone. Lincoln's initial resolve to end the fighting with as little bloodshed as possible to enable reunification was a forgotten dream. Bitterness had hardened into vicious hatred. And any remaining hope that some resolution might soon be reached was ended on the banks of the Tennessee River at Shiloh Church.

The battle began when newly promoted major general U. S. Grant's forty-five thousand troops pursued the Confederates up the Tennessee River to the Mississippi border. He was ordered to stop about twenty miles from the massive railroad junction at Corinth, Mississippi, where A. S. Johnston's forty thousand men had made camp, to await reinforcements. Overly confident that the rebels would not dare leave the safety of their position, the Union relaxed its defenses. This was not the kind of error that either side would make later in the war. General William Tecumseh Sherman would report in his memoir that early in the morning of Sunday, April 6, he was shocked when he "rode out along my lines, and . . . received from some bushes in a ravine to the left front a volley which killed my orderly, Holliday. About the same time I saw the rebel lines of battle in front coming down on us as far as the eye could reach. . . . In a few minutes the battle of 'Shiloh' began with extreme fury."

Johnston, supported by Beauregard, had launched a desperate attack. Sherman's men were stunned at the size of the rebel force and made a valiant effort to hold their ground— killing or wounding 300 of the 6th Mississippi's 425 men—before finally retreating. Union troops dropped back toward the Tennessee River to form a stronger defensive perimeter. "The surprise was complete," wrote one of Johnston's aides. ". . . [The army's] colors, arms, stores, and ammunition were abandoned. The breakfasts of men were on the table, the officers' baggage and apparel left in the tents." The Confederates raced into empty campsites, sometimes pausing to eat warm meals that had been abandoned.

Grant had been absent when the attack began, meeting reinforcements in Savannah, but returned immediately to organize a defensive position at Shiloh Church. Throughout the first day of fighting he rode along the Union lines, rallying his troops; three of his horses were killed under him and he suffered two wounds. Through the day his troops were pushed back and re-formed defensive positions eight different times—but they never ceased fighting. They finally stalled the Confederate advance at an old wagon road that covered about a half mile of the front. The Sunken Road, as it became known, provided cover for Grant's troops as Johnston's army made the mistake of trying to attack through a dense thicket without artillery support. Grant ordered the position held at all costs. Union troops doggedly repulsed numerous attacks, as the bodies of rebel troops piled up. One survivor likened the unforgettable sound of bullets cutting through the brush to a swarm of hornets, causing the attackers to name this deadly half mile the Hornet's Nest.

At midafternoon General Johnston, arguably the Confederates' most able commander at that time, was struck in his leg by a minié ball; the wound initially seemed minimal, but the shot had severed an artery and within minutes he had bled to death. Johnston was the highest-ranking officer to be killed in battle during the entire war. Beauregard assumed command and continued the attack.

In 1885, artist Théophile Poilpot and twelve assistants painted a four-hundred-foot by fifty-foot panorama depicting the Battle of Shiloh, which was displayed in the round in Chicago. It enabled viewers standing in the middle to feel as if they were at the event. This is a chillingly accurate detail from the chaotic fighting at the Hornet's Nest used to advertise that display.

Late in the day the Confederates finally assembled sufficient artillery—sixty-two cannons—to dislodge the defenders of the Hornet's Nest, who ran for their lives under the barrage. But their courageous stand had provided time for Grant to establish a strong defensive line at the riverbank. The rebels made a last charge but Grant said confidently, "Delay counts for everything with us. Tomorrow we shall attack them with fresh troops, and drive them." By the end of the day Union troops had been driven back as far as two miles. But on Monday Grant's reinforced army counterattacked and savaged the outnumbered Confederates. By early afternoon Beauregard ordered his "utterly disorganized and demoralized" troops back to Corinth.

The mountain of casualties staggered both the North and South. The Union suffered 13,047 men killed or wounded, while the rebels lost 10,694 men—among them the president's brother-in-law, Samuel Todd, who had pledged his allegiance to the Confederacy, enlisting in the 4th Louisiana. Both sides had learned a terrible truth. As General Sherman wrote, "The scenes on this field would have cured anybody of war. Mangled bodies, dead, dying, in every conceivable shape, without heads, legs . . . the horrid nature of this war, and the piles of dead gentlemen and wounded and maimed makes me more anxious than ever for some hope of an end but I know such a thing cannot be for a long, long time."

A long, long time.

Music served a vital role in the lives of both Union and Confederate troops, from the popular tunes playing in the background as they marched off to war to those songs played in their honor when they came home or were buried. Soldiers on both sides knew most of the songs; even Lincoln admitted loving the unoffial Southern anthem, "Dixie," claiming, "As we had captured the rebel army, we had also captured the rebel tune." Most regiments had their own bands, and morale-boosting music was often played in camp, when marching, or even, on occasion, during battle—although when fighting started most often musicians were ordered to the rear to assist surgeons in amputations.

In 1863, Union and Confederate bands on either side of the Rappahannock River alternated playing popular songs, and on several occasions these encounters ended with soldiers from both sides joining together to sing an exceedingly wistful version of "Home, Sweet Home."

Many of the most popular songs have survived, among them "The Battle Cry of Freedom," "The Battle Hymn of the Republic," "When Johnny Comes Marching Home Again," "Tenting Tonight on the Old Camp Ground," "Tramp! Tramp! Tramp!," "John Brown's Body," and perhaps the most easily recognized of all, "Taps." In recognition of the importance of music, Union general Philip Sheridan said after the fighting ended, "Music has done its share, and more than its share, in winning this war."

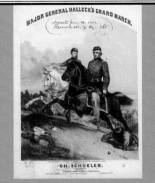

# THREE

# A MARCH TO GREATNESS

## Robert E. Lee Takes Command

The leaders of the Union and Confederate armies knew one another well. Many of them had sat together in the classrooms of West Point. They had trained together, become friends, and fought together. They knew the size of one another's courage, they knew who was bold and who was reticent, they knew whose pride was greater than his good sense, and they knew who let sorrow color his decisions. They knew one another's strengths and weaknesses; they knew one another's secrets. This intimate knowledge made the war even more horrible.

Several of them had first been tested during the Mexican-American War, where they had served together under General Winfield Scott. Joe Johnston was there. Thomas Jonathan Jackson—later to gain fame as "Stonewall" Jackson—saw his first combat there. Jefferson Davis, commander of the 1st Mississippi Rifles, helped prevent an inglorious rout during the Battle of Buena Vista. But it was during the decisive Battle of Cerro Gordo that these future leaders truly proved their mettle.

Only a week after his 1865 surrender at Appomattox, General Robert E. Lee agreed to pose outside his Richmond home for Mathew Brady. The series of six poignant photographs—including this hand-tinted portrait—became quite popular.

In April 1847, Mexican general Santa Anna's twelve thousand well-fortified troops blocked Scott's path to Mexico City. Scott began preparing a frontal assault, which would have resulted in thousands of casualties. But Lieutenant Pierre G. T. Beauregard believed it was possible to flank Santa Anna's dug-in troops by cutting a road through seemingly impassable terrain. Lieutenant George McClellan, a skilled engineer, believed that artillery could not be transported over the steep hills and through deep ravines, but Scott sent Captain Robert E. Lee to determine if passage was possible. Lee found the way and, as Lieutenant U. S. Grant wrote in his memoir, "Under the supervision of the engineers, roadways had been opened over chasms to the right where the walls were so steep that men could barely climb them. Animals could not. . . . The engineers . . . led the way and the troops followed."

Lee's daring, especially contrasted to McClellan's faith in order, overwhelming force, and a direct attack, captured Scott's respect and admiration. "He is," Scott said, "the very best soldier I ever saw in the field." By the end of the Mexican-American War, he had become a close confidant of Scott's and had been promoted to the temporary rank of brevet lieutenant colonel.

Following that victorious war, Lee was appointed superintendent of the Military Academy at West Point, where he trained many of the men who would serve under him—and against him—in the Civil War. Although he had inherited slaves and his own position on slavery has

The Battle of Cerro Gordo in the Mexican-American War brought together many of the young officers who would lead the armies in the Civil War, including Grant and Lee. Mexican leader Santa Anna was so completely surprised by the flanking attack that he was forced to flee, as seen in this lithograph, without his artificial leg, which was captured and put on display.

long been debated, he wrote in 1856, "There are few, I believe, in this enlightened age, who will not acknowledge that slavery as an institution is a moral and political evil." But he was not in favor of secession, adding several years later, "I can anticipate no greater calamity for the country than the dissolution of the Union."

As the nation moved closer to war, it was not at all surprising that Lincoln chose Lee to command the Union army. There could not have been a better choice; in addition to his military experience, few men had deeper roots in the founding of the Republic than Lee. He traced his lineage to Henry Lee, a member of the governing council of the Virginia Colony and for a time its acting governor. Two other relatives, Richard Henry Lee and Francis Lightfoot Lee, were the only brothers to sign the Declaration of Independence. His father was General "Light Horse Harry" Lee, a Revolutionary War hero who was present at Cornwallis's surrender at Yorktown and later became governor of Virginia. His own father-in-law was the adopted grandson of George Washington. It was his father who put down the historic Whiskey Rebellion against taxation; and it was Robert E. Lee who decades later ended John Brown's rebellion at Harpers Ferry and brought him to justice.

Lee's own fate, he knew, was tied to his beloved home state of Virginia. In anticipation of the war he told a friend, "If Virginia stands by the old Union, so will I. But if she secedes . . . then I will follow my native state with my sword and, if need be, my life."

The day after Virginia seceded Lincoln offered Lee the command of the United States Army. Undoubtedly Scott pointed out to him that Scott, too, was the son of a Virginian but that he had chosen to honor the oath of allegiance to the federal government he had taken more than fifty years earlier, "with my sword, even if my own native state assails it." Although Lee had anticipated this agonizing situation, his wife, Mary Lee, described making this decision as "the severest struggle" of his life. How could he take up arms against the South? Even so, Winfield Scott must have been shocked when Lee ended his thirty-two-year career by resigning his commission. "Lee," Scott snapped, "you have made the greatest mistake of your life."

Three days later Virginia's governor appointed Robert E. Lee commander in chief of that state's military and naval forces. A month later, when those forces were absorbed into the Confederate army, President Jefferson Davis, who while serving as secretary of war a decade earlier had appointed Lee superintendent of West Point, made him his chief military adviser. Like McClellan, Lee initially set about transforming an array of state militias into an army, relying on their common purpose to bring them together as a unified fighting force. His first few months were spent working behind a desk in Richmond. It wasn't until September that he took command in the field, which proved to be a dismal failure.

General Winfield Scott, who led the American assault on Mexico City, served as an active duty general longer than any man in history. The "Grand Old Man of the Army" was its general in chief for two decades.

Lee's objective was to rally support for the Confederacy in western Virginia, which did not support secession and within months would form its own government pledging support to the Union. In September 1861, Lee launched an attack on outnumbered Union forces occupying the fort on Cheat Mountain. In his overly complex plan, five columns were to follow different paths up the four-thousand-foot mountain and converge on the fort at the same time. Everything went wrong, there was no communication between those columns, and the attack was called off. Lee barely escaped capture, his son was wounded, and his close friend and relative John Washington was killed. Lee stumbled around western Virginia for the next three months without achieving a single victory.

Lee's sterling reputation had been badly tarnished. When he was recalled to the capital, the *Richmond Examiner* reported he had been "outwitted, outmaneuvered and outgeneraled." Critics began referring to him as "Granny Lee," "The Great Entrencher," even the "King of Spades" because his troops too often seemed to be devoted to digging defensive earthworks rather than attacking. Davis reassigned him to supervise the coastal defense of South Carolina.

Redemption came the following spring. The whispers questioning McClellan's loyalties had grown louder and Lincoln demanded a campaign against Richmond. The president proposed a second overland offensive through Manassas, but McClellan had a more audacious plan. Plagued by poor intelligence from Allan Pinkerton that warned him, woefully inaccurately, that Joe Johnston was waiting at Manassas Junction with as many as 150,000 men, he elected to go around them. McClellan bypassed Manassas entirely by loading his Army of the Potomac on transports and landing 130,000 troops, 15,000 horses and mules, 44 artillery batteries, and sufficient ammunition and supplies at Fort Monroe, intending to march up the peninsula formed by the York and James Rivers to Richmond. Confederate general John Magruder's small army on the peninsula was badly outnumbered, but, aware of McClellan's reputation for caution, he marched the same troops back and forth and set decoy campfires to create the impression that many more soldiers were in camp. Captured Confederate prisoners continued the deception, claiming that "Prince John" (as Magruder had been nicknamed at West Point for his acting ability) had 40,000 men and Johnston was only a day away. The ploy worked and, rather than smashing through a weak defensive line and racing to Richmond, McClellan besieged strategically unimportant Yorktown. Lincoln urged him to attack, warning him, "It is indispensable to you that you strike a blow." The president's secretary John Hay wrote that the general "sits trembling before the handful of men at Yorktown, afraid either to fight or run."

Deceived by faulty intelligence, McClellan moved agonizingly slowly against Yorktown, waiting for promised reinforcements. "He is an admirable engineer," Lincoln once said in frustration, "but he seems to have a special talent for a stationary engine." While he stalled, Stonewall Jackson was building his own legend in the Shenandoah Valley, marching his small but highly mobile "foot cavalry" as much as thirty miles a day in a brilliant campaign that once again threatened Washington. Secretary of War Edwin McMasters Stanton received intelligence that "leaves no doubt that the enemy in great force are marching on Washington." "The Great Scare" proved entirely false; the reinforcements McClellan expected were instead ordered to the valley.

But Lincoln was done waiting, ordering McClellan to "either attack Richmond or give up the job." The day before McClellan launched his assault on Yorktown the fifteen thousand Confederates in that city slipped away, preparing for the defense of the capital. As McClellan's Army of the Potomac moved cautiously closer to Richmond, the outnumbered Johnston decided to attack before all of McClellan's forces crossed the treacherous Chickahominy River. It was a fight that changed the war, although no one could have imagined it. Johnston's plan worked, pushing Union forces back, until reinforcements were able to make it across the river. In a hectic battle at Fair Oaks, Johnston rode along his lines—and was hit by two shots and knocked unconscious; he fell from his horse.

The battle continued into a second day. Union troops pushed to within four miles of Richmond, then paused and withdrew to an earlier position. Once again, McClellan camped to await reinforcements.

The injured Johnston could no longer command the army. Davis put Robert E. Lee in charge. That little twist of fate, born of necessity, would make all the difference. Lee had spent his life preparing for this command; he had a genius for military strategy, he had the respect

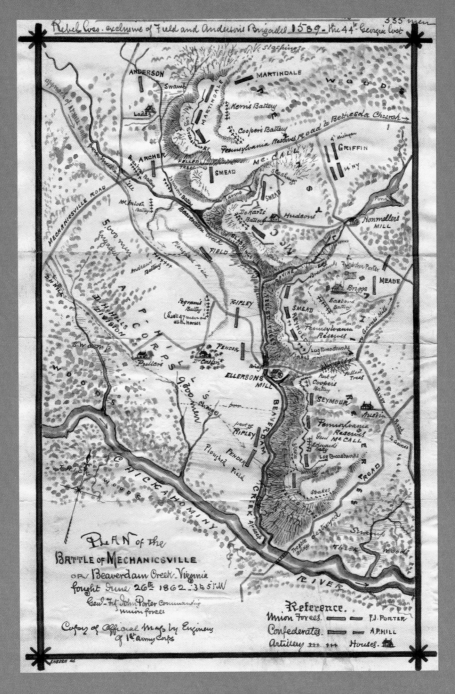

During the war publishers in both the North and South
produced maps of the battles for a public with an almost
insatiable desire for the latest news. So many families had
relatives in the war that there was a widespread hunger for
any reports. This is a map of the second day's fighting in the
Seven Days' Battle of June and July 1862.

of his army, and he was supremely confident. Within months he would fight his way into American history.

Lee inherited a dispirited army. Morale and supplies were low and his army was facing a far superior force. After securing his defenses to make certain the bluecoats would pay in blood for every yard of dirt they gained, Lee attacked the Union left flank at Mechanicsville. That attack failed, at least partially because once again his generals were not yet able to carry out his strategy, and he suffered grievous casualties. But rather than settling for the temporary safety of Richmond, he quickly launched another attack, and another, and yet another. The rebels attacked McClellan's men at Gaines's Mill, at Garnett's and Golding's Farm, at Savage's Station, and at White Oak Swamp. He suffered tremendous casualties but continued to attack, threatening to sever McClellan's supply lines. In fact, Lee remained so calm and proud throughout the entire Seven Days' Battle, never showing the slightest emotion, that his men began calling him the Marble Man.

Unlike McClellan, who rarely appeared on a battlefield, both Lee and Stonewall Jackson liked to be in the thick of the fighting. In fact, later in the war, when Lee's men urged him to stay safely in the rear, he uttered his famous words of caution, "It is well that war is so terrible, lest we should grow too fond of it."

Lee had taken a great gamble with his audacious strategy: by attacking he had left Richmond vulnerable. But he had the measure of his opponent, feeling confident that McClellan would not risk an all-out assault on the city. He was right. McClellan was convinced that Lee had positioned 110,000 men between the Union army and the city—while in fact there were fewer than 30,000. The war might have been won that week, but McClellan instead protected his army. Union general Philip Kearny begged McClellan to allow him to march on the Confederate capital, telling him, "I can go straight into Richmond! A single division can do it, but to play safe, use two divisions."

Finally, relentless rebel attacks pushed the Union troops back across the Chickahominy, back down the Virginia Peninsula, and away from the capital. Richmond was saved. As McClellan retreated, the irate Kearny laced into him, telling him in front of other officers, "I . . . protest against this order for retreat. We ought, instead of retreating, to follow up the enemy and take Richmond; and, in full view of all the responsibility of such a declaration, I say to you all, such an order can only be prompted by cowardice or treason."

McClellan still did not understand how badly he had been outmaneuvered by Lee, telegraphing Stanton, "I have lost this battle because my force was too small. . . . I have seen too many dead and wounded comrades to feel otherwise than that the government has not

General Scott called General Philip Kearny, seen here leading a charge at the Battle of
Chantilly on September 1, 1862, "the bravest man I ever knew." When Kearny was
killed several hours later, after encountering a rebel patrol, Confederate general A. P.
Hill said sadly, "He deserved a better fate than to die in the mud."

sustained this army. . . . I owe no thanks to you or to any other persons in Washington. You have done your best to sacrifice this army."

Lincoln responded diplomatically: With Stonewall Jackson victorious in the Shenandoah Valley, he said, he needed sufficient troops to protect Washington. But he was done with McClellan's incessant requests for more and more troops.

Lee emerged from the Seven Days' Battle a Confederate hero, although personally he was extremely disappointed he was not able to pursue and destroy McClellan's army. It is difficult to appreciate the awe in which Robert E. Lee was held throughout the South. The Confederacy was at war with a substantially larger force from a far more industrialized region capable of properly supplying its army, while the Southern agrarian economy was stagnating. Most industrial production in the South fell into Union hands early in the war. But what they lacked in resources they made up for in determination. While many Northerners wondered why they were fighting this war, Southerners knew they were defending their unique culture. For them slavery was both an economic necessity and the symbol of white racial superiority. What Lee gave them was hope and the noble sense that they were fighting to protect their homes and history rather than slavery. Winning a war against a larger, better-equipped army required the kind of courage, tactical skill, and inspired leadership that Lee had demonstrated. He exemplified the Southern man of honor who had given up his home and his career to fight for the cause. Robert E. Lee literally was a man for whom his troops would give their lives. Faith was an important weapon, and the South believed in him.

With each battlefield success Lee's legend grew larger. Part of that legend was his relationship with his noble horse, Traveller. In those times, a man's horse could make the difference between living and dying. A horse that responded quickly, that wasn't spooked by battle sounds, that could be ridden long and hard was invaluable. That was Traveller, who himself became such a celebrity that his tail and mane were thinned by people plucking hairs as souvenirs. Stephen Vincent Benét described him in an excerpt from his epic poem *John Brown's Body*, titled "Army of Northern Virginia":

And now at last,
Comes Traveller and his master. Look at them well.
The horse is an iron-grey, sixteen hands high,
Short back, deep chest, strong haunch, flat legs, small head,
Delicate ear, quick eye, black mane and tail,
Wise brain, obedient mouth.

Few images inspired more pride and confidence throughout the Confederacy than that of Robert E. Lee astride his noble steed Traveller. This is from an oil painting by L. Valdemar Fischer.

Lee had purchased the four-year-old American Saddlebred, who had been named Jeff Davis at birth, for $200 in 1861. He was a high-spirited horse, and Lee named him Traveller because he moved so beautifully. While he was not Lee's only horse, he was the one Lee rode throughout the major battles of the war, from the Seven Days' Battle through to the end.

Lincoln's admiration for Lee had led him to offer him command of the Union army, so he must have watched in dismay as Lee took charge of the Confederate army. Lee's boldness served to magnify McClellan's reticence. His bravado made McClellan's steady but dull nature appear even more lackluster. Lincoln searched his officer corps for a man who would stand up against Lee, and he thought he'd found him in General John Pope.

Lincoln and Pope had known each other in Illinois, where the president had argued cases in front of the general's father, Judge Nathaniel Pope. After being named commander of the Army of the Mississippi early in 1862, John Pope had distinguished himself with a victory at Island No. 10 in which he'd lost only twenty-three men while taking five thousand Confederate prisoners, successfully opening the upper Mississippi to the federal army. After being ordered east and given command of the Army of Virginia, he undoubtedly earned

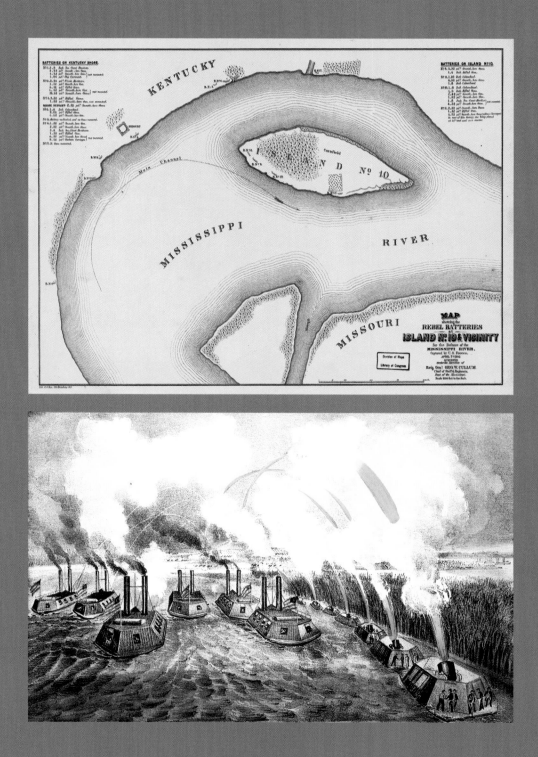

Lincoln's favor when he told the Joint Committee on the Conduct of the War, "I mean to attack . . . at all times that I can get the opportunity."

Finally.

While John Pope had indeed enjoyed military success, his true gift was self-promotion. Almost immediately he earned the disdain of the veteran soldiers in his new command, belittling their sacrifices and their courage while severely criticizing McClellan, telling them,

> I have come to you from the West, where we have always seen the backs of our enemies; from an army whose business it has been to seek the adversary and to beat him when he was found; whose policy has been attack and not defense. . . . I am sure that you long for an opportunity to win the distinction you are capable of achieving. That chance I shall endeavor to give you. Meantime I desire you to dismiss from your minds certain phrases which I am sorry to find so much in vogue amongst you. I hear constant talk of "taking strong positions and holding them," of "lines of retreat" and "bases of supplies." Let us discard such ideas. . . . Success and glory are in the advance; disaster and shame lurk in the rear.

Pope also had brought east with him a military style considered unusually harsh. He warned civilians that they would be responsible for "attacks upon trains or straggling soldiers by bands of guerrillas in their neighborhood," threatening that any home from which shots were fired would be razed and its residents imprisoned, and anyone involved in that type of attack "shall be shot, without awaiting civil process." He told his commanders that their troops could confiscate whatever food or supplies were needed to successfully prosecute the war if Southern farmers refused to sell to them. He went so far as to threaten that anyone corresponding with a member of the Confederacy, even a family member, could be executed.

His proclamations were signed, pompously, "from headquarters in the saddle," which caused people to suggest that perhaps his headquarters actually were in his hindquarters.

Lincoln shrewdly did not replace the popular McClellan with Pope; rather, he detached specific units from McClellan's command and transferred them to the newly created Army of Virginia under Pope.

**War news spread slowly, but each battle seemed monumentally important. The weeklong Battle of Island No. 10, fought on land and river, opened the upper Mississippi to the Union navy and threatened to cut the Confederacy in half.**

To the distress of many soldiers, General John Pope's victory at Island No. 10 caused Lincoln to give him command of the Army of Virginia. "His pompous orders . . . greatly disgusted his army from the first. . . . All hated him," wrote General A. S. Williams, who served on his staff. Pope held his command for less than six months, being relieved after his defeat at the Second Battle of Bull Run.

As much as officers and troops respected McClellan, they grew to despise Pope. Brigadier General Samuel D. Sturgis summed up those feelings quite accurately when he said, "I don't care for John Pope one pinch of owl dung." McClellan himself was furious, writing Lincoln that this was a war that should be fought "against armed forces and political organizations. Neither confiscation of property, political executions of persons, territorial organization of states or forcible abolition of slavery should be contemplated for a moment."

But to Lincoln none of this mattered. Pope said all the right things. He told the president that if ordered he would march directly toward Richmond—even if he had to go through Confederate defenses. His only demand was that Lincoln direct McClellan to attack as soon as Pope's troops were engaged. This was exactly the kind of audacity Lincoln had been longing to hear from his commanders.

Pope's Army of Virginia eventually numbered seventy thousand men, bringing together elements from the armies of the Shenandoah Valley, Northern Virginia, and the Potomac. Among the officers placed under his command was General Fitz John Porter, who loathed him, commenting at one time that "Pope could not quote the Ten Commandments without getting ten falsehoods out of them." Pope intended to attack Lee's troops from the east while they were fighting McClellan on the peninsula. But as the threat on Richmond from McClellan was blunted, Lee sent generals Stonewall Jackson and A. P. Hill north to Manassas to stop Pope's advance.

They made contact with Union troops on August 9 at Cedar Mountain. Jackson's vaunted Stonewall Brigade was taking devastating casualties when Jackson raised his sword and

This camp photo of General Fitz John Porter (seated, center) obviously was taken before November 1862. Note the "contraband," probably former slaves employed by the army to cook and clean. After the Second Battle of Bull Run, Porter was convicted of deliberately disobeying the orders of his commander, John Pope, but decades after the war a commission found that his actions may have saved the Army of Virginia, and an act of Congress restored his commission—and his reputation.

personally rallied his troops. As one eyewitness later wrote, his men "would have followed him into the jaws of death itself; nothing could have stopped them, and nothing did." Both sides broke off the fighting with nothing settled.

While Pope prepared for a major battle, Lee continued pecking away at him. The two sides sparred over the next few days as they each probed for a weakness. The armies remained in such close quarters that Union cavalry successfully raided Confederate cavalry commander Jeb Stuart's camp, capturing Stuart's famed plumed hat—and dispatches from Lee outlining his battle plan. Stuart's men, meanwhile, raided a federal supply depot at Catlett's Station, seizing Pope's dress uniform—and dispatches confirming that reinforcements were on the way to support him.

Lee had little respect for Pope, referring to him disdainfully as a "miscreant" who "must be suppressed." So he must have taken special delight when his scouts discovered an unguarded crossing beyond Pope's right flank. Jackson's 24,000-strong foot cavalry covered fifty-four miles in only thirty-six hours, successfully moving behind the Bull Run Mountains, driving twenty miles deep into the Union rear. His men ripped up railway lines and cut telegraph wires, severing Pope's supply line and communications with Washington—and then attacked the Union army's principal supply depot at Manassas Junction.

The supply depot was a hungry army's dream come true. Jackson's men feasted on fruit, meat, oysters, and lobster—and hundreds of barrels of liquor. They found wine and whisky, beer and brandy. But just as they started to taste their victory, Jackson ordered the barrels smashed open and the contents dumped, fearing "that whisky more than I do Pope's army."

"I shall never forget the scene when this was done," wrote Major W. Roy Mason. "Streams

New York publisher Charles Magnus was one of Currier and Ives's few rivals. His prints, like this one illustrating the chaos and brutality of the Second Battle of Bull Run, were known for their vivid coloring, often achieved by using uncommon paints stenciled by a line of artists each responsible for only one color.

of spirits ran like water through the sands of Manassas, and the soldiers on hands and knees drank it greedily from the ground as it ran." But liquor was not the greatest prize.

In addition to food and clothing, the depot contained forty-eight pieces of artillery, ten locomotives, two railway trains loaded with fifty thousand pounds of bacon, twenty thousand barrels of pork, thousands of barrels of flour, clothing, tents—all the stuff of a well-fed and well-equipped army. Wrote another witness, "To see a starving man eating lobster salad and drinking Rhine wine, barefooted and in tatters, was curious. The whole thing was indescribable." Jackson knew his time there was short, so most of it was burned in a huge bonfire. And then, before the outraged Pope could get there, Jackson's men slipped away. His three divisions took defensive cover behind an uncompleted railway embankment on the old Bull Run battlefield, which a year later still bore the scars of that fight.

Pope's army flailed around blindly, unable to find Jackson. Pope was accustomed to fighting traditional battles, but Lee refused to provide a conventional target for him.

As Lee and General James Longstreet rode north to support Jackson's army before Pope's much larger force could destroy it, fate once again dictated terms. As they approached Groveton, about thirty-five miles from Manassas, Lee rode forward to get a look at the terrain. Within a few minutes Lee returned, a small cut sliced into his cheek. An aide, Major Charles S. Venable, reported that the general had said quietly, "A Yankee sharpshooter came near killing me just now."

That sharpshooter had come within an inch of changing history. Lee had escaped death, perhaps because a gust of wind affected the shot, and his calm response only added to his legend. Lee ignored his superficial wound and continued toward Manassas.

The Second Battle of Bull Run—or as it was known in the Confederacy, Second Manassas—began late in the afternoon of August 28, when Jackson's troops surprised General John Gibbon's Iron Brigade marching to join Pope, who was utterly confused by Jackson's tactics. The Iron Brigade was formed by four western regiments, the only all-western brigade in the Army of the Potomac. These well-drilled troops proudly emphasized their distinctiveness by retaining the formal dress black "Hardee" or "Jeff Davis" hat. Whether it was their endless training or pride in their black hats, it worked. When Jackson's men let loose a rebel yell and swooped down the hillside at Brawner Farm, the Black Hats stood their ground and began pouring fire into the attackers' lines.

The battle raged into the early evening. Having given up their defensive position on the railway embankment when they launched the attack, Jackson's outnumbered troops had to fight it out on equal ground. Gibbon, along with a second brigade under General Abner Doubleday,

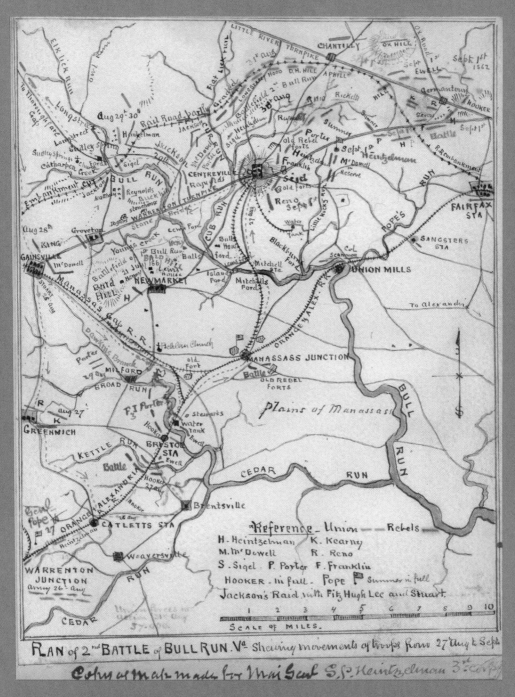

After fighting in the Second Battle of Bull Run, Union soldier Robert Knox Sneden drew this map for his personal diary, which was discovered decades later. Sneden was captured and imprisoned at Andersonville but survived, and almost a century later his words and beautiful sketches would bring the war to the public.

skillfully maneuvered their troops. Eventually the outcome came down to courage and bloodshed. Much of the fight took place at close quarters. As one Union veteran wrote, "The two crowds, they could hardly be called lines, were within, it seemed to me, fifty yards of each other, and they were pouring musketry into each other as rapidly as men could load and shoot."

Jackson ordered an attack at dusk. As another Union soldier remembered, "Our boys mowed down their ranks like grass; but they closed up and came steadily on."

In only a few hours of fighting each side had suffered an estimated thirteen hundred casualties. One of every three men were killed or wounded. As the sun fell behind the Bull Run Mountains and the shadows darkened into night, men searched the battlefield for the still living. The dead lay where they fell. At that time there wasn't much that could be done for wounded soldiers; amputation was the only known means to prevent deadly infections. Because so many men had died for lack of care in the Peninsula Campaign, a rudimentary ambulance corps was in the process of being created; two wagons were to be assigned to each regiment, one to carry medical supplies, the second to transport the wounded to the relative

The placid Potomac River, drawn near Williamsport on the morning General Lee's army crossed and began its invasion of the North.

safety of field hospitals. But they were not yet in service and some wounded men would lie in the fields for more than a week before they received care. And this was just the beginning of the carnage.

It wasn't until much later in the night that Pope learned about the battle. He was elated, believing Jackson's twenty-five thousand men were caught between major Union forces. He immediately requested that Lincoln dispatch the reinforcements he had been promised, then ordered his commanders to attack in the morning, telling them, "I do not see how it is possible for Jackson to escape without very heavy loss, if at all."

McClellan had given up the fight on the peninsula and returned to Washington, allowing Lee and General Longstreet the freedom to turn and march to Manassas. But he resisted Lincoln's request that he commit his remaining troops to Pope's battle, arguing that the men were needed to protect Washington. "I do not regard Washington as safe against the rebels," he wrote to his wife. "If I can quietly slip over there I will send your silver off."

The armies punished each other brutally for the next two days. The fighting was so intense that some members of the Stonewall Brigade ran out of ammunition—and rather than retreating, they stayed in their position and started throwing rocks at the enemy. On the afternoon of the twenty-ninth, Pope, who did not yet know that Longstreet's army had arrived, ordered Fitz John Porter to attack Jackson's right flank. But Porter collided with General James Longstreet and defied that command. Meanwhile General Philip Kearny attacked Jackson's left flank, ordering his men to "fall in here, you sons of bitches and I'll make major generals of every one of you!" As one of his men wrote, when they charged forward, "The slope was swept by a hurricane of death, and each minute seemed twenty hours long." By the morning of the thirtieth a very confident Pope informed Lincoln that he had won a significant victory. Jackson was in retreat, he reported, and he intended to pursue his army and, if possible, destroy it.

But like McClellan, he had fatally underestimated Lee's cunning. Misguided by poor intelligence and ignoring warnings that the rebels had arrived in force, Pope mistakenly concluded that Lee and Longstreet intended only to provide protection for Jackson's army as it withdrew. Determined to prevent that retreat, he once again ordered Porter to attack. Reluctantly, Porter formed his column and began his pursuit of Jackson—and marched right into a trap.

Lee had come to Manassas to fight and had played Pope's tune to perfection. He had shown him what he expected to see, using the man's own confidence to set him up for the slaughter. Longstreet's twenty-five thousand men were lying in wait for Porter's five thousand troops. When the Yankees launched their attack on Jackson, rebel artillery and muskets brought thunder down on them. As one of Longstreet's men remembered, "The first line of the attacking column looked as if it had been struck by a blast from a tempest and had been blown away." Porter's men charged right into their guns, waging a heroic struggle. But against "a perfect hail of bullets," as Private Alfred Davenport described the scene, they could not sustain the offensive. "We broke and run," wrote fifteen-year-old William Platt, and "they shot us down by hundreds."

As the Union line disintegrated, Longstreet's troops attacked. His men fought through the remnants of Porter's troops and pressed the attack deep into Pope's lines. The Johnny Rebs moved forward steadily for almost four hours, creating a relentless hailstorm of bullets and artillery. Longstreet's batteries could barely keep pace with the infantry and had to continuously move forward after firing only a few shells.

To their credit and honor, the Billy Yanks fought gamely and bravely. They conceded nothing. But when the sun mercifully went down, Pope ordered his men back across Bull Run. As Confederate reports described the scene, "In its first stages the retreat was a wild frenzied rout—the great mass of the enemy moving at a full run, scattering over the fields and trampling upon the dying and the dead in the mad agony of their flight."

Pope had suffered a humiliating defeat.

The human cost of the war was growing beyond normal comprehension. The Union suffered 13,824 killed, wounded, or missing at Second Bull Run—more in this one battle than the new nation had borne during the entire Revolutionary War. The Confederates lost 8,353 men killed, wounded, or unaccounted. Soldiers who only a year earlier had marched proudly through the main streets of towns and villages, sent off to war to the cheers of men and the swoons of women, were coming home missing arms and legs or too often in wooden boxes.

A war that few people had wanted but no one could prevent was now raging out of control. Some Northern newspapers and Democratic politicians began suggesting that a negotiated settlement with the South might be possible. In fact, in the midterm elections several months later, the Republican Party suffered substantial losses, evidence that the Union was quickly growing weary of the war. The thousands of deaths at Bull Run and subsequent battles had soured the patriotic fervor.

Pope was relieved of his command within a week and ordered to Minnesota to put down a Sioux Indian uprising. He settled blame for his loss partially on Lincoln, whom he called "feeble, cowardly, and shameful," and McClellan, but mostly on Fitz John Porter, who had refused his order to attack on the first day of the battle. Three months later Porter was arrested

Mathew Brady's 1861 studio portrait of thirty-five-year-old general George McClellan, one of the most beloved and controversial figures of the war.

and charged with disobeying a lawful order and misconduct. His court-martial was a major news event, as the often bitter rivalries between Union officers that so plagued Lincoln were finally exposed to the public. The court-martial had serious political implications; Democrats wanted to use it to place the blame for the growing disaster on Lincoln and the Republican Party. Porter's defense contended that Pope was incompetent and argued that by disobeying his order, Porter had actually saved his army. A slew of generals testified, many of them using the opportunity to buttress their own standing. McClellan took the opportunity to once again disparage Pope. But the court-martial, apparently swayed by those political considerations, found Porter guilty and dismissed him from the army. While signing the order ending Porter's military career, a furious Lincoln said, "In any other country but this, the man would have been shot."

For a nation at war, the verdict proved extremely controversial. Porter was incensed at being branded a traitor and immediately began a campaign to restore his honor. Those people who believed he was guilty claimed he was undermining morale by continuing to attack the army and administration. The *New York Times* suggested his efforts promoted dissension among the troops, even suggesting that perhaps he should have been executed for his disobedience. But Porter persisted and sixteen years later President Rutherford B. Hayes agreed to permit an investigation. In the prolonged hearing Porter presented maps, telegrams, and numerous witnesses from both armies. The commission finally reported that the court-martial had not had access to the information it needed and that rather than a coward or a traitor, Porter was "obedient, subordinate, faithful, and judicious" and that his actions probably "saved the Union army from disaster on the 29th of August." Finally, in 1886 he was granted a full pardon by Democratic president Grover Cleveland.

After smashing through Pope's army Lee once again threatened Washington. In early September 1862, his army crossed the Potomac into Maryland, coming within twenty miles of the Union capital. Lincoln once again handed authority—and the responsibility for stopping Lee—to George McClellan. He did so reluctantly and against the specific wishes of a majority of his cabinet, who handed him a letter stating flatly that they felt strongly that it was "not safe to entrust to Major General McClellan the command of any Army of the United States." In fact, Secretary of the Treasury Salmon P. Chase was infuriated by the decision, believing that McClellan's failure to send reinforcements to Pope, as had been promised, amounted to treason, and "giving command to him was equivalent to giving Washington to the rebels."

Lincoln believed he had no choice, responding, "We must use the tools we have. . . . Unquestionably he has acted badly toward Pope. He wanted him to fail. That is unpardonable. But he is too useful now to sacrifice." The greatest weapon McClellan possessed was the respect of his troops. He retained their loyalty, having proved to them that he valued their lives far more than many other officers did, some of whom were thought to put their own career ahead of the welfare of their troops. As Lincoln pointed out ruefully, "If he can't fight himself he excels in making others ready to fight."

When the defeated and dispirited army learned that McClellan had been returned to command, they responded with wild "huzzahs!" The politicians might despise him, but his men loved him. "The reinstatement of McClellan has inspired strength, vigor, and hope in the army," wrote Navy Secretary Gideon Welles. McClellan, too, was elated, his contempt for Pope's ability having been shown to be justified. "Pope has morally killed himself and is relieved of command," he boasted. "I have done nothing toward this. . . . I have now the entire confidence of the government and the love of the army. If I defeat the rebels I shall be master of the situation."

As McClellan began reorganizing the tattered army, the city of Washington prepared for an attack. Clerks and employees in government offices were enlisted to provide support. Gunboats were anchored in the Potomac. The sale of liquor was suspended. Secretary of War Stanton pleaded with Northern governors for more soldiers. Rumors spread quickly. The lack of communications caused many people to reach the darkest conclusion: Lee was marching on Washington.

In fact, Lee had no intention of attacking Washington. He knew his army lacked the strength or firepower to overcome the well-fortified city; in fact, it was, as Lee informed President Davis, "lacking much of the material of war." His men were in desperate need of food and ammunition and he hoped he might find those supplies in "the fields of Maryland laden with ripening corn and fruit."

Lee also believed his advancing army might be welcomed by people sympathetic to the Confederate cause. Maryland was a border state in which slavery was legal—and public opinion there was mixed. It was even possible that the presence of his army could spark an uprising. On September 4, Lee's troops began crossing the Potomac near Leesburg, Virginia, singing the pro-secession, anti-Lincoln song "Maryland, My Maryland" as they climbed up an embankment into Northern territory at White's Ford. This was the farthest north they had been able to penetrate. But several thousand of the troops, feeling strongly that they had enlisted to defend their homes and not invade the North, simply turned around and went home, while many others straggled behind, lacking shoes and other equipment. Lee was at the front of his army, carried by ambulance. After the battle at Manassas, he had dismounted and was holding Traveller's reins when the horse was spooked. Traveller had reared, spraining both of Lee's wrists on a tree stump, preventing him from leading his men from horseback for several months.

As his men marched into Maryland, Lee issued a proclamation calling for an uprising. It read:

> The people of the Confederate States . . . have seen with profound indigna-
> tion their sister State [Maryland] deprived of every right, and reduced to the
> condition of a conquered province. . . . The people of the South have long
> wished to aid you in throwing off this yoke, to enable you to again enjoy the
> inalienable rights of free men, and restore independence and sovereignty to
> your State. . . . In obedience to this wish, our Army has come among you, and
> is prepared to assist you with the power of its arms in regaining the rights of
> which you have been despoiled. . . . It is for you to decide your destiny, freely
> and without constraint.

Lee's call to arms was met mostly with indifference. Western Maryland was an area of small farms with few slaves, and most of the residents who took a stand in the war remained loyal to the United States. Rather than receiving a hero's welcome, people greeted his invading army with suspicion. A man watching them march into Frederick, Maryland, on September 6 wrote that he was surprised to see "dirty, lank, ugly specimens of humanity, with shocks of hair sticking through holes in their hats, and the dust thick on their dirty faces." Many residents simply hid their Union flags and stayed inside their homes. But one person did not.

The Confederate arrival in Frederick was immortalized a year later with the publication in the *Atlantic Monthly* of John Greenleaf Whittier's poem "Barbara Fritchie," which relates the supposedly true story of a ninety-year-old woman who defiantly hung out a Union flag when the rebels marched into the city. After its staff was shot down, she picked up the flag and . . .

> She leaned far out on the window-sill,
> And shook it forth with a royal will.
> "Shoot, if you must, this old gray head,
> But spare your country's flag," she said.

The poem's patriotic message—an elderly woman offering her life to protect the American flag—was embraced by Northerners and became such an enduring part of American culture that three silent movies were made about it. During World War II British prime minister Winston Churchill quoted these very lines. While the essence of this legend may be true, the crucial details are disputed. One thing most historians agree upon is that the woman who stood tall against the Confederates wasn't Barbara Fritchie.

Barbara Fritchie was a slave-owning widow who supported the Union. While she was in Frederick during the invasion of 1862, she apparently was ill; in fact, she would die three months later. But there were several other women who might well have waved a Union flag in the face of the rebels, including schoolteacher Mary Quantrill, whose husband's uncle formed the notorious gang Quantrill's Raiders. Quantrill supposedly was waving a small handheld flag; when an officer attempted to take it away, she fought back, and he eventually left her alone, telling her he admired her spirit. The poem also might have referred to seventeen-year-old Nancy Crouse, who lived in Middletown, Maryland. She owned a large flag, and when the soldiers tried to take it away, she apparently wrapped herself in it, although she did surrender it when they threatened her at gunpoint. It could also have been referring to Susan Groff, a Frederick hotelkeeper who had gained renown by hiding ninety rifles in a Main

The legendary story of ninety-year-old Barbara Fritchie waving a tattered American flag as Stonewall Jackson marched into Frederick was so successfully memorialized by poet John Greenleaf Whittier that sixty years later artist N. C. Wyeth painted his vision of the incident.

Street well to prevent them from falling into rebel hands, and who owned and often displayed a very large American flag.

Whatever the real story behind the legend is, it is undoubtedly true that the residents of western Maryland offered little cooperation and at least some resistance to Lee. When he offered to buy their farm products, they refused to accept Confederate currency; the farmers wouldn't pick crops, the millers wouldn't grind wheat, shopkeepers didn't open their shops, and cattle owners saved their herds by moving them into Pennsylvania.

By crossing the Potomac into Maryland, Lee had uncorked another complicated problem: what do to about the free blacks living in peace there? The rights of slaves, escaped slaves, and free blacks—and their owners—living in Virginia and Maryland were unsettled and uncertain. Their situation appeared to change depending on which army controlled which territory. Throughout the North, governors and state legislators debated allowing black men to join the armies and fight. But the single greatest unanswered question was what would happen to them, whatever their current status, when one side emerged victorious? It was a question that the leaders on both sides did not want to answer.

Robert E. Lee's inconsistent conduct regarding the question of slavery exemplified its ongoing complexity. The commander of the Confederate army had said publicly that slavery was abhorrent and yet he held a confusing position about slavery himself. In that same often-quoted letter in which he called slavery immoral, he also wrote that slavery somehow was ordained by God for the slaves' own future benefit. "The blacks are immeasurably better off here than in Africa. The painful discipline they are undergoing is necessary for their instruction as a race. . . . How long their subjugation may be necessary is known and ordered by a wise Merciful Providence."

Native Americans called the beautiful Shenandoah Valley, seen in this 1864 Currier and Ives print, the "Daughter of the Stars." Its value as a route between north and south for centuries was emphasized during the Civil War, when three major campaigns were fought there.

While Lee owned no slaves in his own name, he and his wife, Mary Custis Lee, inherited slaves from her father, George Washington Parke Custis. But according to a provision in Custis's will, those slaves were to be set free only after all of his plantation debts had been settled or five years passed. Lee was the administrator of the estate and kept those slaves in bondage to try to save the plantation. In 1859, three of those slaves, Wesley Norris, his sister Mary, and his cousin, believing they had been promised their freedom after Custis's death, escaped and were caught at the Pennsylvania border. What happened next has long been debated. According to an account given by Norris to the *National Anti-Slavery Standard* in 1866, they were returned to Arlington, where Lee ordered the men to receive fifty lashes and Mary Norris twenty lashes. When the overseer refused, Lee recruited the county constable to carry out the punishment. Norris claimed that "General Lee . . . stood by, and frequently enjoined Williams [the constable] to 'lay it on well,' an injunction which he did not fail to heed; not satisfied with simply lacerating our naked flesh, General Lee then ordered the overseer to thoroughly wash our backs with brine, which was done."

An anonymous letter that was published in the *New-York Tribune* in June 1859 about the incident went further, claiming that Lee himself actually had put the whip to Mary Norris. Lee eventually denied the entire story, stating, "There is not a word of truth in it." There isn't sufficient evidence to determine what really happened that day. But an even more confusing footnote to the story is that on January 3, 1863, two days after Lincoln's Emancipation Proclamation went into effect in the North, Lee legally declared that Custis's slaves were "forever set free from slavery."

Historians have never been able to agree on Lee's motivations, but the general certainly must have been aware that a Confederate victory, or even a negotiated settlement, would mean that slavery would continue to exist and might even be extended to new states and territories. And when his army marched into Maryland, the prospect of victory had never been more real. Lincoln's Army of the Potomac was reeling, and cities as far up the coast as New York were watching Lee with great anxiety. In the west, Confederate troops had occupied Lexington, Kentucky, and were pressuring Louisville and Cincinnati with the goal of enlisting Kentucky in the cause—either by choice or by force. While Lee did not believe an attack on Washington was feasible—at least not at this time—he certainly planned to carry his campaign into Pennsylvania in hopes that people might despair of fighting and elect a Democratic Congress disposed to ending the war with a treaty that recognized the rights of Southern states to self-determination. Finally, he wanted Britain to recognize the Confederacy as an independent nation.

British manufacturers were growing desperate for Southern cotton and the large markets cut off by the Union blockade. The sticky issue of slavery was standing in the way of profit. These cautious English politicians simply needed a little bit more assurance that the Confederacy could continue to dominate the larger Yankee forces. A few more impressive victories like Second Bull Run would ensure recognition and with it a demand that Lincoln accept British mediation to end the war.

Disappointed at the inability of his army to survive by foraging, Lee knew he had to secure his lines of supply and communications from the Shenandoah Valley. To accomplish that he once again split his forces, dispatching Stonewall Jackson to attack and capture Harpers Ferry, which was defended by about twelve thousand federal troops. The army would reunite at Boonsboro after achieving its objectives. Although splitting his already weakened army was a dangerous gamble, Lee was certain that the always cautious McClellan wouldn't dare leave Washington poorly defended.

But once again, fate played an unexpected hand. Lee had prepared three copies of his top secret Special Order No. 191 to be delivered to his generals. These plans included the routes to be taken by each force and the timing of the attack on Harpers Ferry. "The army will resume its march tomorrow," it read. Then he outlined precisely what he expected of his commanders—for example, "General McLaws . . . will take the route to Harpers Ferry, and by Friday morning possess himself of the Maryland Heights and endeavor to capture the enemy at Harpers Ferry and vicinity." They were each signed by Lee's adjutant, General R. H. Chilton.

One general who received the order pinned it securely to an inside pocket. Longstreet memorized his copy, then reportedly chewed it up. Major General Daniel H. Hill, Jackson's rear guard commander, also received a copy. On the morning of September 13, Union corporal Barton W. Mitchell of the 27th Indiana Volunteers was walking around a campsite just outside Frederick that rebel troops had recently abandoned. He spotted a thick envelope the rebels had lost or left behind. Inside he found three cigars wrapped in paper—and was stunned as he began reading it. Mitchell handed it to Sergeant John W. Bloss, who sent it forward through the chain of command until it reached headquarters. Incredibly, one of the adjutants at headquarters, Samuel E. Pittman, had worked in a Detroit bank when Chilton was the paymaster at a nearby army post—and recognized his signature.

McClellan had been handed Robert E. Lee's secret plans. If he moved quickly and struck firmly, he might drive a stake through the heart of the Confederate army. The outcome of the war could be determined in the next few days if he found the courage.

If.

Among the early attempts to adapt technology to weaponry was the Winan's Steam Gun, a mounted gun about the size of a steam engine that used centrifugal force rather than gunpowder to fire about 250 rounds a minute.

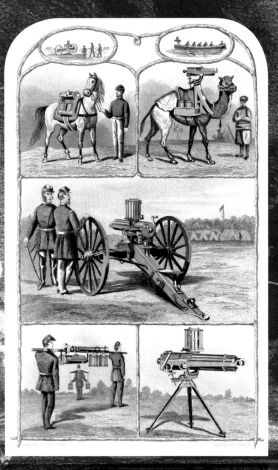

In some ways, the Civil War was the first modern war, giving the world a view of the terrifying weapons of the future.

The Gatling gun, the forerunner of the machine gun, was capable of firing several hundred bullets a minute. Patented in 1862, it was used for the first time in battle during the 1864 siege of Petersburg.

The Union made a further attempt to adapt this protective technology by building an ironclad battery equipped with 18-cannons. This 700-foot long floating fort, which would be moved by steam engines, was still being built when the war ended.

Ironclad warships were used in battle for the first time on March 9, 1862, at the Battle of Hampton Roads when the Union Monitor and the Confederate Merrimac, carrying traditional cannon, fought to a draw.

The Confederacy experimented with contact mines, known as "torpedoes." Surprisingly, inventor Robert Fulton had pioneered development of these devices, which were considered unethical. For a time, even the rebels banned their use. The rebel torpedo at right was anchored in the Tennessee River. Confederate torpedoes proved very successful, sinking and damaging numerous Union vessels.

After iron- or steel-clad ships proved their value, an attempt was made to extend the concept to the railroads; "Railroad Monitors," as they were known, were described as "iron-clad railroad batteries," and proved effective in limited use.

# FOUR

# UNBOUND FOR GLORY

## Frederick Douglass on the Road to Freedom

Like most slaves, Frederick Douglass never knew precisely how old he was. "I have no accurate knowledge of my age," he wrote, "never having seen any authentic record containing it." He was born as property on Maryland's Eastern Shore. He never learned the identity of his father, only that he was white. His only memory of his mother was being held by her in the night, adding, "I do not recollect of ever seeing my mother by the light of day."

There was no reason to believe he would eventually become one of the most important figures of the century.

His name at birth was Frederick Bailey and he lived his young life in a cabin with his grandparents, but he summed up the fate of every slave when he wrote, "I knew the taller I grew the shorter my stay." He was separated from his family when he was about seven years old and sent to live on a plantation. It was there that the wife of his owner taught him the fundamentals of reading and writing, but his desperation for knowledge

By the time this hand-colored photograph of Frederick Douglass, who had been born a slave, was taken in 1866, he was a free man and slavery had been abolished in the United States.

continued long after she was compelled to stop. Slave owners knew that educating slaves was dangerous.

Bailey refused to be easily tamed. His body was owned but not his mind. Frustrated, his masters finally sent him as a teenager to live with a farmer named Edward Covey, who was known as a Negro-breaker. After numerous beatings, food and sleep deprivation, and long days and nights of hard labor, "the snake," as Frederick referred to him, "succeeded in breaking me. I was broken in body, soul, and spirit . . . the dark night of slavery closed in upon me; and behold a man transformed into a brute!"

After one terrible beating Bailey attempted to escape. In response Covey tried to loop ropes around his legs—but this time, "I was resolved to fight, and, what was better still, I was actually hard at it. The fighting madness had come upon me," and it never went away. It took extraordinary courage for a slave to stand up to a white man, and a rebellious slave who attacked an overseer would be brutally flogged till near death. Bailey knew the risk but had gone beyond fear. He beat Covey bloody, he hit him again and again, and then again, and harder; the fight lasted two hours and afterward the Negro-breaker Covey never again "laid the weight of his finger upon me." This was the lesson Frederick would never forget. While still physically enslaved, for the first time he had experienced the scent of freedom.

Bailey's escape in September 1838 was considerably less dramatic. By that time he was working at a shipyard in Baltimore, living somewhat independently as long as he paid part of his weekly salary to his owner. Carrying the papers of a retired free black sailor that he'd either purchased or borrowed, he dressed in the proper sailor's uniform and boarded the Negro car of an aboveground railroad headed to freedom in the North. He had no specific destination, like most slaves. "I really did not, at that time, know that there was a state of New York, or a state of Massachusetts. I . . . was ignorant of the free states, generally."

While the punishments for attempting to escape varied, it was probable that if Bailey had been caught he would have been sent to work in the Deep South. Early in his journey an armed conductor asked to see his papers proving he was a free man. Instead of those papers he showed him the seaman's document he had obtained—although he did not at all resemble the man described on it. It was a moment that changed American history. The conductor noted the printed American eagle and barely looked at the description. "Twenty-five cents," he demanded. Twenty-five cents was the cost of a trip to freedom.

After other close calls Bailey eventually settled in New Bedford, Massachusetts, and married a free woman he'd met in Baltimore. Still in jeopardy, he changed his name to Frederick Douglass, picking the name of a main character in Sir Walter Scott's narrative

NARRATIVE

OF THE

LIFE

OF

FREDERICK DOUGLASS,

AN

AMERICAN SLAVE.

WRITTEN BY HIMSELF.

BOSTON:
PUBLISHED AT THE ANTI-SLAVERY OFFICE,
No. 25 CORNHILL.
1845.

Douglass lived such a dramatic life, three autobiographies were required to tell his entire story. This first book, which told the often-brutal story of a slave's life, was published in 1845 and became an international best-seller—while he was still legally an escaped slave subject to being put into chains.

poem "The Lady of the Lake." And it was as Frederick Douglass that he made his indelible imprint on American history.

Frederick Douglass became the century's most influential black man and a leader in the fight for all individual rights—but especially the battle to abolish slavery in America. He was about twenty-eight years old when his autobiography, *Narrative of the Life of Frederick Douglass, an American Slave*, was published in 1845, and by that time he already was gaining a reputation as a stirring speaker. When the publication of his best-selling book put his freedom in jeopardy he fled to Europe, where he could travel without fear. He was received in Britain as a celebrity, welcomed to high society, and even dined with the Lord Mayor of Dublin. In Ireland he often appeared with the "Irish Liberator," Daniel O'Connell, whom he often quoted in his speeches: "I am the foe of the tyrant . . . wherever slavery rears its head, I am the enemy of the system, or the institution, call it by what you will. I am the friend of liberty." After he spent two years abroad speaking fiercely against American slavery,

English Quakers helped him raise enough money to purchase his freedom, and he returned to America, now legally a free man, to continue his crusade. Several years later, as the British government contemplated recognizing the Confederacy, Douglass's words still resonated and perhaps added to the British reluctance to support a slave nation.

It was as much his presence and eloquence as his book that gained him international recognition. It was sometimes difficult for people who had little direct contact with slaves to accept the fact that they were human beings with all the potential, the intelligence, and the foibles of anyone else. It was Frederick Douglass who stood tall and spoke passionately to represent the millions of men, women, and children then living in slavery—and made it impossible for many Americans to ignore their plight.

In 1852, the leading citizens of Rochester, New York, where he had settled to publish an abolitionist newspaper, the *North Star*, invited him to give a Fourth of July speech at Corinthian Hall. By choice, on the fifth of July he spoke to a hall packed with six hundred abolitionists, and rather than celebrating the anniversary of the nation's freedom he issued a memorable attack on its toleration of slavery. "Why am I called to speak here today?" he asked.

> This Fourth of July is yours, not mine. You may rejoice, I must mourn. . . . Do you mean, citizens, to mock me by asking me to speak today? . . .
>
> What to the American slave, is your Fourth of July? I answer, a day that reveals to him more than all other days of the year, the gross injustice and cruelty to which he is the constant victim. To him, your celebration is . . . mere bombast, fraud, deception, impiety, and hypocrisy—a thin veil to cover up crimes which would disgrace a nation of savages. There is not a nation of the earth guilty of practices more shocking and bloody than are the people of the United States at this very hour.

Douglass told his audience that what was needed to make this truly a free country was "fire," not light, and "thunder," not reason. If this speech was not perceived to be a call to take up arms, it was at least a bitter reminder that the guarantees of the Declaration of Independence and the Constitution were still limited by the color of a man's—or woman's—skin.

Years later, as that war came closer, Abraham Lincoln and Frederick Douglass were not allies: Lincoln needed to avoid alienating any potential supporters. Whatever his personal beliefs, he argued vehemently that the war was being fought to hold the Union together. As he wrote to *New-York Tribune* editor Horace Greeley, in response to Greeley's 1862 editorial criticizing his lack of direction or resolve, "My paramount object in this struggle is to save the Union, and is not either to save or to destroy slavery. If I could save the Union without freeing any slave I would do it, and if I could save it by freeing all the slaves I would do it. . . . What I do about slavery, and the colored race, I do because I believe it helps to save the Union."

In response, a contemptuous Douglass referred to Lincoln as "an excellent slave hound," at least in part because he continued to support the Fugitive Slave Act as well as rescinding proclamations by Major General John C. Frémont in Missouri and General David Hunter in Georgia, Florida, and South Carolina freeing the slaves in those states. Consistently, Lincoln refused to take the moral stand on the most divisive issue in the nation's brief history.

But events were forcing the president to reconsider his position. The Union army had been beaten back to Washington and popular support for the war was waning. It was becoming increasingly more difficult to enlist soldiers to fight for a cause they couldn't quite understand. Lincoln was being pressured to allow black men to participate in the war. His own generals pointed out that the Confederates were using slave labor to do the work being performed by federal troops. A Union officer complained that throughout McClellan's Peninsula Campaign, soldiers had been exhausted doing manual labor and building fortifications, entrenchments, and bridges while "the same kind of work in the Southern army was performed by negro labor almost wholly." There also were some soldiers who claimed to have seen black men actually fighting for the Confederacy. A soldier writing in the *Indianapolis Journal* argued, "Fighting and marching does not wear the soldiers half so fast as ditching and fatigue duty, and the prevalent opinion in the army is in favor of negroes doing that kind of work," adding that troops were writing to friends and telling them not to enlist "as long as this state of things exists." Many Northern newspapers agreed; the *Boston Herald* editorialized, "We were not beaten by the arms of the enemy, but rather by the picks and spades in the hands of our own soldiers, with which they have wasted their vigor." No one questioned either the availability or the desire of the growing number of contraband blacks to do this work. Many battalions were trailed by large numbers of men and women who had simply walked off plantations. The army was feeding them whenever possible but it had become a substantial problem with no easy solution.

From other corners came stronger appeals for abolition. After suffering thousands of killed and wounded in the first year of the war, Northerners had little interest in placating the Confederacy in hopes of a negotiated settlement. If the North was going to fight, the abolitionists argued, here was a noble objective to fight for. Susan B. Anthony toured upstate New York gathering support. Henry Ward Beecher wrote impassioned editorials, and

Frederick Douglass thundered that it had "never been more palpable . . . that the only choice left to the nation is abolition or destruction."

But still, Lincoln resisted. Slavery was a constitutionally protected right in states where it was legal; abolishing it would mean violating the Constitution. He also was deeply concerned about how his officers would react if he emancipated the slaves. An increasingly belligerent McClellan was strongly against it, warning the president—whom he described to his wife in a letter as "an idiot" and "the original gorilla"—that "a declaration of radical views, upon slavery, will rapidly disintegrate our present Armies." McClellan made it clear that he was fighting the war to save the Union and that abolishing slavery would be detrimental to the possibility of reconciliation. The general was far from alone and Lincoln weighed the risks of telling white soldiers that they were endangering their lives to free black men and women against the obvious military benefits of allowing black men to support the fight for their own freedom.

Clearly there was not universally strong support for abolition in the North. In Cincinnati, the nation's third-largest industrial city, Irish dockworkers, fearful that freed black men would take more of the diminishing number of stevedore jobs, rioted for a week in early July 1862, tearing through Bucktown, beating people and destroying property. Race riots ignited in several other cities, among them Brooklyn, New York, and New Albany, Indiana, and tensions simmered in other cities as the debate became increasingly loud and angry.

Among those people who may have been trying to sway Lincoln was a remarkable black woman named Elizabeth Keckley, whose talent as a dressmaker and seamstress enabled her to become a companion, confidante, and traveling partner to Mary Todd Lincoln. Born about

Born into slavery, Elizabeth Keckley, after using her sewing skills to earn sufficient funds to buy her freedom, became a modiste, or custom dressmaker, to the leading ladies of Washington, and eventually Mary Todd Lincoln's best friend.

For six months in 1864 painter Francis Bicknell Carpenter was permitted to set up a studio in the White House, becoming a very early version of the White House photographer. This painting, *The Lincoln Family in 1861*, was painted from memory in 1872.

1818, Keckley was the daughter of a house slave and a then-unidentified white man. She was moved to Saint Louis with her owners in the 1840s and there discovered her sewing skills. "With my needle," she recalled in her autobiography, "I kept bread in the mouths of seventeen persons for two years and five months." She also was able to save enough money—$1,200—to purchase freedom for herself and her son. Eventually she moved with her husband and child to Washington, DC, where her list of clients eventually included the wives of Jefferson Davis and Robert E. Lee. When Varina Davis and her husband left Washington in January 1861, she invited Keckley to come with them, telling her she was fearful that should war occur, Northerners might blame blacks and "in their exasperation . . . treat you harshly." Keckley refused politely.

Keckley met Mrs. Lincoln on Inauguration Day and spent the next four years working in the White House, designing and sewing for the president's wife, whom she also dressed, and caring for Tad Lincoln while becoming, as Mary Lincoln once described their relationship, "my best friend." During that time thousands of contrabands poured into Washington, "fresh from the bonds of slavery," Keckley wrote. "Fresh from the benighted regions of the plantation, they came to the Capital looking for liberty, and many of them not knowing it when they found it." In fact, many of them suffered. To provide relief and educational opportunities for these fugitives, Keckley created the Contraband Relief Association. Among her first contributors were Mrs. Lincoln and Frederick Douglass, each of whom donated $200.

During her time in the White House, Keckley's son, who easily passed for white, enlisted in the Union army and was killed at the Battle of Wilson's Creek in August 1861. Their shared grief over the death of their sons brought Mary Lincoln and Elizabeth Keckley even closer. There is no evidence to show that Keckley had any influence over President Lincoln while he was considering his momentous decision about emancipation, but given the nature of her relationship with the First Lady, it certainly is possible to assume that she played a role.

Joining McClellan in his disdain for Lincoln was Frederick Douglass, but obviously for precisely opposite reasons. He had consistently been disappointed by the president's position, writing that Lincoln's first inaugural address was "a weak and inappropriate utterance" that presented a policy of "complete loyalty to slavery in the slave States."

But Lincoln was searching desperately for some compromise on the issue. When he found no support for his suggestion that loyalist slave states agree to a slow, compensated emancipation, meaning that owners would be paid for their property, he seriously embraced the possibility of separating the races by establishing a black colony outside the United States. In August 1862, he invited a delegation of five black clergymen to the White House to try to drum up support for his plan to send emancipated slaves to a region in what is now Panama to work there in coal mines. Douglass was incredulous, writing in his abolitionist newspaper that Lincoln "seems to have an ever increasing passion for making himself appear silly and ridiculous." But rhetoric, which worked so well for Douglass, would not work for Lincoln. The "Great Emancipator" had to learn how to become the "Great Compromiser."

While Lincoln was equivocating, the Republican Congress acted, passing bills in July 1862 that freed the slaves of anyone who had joined the rebellion against the United States and permitted the president to utilize those freed slaves in any military capacity—including allowing them to serve in the army. But before these laws could be enacted, Lincoln finally found an acceptable solution. He presented to his cabinet a version of the document that became known as the Emancipation Proclamation. This preliminary version freed the slaves in any state still in rebellion—although not in those slave states that had remained loyal—and those slaves "shall be then, thenceforward, and forever free; and the Executive Government of the United States, including the military and naval authority thereof, will recognize and maintain the freedom of such persons." In addition, he wrote, "such person of suitable condition will be received into the armed service of the United States to garrison forts, positions, stations, and other places, and to man vessels of all sorts."

It was a very practical document, designed to cripple the Confederacy by stripping it of the slaves who performed the menial tasks that allowed soldiers to fight. Its goal was to win the war by freeing the slaves rather than making the abolition of slavery the objective of the war. Lincoln hoped that by limiting its purview to regions in rebellion, he might satisfy both his supporters and detractors. But legally, he could not include border states like Kentucky or Maryland since the "war powers" granted by Congress applied only to slave states at war with the federal government. Lincoln's cabinet was divided. Several secretaries felt it was far too radical, while others believed it would make little difference. Secretary of State William Seward, a strong abolitionist, urged him to wait for a Union military victory before issuing it, arguing that releasing it at the present time, after a defeat, would make it appear to be a desperate move. Seward felt strongly that it needed to be "borne on the bayonets of an advancing army, not dragged in the dust behind a retreating one."

Lincoln's original draft also contained a reference to support colonization, but Seward suggested a modification that made it voluntary. Eventually that clause was removed completely.

The president agreed with Seward, recognizing that if he issued the proclamation after a military defeat, "it would be considered our last shriek." He agreed to wait until McClellan gave him a military victory. The presumption was that it would not be too long a wait. McClellan had been handed a copy of Lee's Special Orders No. 191, the most valuable piece of intelligence of the war, on September 13. He held in his hands Lee's plans to split his army. After completing their missions, the army was to reassemble behind Antietam Creek, near the village of Sharpsburg, Maryland, where Lee waited with his remaining force.

McClellan moved swiftly, without pressing the fight. On September 14, General Jesse Reno's troops broke through Turner's Gap and pushed the dazed rebels back. A key moment in the battle came when greatly outnumbered federal troops allowed the Confederates to get "within fifteen paces," as John C. Abbott wrote in his 1863 *History of the Civil War in America*. "When the patriots sprang to their feet and poured in upon the rebel ranks such a staggering storm of lead, that the whole line reeled, as if smitten by thunderbolts, turned and fled. The ground behind them was covered with their slain."

After the debacle at Second Bull Run, this vitally important victory boosted flagging morale and opened a passage to Antietam. Unfortunately, in the fighting, popular general Jesse Reno was mortally wounded. As he lay on the ground he told his soldiers, "Boys, I can be with you no longer in body; but I am with you in spirit."

But even with Lee's campaign orders in hand, McClellan was still cautious. Rather than pressing forward to reinforce the garrison at Harpers Ferry before the rebels got there, he hesitated, and as a result Jackson's forces captured the strategic town. Meanwhile, McClellan didn't know that his own battle plan had been compromised: a Confederate sympathizer had learned of his intent and gotten a warning to Lee. General Lee responded by ordering his army to concentrate behind Antietam Creek in western Maryland as rapidly as possible. Had McClellan attacked immediately, his ninety thousand men might have overwhelmed Lee's fifty thousand troops. But he didn't, and by the time he launched his offensive, Jackson's divisions had arrived carrying large supplies of ammunition captured at Harpers Ferry, and additional troops were marching double-quick to support him.

On the morning of the sixteenth, 170,000 men looked across Antietam Creek as they

Union captain James Hope's panoramic painting,
*A Fateful Turn*, depicts the fighting at Antietam moments
before the old sunken farm lane became known forever as
Bloody Lane. There were five paintings in the series; each
one weighed more than two hundred pounds.

waited anxiously for the fighting to begin. Minor skirmishing broke out that afternoon as McClellan probed Lee's northern flank, serving mostly to give away his own strategy.

The Battle of Antietam, or the Battle of Sharpsburg, as it is also known, commenced at daybreak on the seventeenth when General Joseph Hooker launched an attack on Lee's left flank. It raged throughout the entire day. As the *Charleston Courier* described the carnage, "From twenty different standpoints great volumes of smoke were every instant leaping from the muzzles of angry guns. . . . Men were leaping to and fro, loading, firing, and handling the artillery, and now and then a hearty yell would reach the ear, amid the tumult, that spoke of death or disaster from some well-aimed ball."

By early afternoon almost two hundred artillery pieces were firing at close range. An eyewitness reported that "every hilltop, ridge and woods along the whole line was crested and veiled with white clouds of smoke. . . . Four miles of battle, its glory all visible, its horrors all hidden, the fate of the Republic hanging on the hour." Throughout the day both sides launched attacks that were repulsed, then countered. The casualties were horrendous; in less than an hour General John Bell Hood's division lost fourteen hundred men in Miller's Cornfield. When Hood was asked later, "Where is your division?" he replied, "Dead on the field." One of his regiments, the 1st Texas, lost 186 of its 226 men.

The Union forces gained ground in the morning but lost much of it in the afternoon. The fighting became so confusing that at one moment a future Supreme Court justice, Captain Oliver Wendell Holmes, saw one of his men firing backward, into what appeared to be his

For decades following the war an untold number of illustrations were produced to fill the demand from patriotic veterans and families. *The Battle of Antietam* is one of the thirty-six chromolithographs published by **Kurz and Allison**. Supposedly depicting the fighting at Burnside Bridge, like most fanciful prints, it is highly melodramatic.

own lines. Holmes smacked him with the side of his sword—until he realized the rebels had managed to get around behind him. By late afternoon Lee had committed all of his troops to the battle and had none left in reserve; Union troops broke through the center of the rebel line but McClellan refused to commit his twenty thousand fresh troops, believing that Lee still held thousands more men waiting to counterattack—and then during those few desperate hours General A. P. Hill arrived with about three thousand fresh troops to reinforce Lee.

Late in the afternoon Lee made one last attempt to push back the federal army. Hill's fresh troops attacked General Ambrose Burnside, whose men had fought their way over a narrow stone bridge and onto the Sharpsburg Road. Burnside's lines wavered under the relentless assault and were driven back. When Burnside requested reinforcements, McClellan sent him a message. "I can do nothing more. . . . Tell him if he cannot hold his ground, then the bridge, to the last man!—always the bridge! If the bridge is lost, all is lost." But as the sun set, Lee halted his attack.

There was no clear victor. The Union held control of the battlefield but neither side had gained anything substantial while suffering tremendous losses. More Americans were killed, wounded, or missing in battle on that day, September 17, 1862, than on any single day in our history. McClellan had suffered 12,410 casualties, including 2,108 dead, while Lee had lost 10,316 men, including 1,546 killed. As many as 5,000 men were killed or wounded in repeated attacks on a sunken farm road that became known as Bloody Lane. In the next few days, an additional 2,000 federal troops and 1,500 rebels would die of their wounds.

Among the heroes that day was Clara Barton, who had spent more than a year lobbying the army for permission to bring her medical supplies onto the battlefield. She arrived at

Among the first women to gain recognition in the war was Clara Barton, an educator and US Patent Office clerk, who became known as "The American Nightingale" and "The Angel of the Battlefield" for her efforts to bring medical care to wounded soldiers.

Sharpsburg around noon with a wagon filled with supplies she had collected and spent the next few days treating the dying and wounded, binding their wounds, bringing them food and water, assisting surgeons as they amputated limbs, and in at least one instance actually cutting a ball out of a wounded soldier's face. During the fighting she was holding a wounded soldier when she felt a stir in the sleeve of her dress—and discovered a bullet had ripped through it and killed the man she was treating. As army surgeon Dr. James Dunn later wrote of her service at Antietam, "In my feeble estimation, General McClellan, with all his laurels, sinks into insignificance beside the true heroine of the age, the angel of the battlefield."

Lee had gambled his entire army in the fight, while McClellan held almost a quarter of his men in reserve. Although there were numerous skirmishes the next morning, neither side could sustain a battle and Lee withdrew his army, retreating into Virginia. Generals Burnside and Franklin pleaded with McClellan to attack. As Abbott wrote four years later, McClellan "had the opportunity either of driving the rebels into the Potomac and of capturing a large portion of their army, or of pushing them, in a demoralized state, farther into hostile country, where their communications with Virginia could easily be severed." Instead, the always cautious commander allowed Lee to save his army, reporting, "I felt that my duty to the army and country forbade the risks involved in a hasty movement."

The true horror of that day was soon brought into American homes through photographs published in magazines or displayed in galleries. For the first time Americans could see the bodies piled up for themselves rather than through illustrations. Pictures of the bodies of their sons and neighbors and friends, of boys not yet ready to shave, mesmerized the public. Scottish immigrant Alexander Gardner, who ran Mathew Brady's Washington photo gallery, became a staff photographer under McClellan and his images from Antietam shocked Northerners, putting even more pressure on Lincoln to bring the war to an end.

While Antietam was not the glorious victory needed to fulfill Seward's vision, Union troops had acquitted themselves well, and at the end of the fighting McClellan controlled the battlefield while Lee had been forced to retreat for the first time in the war. His attempted invasion of the North had been repulsed. The president could no longer wait. After telling his cabinet, "I made a solemn vow before God, that if General Lee was driven back from Pennsylvania, I would crown the result by the declaration of freedom to the slaves," on September 22, he issued the preliminary Emancipation Proclamation. He warned the Confederacy that if it did not end the rebellion by January 1, 1863, he would sign this document, legally freeing more than three million enslaved men, women, and children.

As expected, the preliminary document caused great controversy. Many Northerners railed against it, believing this issue had been settled in the Constitution. Copperhead Democrats, for instance, who were against the war and favored ending it by permitting slavery to continue, denounced it as an unconstitutional abuse of presidential power. They warned, as Frederick Douglass said in ridiculing them, "The only effect of the Proclamation is to make the slaves cut their masters' throats and stir up insurrections all over the South.—The same men tell you that the Negroes are lazy and good for nothing, and in the next breath they tell you that they will all come North and take the labor away from the laboring white men here." McClellan made his disgust public, criticizing Lincoln for "inaugurating servile war."

The photographs of Mathew Brady brought the horrors of the Civil War to civilians. For the first time, unburied corpses and smashed field equipment could be seen as they lay, within hours of the battle. Using the equipment seen in this 1864 photograph, Brady's photo outfit at Petersburg captured images of all aspects of the war—except the fighting, as cameras could not yet capture moving images.

Enlistments in the army declined significantly as many men refused to put their own lives at risk to free blacks, while most of those already enlisted were ambivalent. Others believed it was far too drastic and favored a slower, more reasoned approach. Secretary of State William Seward complained that it applied only to those states in which Lincoln had no real power, noting, "Where he could, he didn't; Where he did, he couldn't."

The proclamation was one of several contentious issues in the midterm elections of 1862. In addition to being dissatisfied about the conduct of the war, Northern Democrats were also unhappy with rising taxes and Lincoln's suspension of the constitutionally guaranteed right of habeas corpus and were fearful that newly freed slaves would flood the labor market. The Democrats gained 28 seats in the 185-member House of Representatives, although Republicans managed to retain control. Senators at that time were elected by state legislatures rather than by popular vote, so Republicans managed to slightly increase their majority. The elections demonstrated that there existed no great reservoir of support for Lincoln's proclamation. People accepted it, but clearly they did not like the fact that a war they had believed was being fought for union now was being waged to free the slaves.

While Lincoln claimed the right to issue this order as one of the executive's undefined "war powers," he still appealed to legislators for support. In his annual message to Congress in December he renewed his request for voluntary colonization of freed slaves and "compensated emancipation," the plan to pay slave owners for releasing their property. He went so far as to suggest that slavery should be eliminated by January 1, 1900, to spare "both races from the evils of sudden derangement." But he also made an impassioned plea for congressional backing for his proclamation, writing:

> We can succeed only by concert. . . . The dogmas of the quiet past, are inadequate to the stormy present. The occasion is piled high with difficulty, and we must rise—with the occasion. As our case is new, so we must think anew, and act anew. . . .
>
> Fellow-citizens, we cannot escape history. . . . We know how to save the Union. . . . We—even we here—hold the power, and bear the responsibility. In giving freedom to the slave, we assure freedom to the free—honorable alike in what we give, and what we preserve. We shall nobly save, or meanly lose, the last best hope of earth. Other means may succeed; this could not fail. The way is plain, peaceful, generous, just—a way which, if followed, the world will forever applaud, and God must forever bless.

Carpenter's 1864 oil painting *First Reading of the Emancipation Proclamation of President Lincoln*, which depicts the president and his cabinet, was re-created from sketches and photo portraits of each man. Lincoln worked with the artist to put each man in his proper position.

Precisely one hundred days after issuing the preliminary document, on January 1, 1863, Abraham Lincoln signed the Emancipation Proclamation, liberating the slaves in the Confederate states. "I never, in my life, felt more certain that I was doing right," he said, "than I do in signing this paper." It was done without celebration. As his private secretaries, John Nicolay and John Hay, later described the low-key event that changed America forever, "Vast as were its consequences, the act itself was only the simplest and briefest formality. It could in no wise be made sensational or dramatic. . . . Those who were in the house came to the executive office merely from the personal impulse of curiosity joined to momentary convenience. His signature was attached to one of the greatest and most beneficent military decrees of history in the presence of less than a dozen persons."

That first day of 1863 had been cautiously anticipated by both black and white abolitionists.

Despite great efforts by Southern whites, news of the preliminary proclamation had spread throughout the Confederacy. Months before it was to go into effect, escaping slaves had been citing it to claim their freedom. Abolitionists declared January 1 a day of jubilee and scheduled prayer meetings, concerts, and gatherings of all types. An estimated five thousand slaves, some of them walking off plantations, gathered in Norfolk, Virginia, to await news of the signing. But no one waited for official word that Lincoln had emancipated the slaves more anxiously than Frederick Douglass, who spent the day listening to lectures in Boston's Tremont Temple ready "to receive and celebrate the first utterance of the long-hoped-for proclamation." The day stretched into the early evening, but still there was no word from Washington. Douglass wrote later, "It was by no means certain. The occasion, therefore, was one of both hope and fear. . . . Every moment of waiting chilled our hopes, strengthened our fears. . . . We were watching, as it were, by the dim light of the stars for the dawn of a new day." It was after ten p.m. before the news arrived by telegraph. "The effect of this announcement was startling beyond description, and the scene was wild and grand. Joy and gladness exhausted all forms of expression from shouts of praise, to joys and tears."

While legally the Emancipation Proclamation did not immediately liberate any slaves, unless they were already in Union hands, its effect was enormous.

In addition to its impact on the military outcome of the war—eventually more than two hundred thousand black men would join the fight for their freedom—it also had vitally important international political implications. In Europe, many politicians had framed the war as an attempt by courageous Southerners to gain their freedom from the oppressive North. In late 1862, British leaders had proposed a peace agreement in which the North would recognize Southern rights—and warned that if this proposal was rejected they would support the Confederacy. But there was a strong antislavery sentiment in England, and the Confederacy was now cast as fighting to protect slavery while the North was viewed as fighting for human rights. That made it difficult for European nations, where slavery had been eliminated, to offer any assistance to the South. This was a major blow to President Jefferson Davis, who had been courting those governments for several years. The Emancipation Proclamation's real purpose, Davis said, was to provide European nations "justification in withholding our just claims to formal recognition."

Abolitionists rejoiced. The headline of Horace Greeley's *New-York Tribune* was simply,

To celebrate the Emancipation Proclamation, the vignettes on the left of this popular lithograph, published in 1864 in Madison, Wisconsin, by Martin and Judson, show scenes related to slavery, while those on the right illustrate the benefits of freedom. ☞

EMANCIPATION
Proclamation
Whereas on the 22d day of September in the year of our Lord 1862 a Proclamation was issued by the President of the United States containing among other things the following to wit
That on the first day of January in the year of our Lord 1863 all persons held as slaves within any State or designated part of a State the people whereof shall then be in rebellion against the United States, shall be then thenceforth and forever free and the Executive Government of the United States including the military and naval authority thereof will recognize and maintain the freedom of such persons and will do no act or acts to repress such persons or any of them in any effort they may make for their actual freedom.
That the Executive will on the first day of January aforesaid by proclamation designate the States and parts of States if any in which the people thereon respectively shall then be in rebellion against the United States, and the fact that any State or the people thereof shall on that day be in good faith represented in the Congress of the United States by members chosen thereto at elections wherein a majority of the qualified voters of such State shall have participated, shall in the absence of strong countervailing testimony be deemed conclusive evidence that such State and the people thereof are not then in rebellion against the United States
NOW THEREFORE I
ABRAHAM LINCOLN
PRESIDENT OF THE UNITED STATES
BY VIRTUE OF THE POWER IN ME VESTED AS
COMMANDER IN CHIEF OF THE ARMY AND NAVY
in time of actual armed rebellion against the authority and government of the United States and as a fit and necessary war measure for suppressing said rebellion do on this first day of January in the year of our Lord one thousand eight hundred and sixty three, and in accordance with my purpose so to do publicly proclaimed for the full period of one hundred days from the day of the first above mentioned order and designate as the States and parts of States wherein the people thereof respectively are this day in rebellion against the United States the following to wit Arkansas Texas Louisiana except the parishes of St Bernard Plaquemines Jefferson St John St Charles St James Ascension Assumption Terre Bonne Lafourche St Mary St Martin and Orleans including the City of New Orleans Mississippi Alabama Florida Georgia South Carolina North Carolina and Virginia except the forty eight counties designated as West Virginia and also the counties of Berkeley Accomac Northampton Elizabeth City York Princess Ann and Norfolk including the cities of Norfolk and Portsmouth and which excepted parts are for the present left precisely as if this proclamation were not issued And by virtue of the power and for the purpose aforesaid I do order and declare that all persons held as slaves within said designated States and parts of States are and henceforward shall be free and that the executive government of the United States including the military and naval authorities thereof will recognize and maintain the freedom of said persons And I hereby enjoin upon the people so declared to be free to abstain from all violence unless in necessary selfdefense and I recommend to them that in all cases when allowed they labor faithfully for reasonable wages And I further declare and make known that such persons of suitable condition will be received into the armed service of the United States to garrison forts positions stations and other places and to man vessels of all sorts in said service And upon this sincerely believed to be an act of justice warranted by the Constitution upon military necessity I invoke the considerate judgment of mankind and the gracious favor of Almighty God In witness whereof I have hereunto set my hand and caused the seal of the United States to be affixed
Done at the city of Washington this first day of January in the year of our Lord one thousand eight hundred and sixty three and of the independence of the United States of America the eighty seventh
A Lincoln
GIVE THANKS ALL YE PEOPLE, GIVE THANKS TO THE LORD.
ENTERED ACCORDING TO ACT OF CONGRESS IN THE YEAR 1864 BY S. W. MARTIN & N. P. JUDSON, IN THE CLERKS OFFICE OF THE DISTRICT COURT OF THE U. S. FOR THE DISTRICT OF WISCONSIN.
DEL, LITH. AND PRINT. BY L. LIPMAN, MILWAUKEE, WIS.
PUBLISHED & SOLD BY MARTIN & JUDSON, MADISON, WIS.

"GOD BLESS PRESIDENT LINCOLN." Speaking in the great hall at the Cooper Union in New York, where only a few years earlier Lincoln had spoken, Frederick Douglass praised his sometimes foe, calling the signing of the proclamation "the greatest event of our nation's history, if not the greatest event of the century." Describing it as a revolution as great as if the pope had suddenly become Protestant, he added, "Color is no longer a crime or a badge of bondage." Douglass was not upset that the document extended only to the Confederacy, pointing out that "slavery must stand or fall together. Strike it at either extreme—either on the head or at the heel, and it dies. A brick knocked down at either end of the row brings every brick in it to the ground." And he finished his speech by predicting a glorious future, "when we have blotted out this system of wrong, and made this United States in fact and in truth what it is in theory—The Land of the Free and the Home of the Brave."

As Douglass predicted, the slaveholding Northern and border states, while not directly affected by the proclamation, moved steadily to eliminate slavery. Delaware sent an abolitionist to Congress although many of its slaves were already running away to join the Union army; Maryland called a state constitutional convention to abolish slavery and its 1864 constitution prohibited the practice. The constitution of the new state of West Virginia provided for the eventual emancipation of its slaves. In Tennessee, a state with greatly divided loyalties, military governor Andrew Johnson called for immediate emancipation, although it did not come until voters approved a new constitution in 1865. Even the newly elected governor of Louisiana, Michael Hahn, called for the "universal and immediate extinction of slavery," which was abolished by a state constitutional convention.

Not surprisingly, the reaction throughout the Confederacy was quite different. President Davis proclaimed that the "restoration of the Union has been rendered forever impossible by issuing this document," as it "affords our people the complete and crowning proof of the true nature of the designs of the party . . . which sought to conceal its purpose by every variety of artful grace." Far worse, he predicted that slaves would arise and attack their masters. Union officers should bear responsibility for this violence, he wrote, and if captured be handed over to state governors "to be regarded as persons inciting servile insurrection under President Lincoln's emancipation proclamation." The penalty for inciting insurrection was death.

Many Confederates had always believed that the Union's true purpose in fighting this war was to free the slaves and were pleased it finally had been admitted publicly. They felt it would give the rebels a new and resounding cause around which they might rally. But perhaps its most significant immediate impact was to open the military to black soldiers. As Douglass lamented, "It was a measure apparently inspired by the low motive of military necessity." Enlisting black men had long been a controversial issue that Lincoln had artfully avoided, mostly by doing nothing to change existing laws. But the pressure on him had been growing as the number of casualties the Union army had suffered grew larger and larger. There was no doubt that black Americans were ready to enlist. Three years before the war a secret organization called the Loyal League had been established to prepare for that eventuality. John Rock, an African American doctor, lawyer, and teacher, had predicted accurately, "Sooner or later the clashing of arms will be heard in this country, and the black man's services will be needed: 150,000 freemen capable of bearing arms, and not all cowards and fools, and three quarter of a million slaves, wild with the enthusiasm caused by the dawn of the glorious opportunity of being able to strike a genuine blow for freedom, will be a power which the white man will be 'bound to respect.' Will the blacks fight? Of course they will."

A month after Lincoln had signed the proclamation, Massachusetts governor John A. Andrew formed the first black unit in the North, the 54th Massachusetts Volunteer Infantry.

Troops of the Massachusetts 54th Volunteer Infantry, the "Swamp Angels," as they became known, were one of the first official African American units. This photo was probably taken at their training camp just outside Boston.

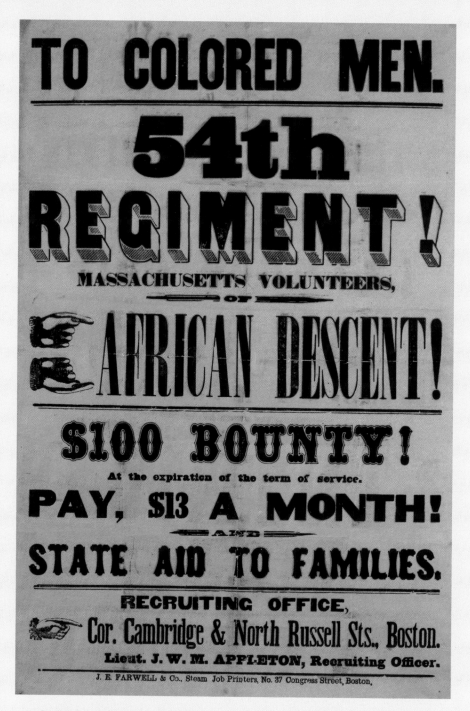

Initially people wondered if African Americans would volunteer
to fight. While at first there was some reluctance because blacks
mistrusted whites in both the North and South, by the time the
war ended it is estimated that African American soldiers
comprised about 10 percent of the Union army.

More than one thousand men from Northern states, Canada, some slave states, and the Caribbean responded to the call to arms, and among the first volunteers to join this unit were Frederick Douglass's sons, Lewis and Charles. Andrew picked twenty-five-year-old Robert Gould Shaw, the son of wealthy abolitionists, to command the unit. Shaw had survived the bloodbath at Cedar Mountain, where a quarter of the men in his 2nd Massachusetts Regiment were killed, and Antietam. Having enjoyed a privileged upbringing, including European travel and a Harvard education, Shaw had found a purpose to his life when he enlisted in the army in 1861 and had served courageously. He wrote of watching in awe at Cedar Mountain as other wealthy young Bostonians stood tall and walked "straight up into the shower of bullets, as if it were so much rain; men, who until this year, had lived lives of perfect ease and luxury." And after they had died in the battle he dutifully collected locks of their hair to return to their families.

Initially he turned down the offer to lead the unit. His reason had nothing to do with the race of the troops. Rather, he did not want to abandon the surviving troops of the 2nd Massachusetts to accept command of what he assumed would be mostly a support unit. He was a combat soldier and it seemed improbable to him that the army would actually allow black soldiers into battle. His parents, primarily his mother, prevailed on him to accept Andrew's request to form the 54th. Finally, reluctantly, he agreed.

Although initially he harbored doubts about the quality of his men, he quickly gained respect for them. In fact, when the army announced that black soldiers would receive less pay than white troops, Shaw led a several-months-long boycott of all payments until the army finally agreed to pay all soldiers equally at the white rate—and pay back wages. He also began lobbying commanders to give his men the opportunity to prove their mettle in battle. News that the Confederate Congress had resolved that all captured black soldiers would be sold into slavery and their white officers would be summarily executed did not temper his resolve. This unit was fighting to free their race; threats could not shake their determination. On May 28, 1863, four months after forming his unit, Shaw proudly paraded his 54th Massachusetts (Colored) Volunteer Infantry Regiment through the streets of Boston, from the Boston Common to the docks, where they boarded a transport to take them into the fight.

Frederick Douglass must have watched with both great pride and parental fear as his sons marched off to war with a thousand other black soldiers.

This war was no longer being fought simply to tie together the old Union; perhaps reluctantly, and certainly out of necessity, it now had a much more noble purpose: the end of slavery in the United States.

And to guarantee that all the Union had to do was win the Civil War.

# FIVE

# THE COMMANDING PRESENCE

## The Genius of Stonewall Jackson

Before the nation fell into war and when it was still being cobbled together state by state, the vast Texas territory was the great prize. The Republic of Texas had declared its independence in 1836, but the Mexican government had refused to acknowledge it. After Mexico rejected an offer from President James K. Polk to purchase the sparsely occupied land between the Nueces River and the Rio Grande in 1845, General Zachary Taylor led American troops into the disputed territory of Coahuila and the Mexican-American War began. In 1847, General Winfield Scott led the first major amphibious landing in American military history, preparing to attack the city of Veracruz. Within months Scott's army was closing in on the Mexican capital, Mexico City.

For many young American soldiers this was to be the great testing ground, the place where they would earn their spurs for the great war they could not know was coming. Among them were Ulysses S. Grant, Robert E. Lee, George Meade, James Longstreet, and a brand-new West Point

Thomas Jonathan "Stonewall" Jackson was second only to Robert E. Lee in the hearts of Confederates. Historians consider him among the most gifted leaders in American military history, and his accidental shooting by his own men changed the course of the Civil War.

graduate, twenty-two-year-old Second Lieutenant Thomas J. Jackson. Initially, Jackson was attached to a rear-echelon artillery battery and his prospects for combat were slim. "I envy you men who have been in battle," he confessed to a soldier who had seen action. "How I should like to be in one battle."

That opportunity finally came during the September 1847 battle for control of Chapultepec Castle, a key point in Mexico City. Ordered to provide artillery support for infantry troops attacking Chapultepec Castle, Jackson's unit struggled to drag their guns across the marshy land that surrounded it. Mexican troops occupying the castle heights raked fire down on the American attackers. Artillery began shelling them. One of Jackson's guns was hit and three men were killed. As his men began breaking, diving for cover, and retreating, Jackson stood tall and defiant. When he was asked about being in battle for the first time, he responded that he had been "afraid the fire would not be hot enough for me to distinguish myself."

It was at this moment that the legend that was to become Stonewall Jackson was born. Supposedly a Mexican cannonball shot right between his legs. Rather than panicking, he looked down disdainfully, as if insulted that death had come so close. He attempted to rally his men with the cry, "There is no danger! You see! I am not hit!" When that failed, when fear and blood proved too much for most of the men and they cowered on the ground, Jackson and one sergeant loaded and fired the fieldpiece, and then did it again. Later, a second American cannon was pulled into position and opened fire. Eventually, the overwhelming

Lieutenant Jackson first gained notoriety during the storming of Chapultepec Castle in the Mexican-American War when he refused an order to withdraw and instead created an opening that reinforcements successfully exploited.

American force was able to take the castle—and Tom Jackson emerged from the smoke of battle as a courageous battle-hardened officer. For his gallant and meritorious service in battle he was promoted to the rank of brevet, or temporary, major.

That's the way the story was told and it brought great attention to the young officer. According to legend, there was one other event during that war that would play an important role in the War Between the States. It was during the Mexican-American War that Tom Jackson befriended Captain Robert E. Lee. In fact, the two men formed such a fast friendship that when Lee responded to a slight by another officer by challenging him to a duel, he asked Jackson to serve as one of his seconds. The first shot was rifles at forty paces—and both Lee and his opponent missed. Lee's opponent then retired and the matter of honor was considered settled; but Lee and Jackson had forged the bond of complete trust that would make a difference years later.

In addition to being a fearless warrior, Stonewall Jackson was a devout Christian, a Calvinist who believed God had planned his fate, which meant he could take great risks because the outcome was already determined. Whether he lived or died was God's will, and therefore standing or hiding in battle made no difference. "My religious belief teaches me to feel as safe in battle as in bed. God fixed a time for my death. I do not concern myself about that, but to be always ready, no matter when it may overtake me."

Initially Jackson was not a supporter of secession. "It seems to me, that if they would unite thus in prayer, war might be prevented and peace restored." And when asked by a friend how he could remain so calm when facing battle, he explained that he found comfort in his faith. "Why should the peace of a true Christian be disturbed by anything which man can do unto him? Has not God promised to make all things work together for good to those who love him?"

When war came in 1861, Jackson, like so many others, was torn between his country and his state. He was born in Clarksburg, Virginia, but his first wife had been born in the North, and his sister was a Unionist, so he spent considerable time in prayer and contemplation before committing himself to the Confederate cause. Believing that the Lord had put him on this path, he never again doubted the righteousness of it. He resigned his teaching position at the Virginia Military Institute and joined Lee's army. This was the war for which he had been preparing his entire life.

Both Jackson's sister and father had died of typhoid while he was still a young child and he was raised by an uncle. He was a big man, bulky, and at six feet considerably taller than most men in that era. He was not especially graceful and was said to be an awkward rider. His

*Cartes de visite*, or visiting cards, predecessors of calling cards, became extremely popular in the 1850s. This *carte* depicts a younger and stern pre-Stonewall, Thomas Jackson. This same image was used in 1863 on a deck of playing cards—Jackson was the four of clubs.

rural western Virginia upbringing did not adequately prepare him for the advanced studies at West Point and initially he fell behind his younger and far better educated classmates, such as George McClellan and A. P. Hill. At times wealthier classmates ridiculed him for his lower-class background. But the tenacity that was to mark his command in battle quickly became evident and he did whatever was necessary to succeed. As one of his classmates later remembered, "All lights were put out at Taps, and just before the signal he would pile up his grate with anthracite coal, and, lying prone before it on the floor, would work away at his lessons by the glare of the fire." He graduated in 1846 near the top of his class. One classmate remarked, "There was no one of our class who more absolutely possessed the respect and confidence of all."

After the Mexican-American War was won, rather than serving in a peacetime army Jackson accepted a position at the esteemed Virginia Military Institute, teaching natural and experimental philosophy—which essentially was physics—and artillery tactics. He was not a gifted teacher; his classroom technique consisted of forcing his students to memorize material and recite it precisely as it was written; his tactics course apparently consisted primarily of his students pulling fieldpieces around the campus. He was thoroughly disliked by many of his students. One of them supposedly challenged him to a duel, and he had restraining orders placed on several others. The institute's superintendent admitted that the man whom students derisively nicknamed Old Jack, Tom Fool, and Square Box, "was no teacher, and he lacked the tact required for getting along with his classes."

In his classroom he would sit "perfectly erect and motionless," remembered one of his students, and when he was asked to explain a complex proposition he would recite from his photographic memory the exact words written in the text. He sucked on lemons and at night he was said to sleep with one arm in the air, which he explained increased circulation.

But there also was something so decent about Jackson that even with these quirks, many students admired him. He might not have been a great teacher, but he was a rare leader. And it simply wasn't possible to ever assume his position on an issue. When VMI's superintendent, Francis Smith, was put in charge of John Brown's hanging, Smith assigned several of his students to provide additional security. Jackson was given twenty-one cadets and two howitzers and was only feet away from Brown as he stood on the scaffold. "It was an imposing but very solemn scene," he wrote to his wife. "I was much impressed with the thought that before me stood a man, in the full vigor of health, who must in a few minutes be in eternity. I sent up a petition that he might be saved. Awful was the thought that he might in a few minutes receive the sentence."

When the war began, several of Jackson's students followed him into the Confederate army and served proudly under his command as he rose in prestige. They were with him on the field at Bull Run when he stood resolute while the lines around him were crumbling—the day he became Stonewall Jackson.

No one ever doubted his courage under fire or his mastery of battlefield strategy. Although he was a harsh disciplinarian, his troops loved him. Whenever he or Lee appeared on a battlefield, the men would start cheering; after several such outbursts federal soldiers finally figured out why. From then on, when they heard the hurrahs being raised they immediately began shelling that part of the line. In response Jackson taught his battle horse, the famed Little Sorrel, to run down the line as fast as she could.

It was after the first fight at Bull Run that Jackson pleaded with President Jefferson Davis to carry the war into the North. Captain Edward Porter Alexander reported in his memoirs that when Davis visited the battlefield only hours after the battle had ended, Jackson shouted to him, "We have whipped them. They ran like sheep. Give me 5,000 fresh men, and I will be in Washington City tomorrow morning."

While President Davis and General Jackson enjoyed a cordial and respectful relationship, Jackson was frustrated by Davis's reluctance to press forward when he had the Union troops on the run. For him, there was only one way to wage war: "War means fighting," he once said. "To fight is the duty of a soldier; march swiftly, strike the foe with all your strength, and take away from him everything you can. Injure him in every possible way, and do it quickly."

The daily life of soldiers at war was brought home to readers through the sketches of Edwin Forbes, which appeared regularly in *Frank Leslie's Illustrated Newspaper.* A closer look at this seemingly tranquil scene, *Officers and Soldiers on the Battlefield of the Second Bull Run, Recognizing the Remains of Their Comrades,* reveals a patrol examining the skulls and bones of the men who died there a year earlier.

Within days of the great Confederate victory at Bull Run, Jackson presented Davis with a strategy that he believed could end the war quickly. McClellan's army had suffered a grievous defeat, Jackson said, and before he had time to heal his wounds and reinforce his army, the Confederacy had to attack. As General Gustavus W. Smith recalled him proposing,

> McClellan's raw recruits could not stand against us in the field. Crossing the Upper Potomac, occupying Baltimore, and taking possession of Maryland, we could cut off the communications of Washington, force the Federal Government to abandon the capital, beat McClellan's army if it came out

against us in the open country, destroy industrial establishments wherever we found them, break up the lines of interior commercial intercourse, close the coal mines, seize and, if necessary, destroy the manufactories and commerce of Philadelphia, and of other large cities within our reach; take and hold the narrow neck of country between Pittsburgh and Lake Erie; subsist mainly on the country we traverse, and making unremitting war amidst their homes, force the people of the North to understand what it will cost them to hold the South in the Union at the bayonet's point.

Jackson's aggressive strategy, which was remarkably similar to the "scorched earth policy" adopted three years later by Union general William T. Sherman as he marched through Georgia, meant declaring war on the people of the region rather than their army. It meant destroying their homes and farms, stores and factories, robbing the enemy of any means of support. Many historians believe that, had it been implemented at that moment, it might have led to a Confederate victory.

But President Davis did not agree with Jackson. Davis wanted to fight a defensive war, confident that as European mills grew desperate for cotton, their governments would intervene to forge a truce, or that the cost of the war would simply be more than the North was willing to bear. The risk of sending his army north without sufficient supplies was far too great for him and he dismissed Jackson's plan.

Jackson returned to the battlefield, frustrated that his commanders could not see the obvious. His firm belief that he was simply carrying out God's plans for him allowed him to accept this rebuff. Besides, General Lee also had plans for him. George McClellan had spent the months following his defeat at Bull Run rebuilding his army. Lincoln's three-month volunteers had been replaced by three-year enlistees. Finally, in the spring of 1862, McClellan was ready to move on Richmond. He launched his Peninsula Campaign by landing troops at Fort Monroe, planning to advance on the Confederate capital from the southeast while McDowell's thirty-five-thousand-man army was to attack from the north. To meet that threat, Lee ordered Jackson to take seventeen thousand men into the strategically vital Shenandoah Valley, which stretches for two hundred miles between the Blue Ridge and Allegheny Mountain ranges and at most points is about twenty-five miles wide, to meet McDowell.

But Jackson had far more ambitious ideas. He intended to get to the Big Valley, as it was known, before the federal troops could get comfortable, fight through them, and march

General Nathaniel P. Banks was the perfect example of a politician at war. Lincoln appointed the powerful former Speaker of the House of Representatives and governor of Massachusetts a major general, and his lack of military experience proved telling in a series of lackluster campaigns. He was criticized for failing to reinforce Grant at Vicksburg and later for being unable to occupy Texas in the Red River campaign.

on Washington. He executed his plan and reached the Shenandoah Valley undetected and launched a surprise attack on General Nathaniel P. Banks's six-thousand-man force, at that time the bulk of the Union forces in the region. Only a skillful retreat under fire by Banks prevented Jackson from annihilating his troops. To meet Jackson's threat, Lincoln immediately ordered McDowell to lay "aside for the present the movement on Richmond . . . to capture the forces of Jackson and Ewell."

Jackson had successfully taken the pressure off Richmond and instead put it on Washington. As Secretary of War Stanton warned, "Intelligence from various quarters leaves no doubt that the enemy, in great force, are marching on Washington."

Even from a Union standpoint, McClellan's failure to capture Richmond might indeed have been "God's plan." As John S. C. Abbott noted in his history of the Civil War, "there are innumerable instances, in the history of this war, in which apparent disasters have proved our choicest blessings. Had Richmond then been taken and the rebel army crushed, it is almost certain that some compromise would have been effected which would have preserved slavery, the fruitful cause of all our troubles."

The truth was that nobody really knew where Jackson's army was at any specific time. His ability to inspire his men to seemingly incredible feats was already inspiring awe. Jackson's army, his "foot cavalry," covered more territory in a day than McClellan's army could manage in a week. He seemed to be everywhere at once. Jackson's Shenandoah Valley campaign began in late March, when his men marched out of Winchester, a prosperous town with gaslit streets that had the misfortune to be set on a natural road in the northern valley, surrounded on all sides by small hills that hid the approach of enemy soldiers. It was seventy miles from Washington and twenty miles from the rail depot at Harpers Ferry, making it strategically important. While few local farmers owned slaves and most residents were against secession, when the fighting started the town supplied four companies of men to the Stonewall Brigade. Throughout the war the town changed hands seventy-two different times. Union troops occupied it for the first time in March when Jackson retreated after the First Battle of Kernstown, only to withdraw two months later when Jackson's reinforced army stormed over those hills from the south. The townspeople were so thrilled to be liberated that many of them joined the Confederate soldiers in fighting the Yankees; one report even described a woman leaning out a second-story window to fire at retreating Union soldiers. Jackson wrote to his wife that the townspeople "seemed nearly frantic with joy. . . . Our entrance into Winchester was one of the most stirring scenes of my life." Townspeople besieged him for his autograph on books or on slips of paper, and with his permission cut the buttons off his uniform—but he refused to allow them to cut a single strand of his thinning hair.

Jackson's strategy of relentless attack, then rapid withdrawal, confounded Union generals, many of whom had studied traditional military strategy at West Point. At one point at the end of March 1862, John Worsham, a proud member of Jackson's foot cavalry, wrote, "We were now retreating and advancing at the same time, a condition an army never undertook before." At one point a back road on which they were traveling had become soft with rain and snow, and, "as an evidence of General Jackson's anxiety and solicitude, I saw him personally getting rocks, and putting them in the holes of this road."

Somehow Jackson had figured out how to hide thousands of soldiers and his supply train in plain sight, moving throughout the valley at will, striking where he was unexpected, pressuring the bluecoats. On May 23, Worsham recalled, "General Jackson, as usual, made an immediate attack on the enemy. . . . The Yanks, finding things getting so hot, set fire to the two bridges, and were immediately charged by our cavalry and skirmishers, who saved the bridges in a damaged condition, crossed and were right in the midst of the enemy, Jackson along with them. The enemy made a bold stand and fought well, but they could not withstand Jackson's mode of warfare, and retreated . . . soon the entire force was killed and captured." The next morning, as Jackson's men marched out of the town, one prisoner shouted out a greeting to a soldier—to everyone's surprise it turned out to be his brother.

John Esten Cooke, a novelist serving in the Confederate army who filed stories with Southern newspapers, wrote about the love and respect that Stonewall Jackson's men held for him. In early August, Jackson's men were entrenched in the thick woods of Cedar Mountain, a small rise known sometimes, and appropriately, as Slaughter Mountain. As Union troops crossed a spacious wheat field, Jackson's artillery opened up on them with crushing fire. The Union troops' only possible salvation was to charge directly into the cannons. With loud cheers they raced into the woods and attacked with their bayonets, succeeding in collapsing the Confederate left flank and threatening the main body. Suddenly, Cooke wrote,

> At this moment of disaster and impending ruin, Jackson appeared, amid the clouds of smoke, and his voice was heard rising above the uproar and the thunder of the guns. The man, ordinarily so cool, silent and deliberate, was now mastered by the genius of battle. . . . Galloping to the front amid the heavy fire directed upon his disordered line—with his eyes flashing, his face flushed, his voice rising and ringing like a clarion on every ear, he rallied the confused troops and brought them into line. At the same moment the old Stonewall Brigade and Branch's Brigade advanced at a double-quick, and shouting "Stonewall Jackson! Stonewall Jackson!" the men poured a galling fire into the Federal lines. The presence of Jackson, leading them in person, seemed to produce an indescribable influence on the troops, and, as he rode to and fro, amid the smoke, encouraging the troops, they greeted him with resounding cheers.

Both sides absorbed as many as three hundred casualties and claimed victory, but the next morning it was reported, "After looking at each other defiantly for a short time," both armies retired from the field without a clear victor.

Jackson had earned General Lee's trust while becoming a Confederate hero. By September, Lee had marched his army across the Potomac into Maryland. But his supply route and lines of communications through the Big Valley were blocked by fourteen thousand Union troops in Harpers Ferry and Martinsburg. This was when he devised his plan revealed by Special Orders No. 191, in which he would temporarily split his army, sending Jackson to spearhead the attack on Harpers Ferry.

It was a complicated strategy. Jackson would command three columns that would have to traverse rough terrain—including recrossing the Potomac—to simultaneously approach Harpers Ferry. Success required an unusual degree of communication, coordination, and perseverance. Union troops were well fortified and resisted the initial heavy barrage, but under the cloak of eleven hours of darkness Jackson repositioned his men and guns. Cannons had been dragged up a mountain. At dawn more than five thousand infantrymen and twenty cannons overlooked Harpers Ferry and more artillery pieces were positioned to fire at point-blank range into the ravines where Union troops had taken cover. The Yankees were forced to surrender. At a cost of 273 casualties, Jackson had captured 12,700 prisoners, seventy-three artillery pieces, and two hundred wagons loaded with supplies. It was to be the most complete victory of the entire war.

Following this great victory, Jackson notified President Davis in Richmond, "Through God's blessing the advance . . . has been successful." His belief that all was preordained never wavered. Watching his men leave the field after defeating Union troops in the Battle of Port Royal, he exclaimed, "He who does not see the hand of God in this is blind, sir, blind!" And following his victory at First Bull Run, he had written to his wife, "Whilst great credit is due to other parts of our gallant army, God made my brigade more instrumental than any other in repulsing the main attack."

By this time Jackson rivaled only Lee as the most admired and beloved Confederate commander. Stories were told about him, some true, many fanciful. For example, it was said that Stonewall was a man of simple tastes who did not imbibe. Yet one cold night during the Shenandoah Valley campaign, when he could not light a fire because the enemy was too close, a staff surgeon, Hunter McGuire, gave him a slug of whisky to warm his insides. "Isn't the whisky good?" McGuire asked. "Yes, very, I like it," the general replied, "and that's the reason I don't drink it!" Poems and songs were written about him. When he rode through towns the citizens would run to get a glimpse of him, to be able to say they had seen Stonewall Jackson. A poem written about the Shenandoah Valley campaign, "Stonewall Jackson's Way," was set to music and became among the most popular songs of the war. Although the publisher originally claimed it was found "written on a small piece of paper, all stained with blood, in the bosom of a dead soldier" long after the war, Northerner John Williamson Palmer claimed credit. The song concludes:

> Ah! Maiden, wait and watch and yearn
> For news of Jackson's band!
> Ah! Widow, read, with eyes that burn,
> That ring upon thy hand;
> Ah! Wife, sew on, pray on, hope on;
> Thy life shall not be all forlorn

Lincoln and General McClellan, shown at Antietam in this 1862
photo, had a difficult relationship. In the first years of fighting,
McClellan's plodding ways saved countless lives and made him
very popular with the Army of the Potomac. But he made
no effort to disguise his anti-Lincoln politics and resisted the
president's insistence that he move more aggressively.

The foe had better ne'er been born
That gets in "Stonewall's way."

By late fall 1862, Lincoln finally was done with McClellan. "He's got the slows," was the
way he described it. McClellan's failure to pursue Lee's wounded army after Antietam had
convinced the president he would not prosecute the war. Lincoln visited McClellan's camp
with his aide Ozias Hatch, who later recalled, "The President, waving his hand towards the
scene before us, and leaning towards me, said in an almost whispering voice: 'Hatch—Hatch,

what is all this?' 'Why, Mr. Lincoln,' said I, 'this is the Army of the Potomac.' He hesitated a moment, and then, straightening up, said in a louder tone: 'No, Hatch, no. This is General McClellan's body-guard.'"

Historian Stephen Sears wrote that the flawed General McClellan "was a man possessed by demons and delusions. . . . He believed with equal conviction that enemies at the head of his own government conspired to see him and his army defeated so as to carry out their traitorous purposes. He believed himself to be God's chosen instrument for saving the Union. When he lost the courage to fight, as he did in every battle, he believed he was preserving his army to fight the next time on another and better day."

Following the early November elections, in which Lincoln's Republicans suffered substantial losses in Congress, the president placed General Ambrose Burnside in command of the Army of the Potomac. Burnside, who was easily recognizable by his unusual facial hair, which gave us the word "sideburns," in fact was a well-respected officer who had won praise for his aggressive tactics at Antietam. He was, as *Harper's Weekly* described him, "a soldier who to the greatest military skill unites dash, energy, and the prestige of success, and a man of the most exalted character and the noblest heart." Far more important to Lincoln was his willingness to fight. The preliminary Emancipation Proclamation had been issued and the

General Ambrose Burnside (left), remembered as much for giving us the word "sideburns" to describe muttonchops as for his wartime achievements, led his men into Lee's trap in the Battle of Fredericksburg (above). Concealed Confederate artillery began shelling exposed Union troops, prompting rebel colonel Porter Alexander to later say, "A chicken could not live on that field when we open on it."

This highly dramatized lithograph, published in 1888, illustrates the difficulty
Burnside faced trying to construct pontoon bridges to get his men across the
Rappahannock River under withering enemy sniper fire.

president hoped to sign it in January following a great Union victory. He needed that victory to silence his political critics and expected Burnside to deliver it to him.

Burnside launched an audacious plan: Lee had retreated across the Rappahannock River, near the town of Fredericksburg. That town was sixty miles from Richmond, connected to it by rail and roadway. Burnside proposed smashing through Lee's lines and marching on the Confederate capital. Lee's army was spread out in a semicircle about seven miles long. A frontal assault on the main body meant passing between General Longstreet's five divisions situated west of the town and Jackson's four divisions in the hills to the south. Instead Burnside decided to attack the flanks, committing sufficient troops to keep Longstreet occupied while launching his real attack on Jackson. Speed was essential; Burnside had to get his men across the Rappahannock on pontoon bridges before Lee discovered the point of his attack and shifted troops to reinforce Jackson.

On November 21, Burnside's 106,000-man army moved into position. Lee's 65,000 men lay camped on the Rappahannock, still unsure about the Union intentions. But the pontoon bridges Burnside needed to cross the river were delayed in arriving, and when they finally got there a massive snowstorm made operations impossible. Any chance of surprise was lost. Burnside's original plan was no longer viable, but he stubbornly refused to alter it to fit the new situation. The delay gave Lee sufficient time to move his troops into strong defensive positions in the hills. As Abbott wrote, "[Burnside's] success would have been entire, except for the unexpected delay in building the bridges, which gave the enemy ample time to concentrate their whole force at the precise point where it would be most effective."

The result was a shooting gallery. As the morning fog lifted on December 11, rebel snipers were firing from inside buildings, behind trees and walls. They "laugh[ed] at us with impunity," remembered a survivor. It took twelve hours before Union troops were able to row two hundred yards across the river and silence the snipers. That was sufficient time for Lee's army to dig into the hills surrounding the town. They took their strong defensive positions— and then they waited.

Burnside's army swept into the deserted town of Fredericksburg. The rebel artillery was oddly silent. Union soldiers suspected that Lee was low on ammunition or that he had ordered a withdrawal. In fact, Burnside's troops were walking into a trap.

At one point Lee considered surprising Burnside by attacking at night, an extremely risky strategy. Among his fears, he confessed, was the difficulty his men would have in identifying enemy soldiers in the dark. Jackson suggested a simple answer: "Strip our men to the waist, and kill every man that has a shirt on." When Lee rejected that idea, Jackson suggested tying a yard of white bandage around each soldier's arm. Lee finally decided the night attack was too risky and abandoned it.

Later that afternoon General Lee stood on the top of a rise with Jackson and Longstreet, watching massive numbers of Union troops crossing the river. Longstreet finally asked Jackson, "General, do not all these multitudes of Federals frighten you?"

Jackson answered confidently, "We shall see very soon whether I shall not frighten them."

A thick fog on the morning of the thirteenth prevented Burnside from launching observation balloons, so he had no idea that Stonewall Jackson was watching every movement. Jackson's men waited until the Yankees began crossing the half mile of open corn and wheat fields between Fredericksburg and the hills. And then they opened fire.

Entrenched in strongly fortified positions, many of them behind a stone wall, Lee's troops had a clear field of fire. Burnside fed his men into the grinder, launching wave after wave of frontal assaults that had little chance of succeeding. As General Longstreet respectfully described them, "A series of braver, more desperate charges than those hurled against the troops in the sunken road was never known and the piles and cross-piles of dead marked a field such as I have never saw before or since."

For a brief time, Union General George Meade's troops had managed to break through Jackson's line and threatened to roll up his forces, but Jackson calmly ordered his reserve into the gap and, when Union reinforcements failed to arrive, Meade withdrew.

Burnside's army paid for every foot they gained with their bodies. By the end of the day they had advanced only five hundred yards. The blood-soaked fields of Mannsfield Plantation would become known forever as the Slaughter Pens and five heroic Union soldiers would earn the Congressional Medal of Honor. More troops fought that day than in any other battle of the war, and the cost reflected that. Slaughtered in the fields, utterly defeated in achieving its mission, the dispirited Union army withdrew from the field as darkness fell mercifully. They had suffered 12,700 casualties that day, compared to the rebels' 5,300.

Still Burnside was not done. During a long war council with his commanders the next day he proposed sending fifteen thousand soldiers into the cauldron, believing that this large number of men would overwhelm rebel defenses. His staff argued against the plan. He then suggested occupying the town while withdrawing most of his army across the river. His officers had no confidence in him, and Burnside finally accepted his defeat. In the middle of the dark night the entire army marched silently away. "The history of wars does not record an instance of a retreat on so large a scale," wrote Abbott, "under the very eyes of the foe, successfully accomplished without the loss of a man, a gun, or a caisson."

Burnside's effort to give Lincoln the victory he so desperately craved had been a disaster. As journalist Murat Halstead of the *Cincinnati Commercial* reported, "It can hardly be in human nature for men to show more valor, or Generals to manifest less judgment, than were perceptible on our side that day. . . . The occupation of Fredericksburg was a blunder." The *New York Herald* wrote bluntly of Burnside that the enemy "had out-Generaled us."

Lincoln did his utmost to find something positive in the events, telling his army, "The courage with which you, in an open field maintained the contest against an entrenched foe . . . show[s] that you possess all the qualities of a great army, which will yet give victory to the cause of the country." But he confided to his aides, "If there is a worse place than hell, I am in it."

As Lee and Jackson became legends, Lincoln searched desperately for a man capable of leading his army to victory. "They say at Washington that we have some thirty-eight to forty major-generals," reported *Harper's Weekly,* "and nearly three hundred brigadiers; and now the question is, have we one man who can fairly be called a first-class general?" At the end of January, Lincoln removed Burnside, replacing him with General "Fighting Joe" Hooker.

By that time, emancipation had been proclaimed, freeing all the slaves in rebel-held territory. While Robert E. Lee was furious about this, Jackson viewed it as more of a military problem, knowing that it would add tens of thousands of men to the Union ranks. In fact, he was quite ambivalent about slavery. While clearly he recognized the immorality of a system that subjugated some of God's children, he also accepted its existence as the Lord's will. It was not for him to question God. But as a good Christian he treated slaves fairly and with

General Robert E. Lee's almost mythical reputation grew even greater after he defeated the much larger force commanded by General Joe Hooker (above) at Chancellorsville. Suffering a concussion from a cannonball's near miss, the usually aggressive Hooker hesitated to counterattack—and as a result almost lost the Army of the Potomac.

as much respect as was possible at that time. It was his task, he believed, to save their souls. As a child, he broke Virginia laws against educating slaves by teaching his cousin's slave to read—and that slave then boarded the Underground Railway and escaped to Canada.

According to some reports, Jackson's family owned six slaves in the late 1850s. Two of them had asked Jackson to buy them after their owner had died and allow them to work off their debt, a not uncommon practice. When he married for a second time, in 1853, his wife already owned several slaves. In 1855, he ignored the loosely enforced educational laws and began a "colored" Sunday school class in Lexington and taught reading and the Gospel to black children. There were people who tried to stop him. As one of his former instructors in that school remembered, "Some of the Bourbon aristocracy criticized his action, and even went so far as to threaten prosecution. But a healthy Christian segment in the community sustained him, and he went forward in the path of duty." He initially held the classes in his home, but when they grew to more than one hundred children, he had to move them to his church, and he awarded books and Bibles to the better students. Jackson actually seemed to be far more respected by the slaves than by the white population of Lexington.

He went to war with a slave named Jim Lewis, about whom little is known other than his complete devotion to Jackson. Jim Lewis was his "body man," meaning he stayed close by him, doing everything necessary to allow Jackson to focus on the war. One widely repeated story described Lewis packing all of Jackson's gear before being told to do so; when asked how he knew when it was time, he replied, "When I see the General get down on his knees and praying three, four times during a night I pack the baggage, for I know he going on an expedition."

Even while commanding a great army, Jackson's black Sunday school class remained vitally important to him. Only days after First Bull Run, his pastor, Rev. Dr. William S. White, received a letter from him. Presuming it included details of the Confederate victory, many people rushed to the church to hear it read. Reverend White mounted a box and opened the letter. "My Dear Pastor," it read. "In my tent last night, after a fatiguing day's service, I remembered that I had failed to send you my contribution for our colored Sunday school. Enclosed you will find my check for that object." Inside the envelope was a $50 donation. The school became so popular and successful that years later Robert E. Lee praised it, admitting, "The negro Sunday school, which he taught with such devotion, exerted an influence on the negroes of Lexington which is felt to this day among the negroes of that whole region."

By the spring of 1863, Stonewall Jackson had been at war for more than a year. It was time to meet his infant daughter, who had been born days before the Battle of Fredericksburg. Stonewall Jackson was married twice. His first wife, Elinor Junkin, whose father was the

The price of victory proved impossibly high for the rebels. As Stonewall Jackson scouted the battlefield in the darkness, his own troops mistakenly shot him. His wife, Mary Anna Morrison Jackson (above), rushed to Chancellorsville with their child to minister to him, and he died with her nearby several days later.

president of Washington College—later Washington and Lee University—had died after giving birth to a stillborn child. He married Mary Anna Morrison three years later—her father was the president of Davidson College—and their infant died less than a month after birth. Jackson stoically accepted these losses as God's will, and so was overjoyed when his first surviving child, a daughter named Julia Laura, was born in November 1862. But as he warned his wife shortly after Julia's birth, "Do not set your affections upon her, except as a gift from God. If she absorbs too much of our hearts, God may remove her from us."

In April, Jackson finally held his daughter. "During the whole of this short visit," wrote Mary Anna Jackson, "he rarely had her out of his arms, walking her, and amusing her in any way he could think of. . . . When she slept in the day, he would often kneel over her cradle, and gaze upon her little face with the most rapt admiration." But while Jackson was resting with his family, Hooker's army was attempting a daring maneuver. This would be the last rest Jackson would have. When he was informed that Hooker was marching, he rushed back to join his men.

General Joe Hooker was the opposite of McClellan; he sometimes moved too rashly and too often expressed undue confidence. In fact, rather than pushing him to fight, Lincoln had to restrain him. Oddly, though, the nickname "Fighting Joe" had been given to him by an overzealous copy editor at the Associated Press, who inadvertently left the punctuation mark out of a headline that was supposed to read, "Still Fighting—Joe Hooker." Personally,

When Lincoln gave Joe Hooker command of the Army of the Potomac in the winter of 1863 (about the time Mathew Brady took this photograph), the confident general boasted, "May God have mercy on General Lee, for I will have none."

he despised it, explaining, "Don't call me Fighting Joe, for that name has done and is doing me incalculable injury. It makes a portion of the public think that I am a hot-headed, furious young fellow, accustomed to making furious and needless dashes at the enemy." That did not prevent Lee from mockingly referring to him as "F. J. Hooker."

Also inaccurate is the belief that the slang term for a prostitute, "hooker," was first applied to the working ladies who trailed his army. In reality, the derivation goes back much further in history and there are several possible explanations—none of them having to do with the general.

Joseph Hooker was another West Point graduate who had served nobly in the Mexican-

American War. He "attracted attention," according to newspapers, "by his gallant and meritorious conduct" at Chapultepec. Early in the Civil War his aggressive tactics had proved successful, although he was loudly critical of Union commanders. He had been especially infuriated at the waste of his men at Fredericksburg; his division had suffered massive losses when ordered to make several frontal assaults directly into Confederate lines.

When given command of the Army of the Potomac he raised morale by improving living conditions; he cleaned up camps and hospitals, substituted fresh food and bread for hardtack, increased security, granted longer leaves, and tried to ensure that his men had serviceable uniforms and equipment. Recognizing that the army too often moved blindly, he established a functioning intelligence service and even authorized a separate cavalry corps to mirror Confederate Jeb Stuart's mounted force. And after doing all of that, he devised a strategy that might have won the war.

Rather than repeating Burnside's fatal mistakes, he planned to circle Lee's flank, forcing him to abandon his secure position around Fredericksburg and retreat or fight in the open field. In early May, it was reported, "the whole region was alive with movement," as about one hundred thousand Yankees soldiers, each man carrying about sixty pounds of equipment, "concealing themselves in the dense growth of woods which lined the stream, and behind the curtain of hills," crossed the upper waters of the Rappahannock and the Rapidan ten miles above the city, successfully flanking Lee's army. Many of them crossed the rivers naked, their clothes bundled up and kept dry on the tips of their bayonets. They made camp near the tiny village of Chancellorsville, which consisted primarily of the Chancellor tavern. To create a diversion, an additional twenty thousand troops staged a clever ruse two miles below Fredericksburg. Under the watchful eyes of rebel spotters, two divisions marched over a hill and down a long bank, then crossed the river. Four more divisions with their artillery and baggage trains followed them—but instead of crossing the river they circled around through a ravine, completely hidden from the spotters, then marched over the hill again and again, creating the impression of a far larger force.

"It is with heartfelt satisfaction," the confident Hooker reported, "that the commanding general announces to the army that the operations of the last three days have determined that our enemy must either ingloriously fly or come out from behind his defenses and give us battle on our own ground, where certain destruction awaits him." But to Hooker's discomfort, rather than the hard ground and open plain he had expected, the land surrounding Chancellorsville was a thick swampy marsh, covered by dense underbrush. The Wilderness, as it was known, "an impenetrable thicket," made maneuvering difficult while providing cover for enemy troops.

Prior to the war Virginian Jubal
Early had been passionately opposed
to secession, but, like Lee, his loyalty
to his state prevailed. Serving under
Jackson at Chancellorsville, he
fought in many of the major battles
of the war, coming within sight of
Washington, DC—but he hesitated and
lost whatever opportunity he may
have enjoyed.

General Lee made a fateful decision. Deciding that the attack below the town was a diversion, he once again split his army, sending Jackson with the bulk of his men to meet Hooker's threat while leaving General Jubal Early to answer the Union attack on Fredericksburg. Dividing an already smaller force was questionable military strategy, but Lee had a not-so-secret weapon: the genius of Stonewall Jackson. Union observers in balloons reported that great numbers of rebel troops were abandoning their positions on the heights and racing toward Chancellorsville. In response, on Friday, May 1, Union general John Sedgwick launched an assault on the rebel fortifications at Fredericksburg, his men racing across the recently blood-soaked field, and this time overwhelming the greatly reduced force there. "The enemy," reported the *New York Times*, "... fled in wild confusion, secreting themselves in the houses, woods, and wherever a place of concealment was afforded." But most important, they continued to engage the Yankees in battle, holding them in place.

That same morning, Jackson ordered an attack on Hooker's troops in the Wilderness, knowing the terrain would make it impossible for Union forces to organize a coordinated attack. As a Union soldier explained, "The passage through the tangled thickets broke up companies and regiments into crowds. Men were separated from their commands and absolutely lost in the woods." By early afternoon the rebels had gained a small advantage, then began withdrawing under heavy fire. General Hooker's officers pleaded with him to mount a massive counterattack that might overwhelm Lee's exposed army, but the suddenly reticent general refused, instead withdrawing his bluecoats into a defensive position.

That night Jackson was told by his topographer that by following back roads his troops could swing around Hooker's right flank and launch a surprise attack from the west. He and Lee sat alone by a fire as Jackson outlined his bold plan. The strategy meant splitting the Confederate army into two smaller forces, leaving the main body completely vulnerable if Hooker attacked. But Lee was willing to take that risk, confident that Hooker, assuming his army remained safe in its camps, would not take the initiative.

On May 2, Jackson led twenty-eight thousand men on the daring raid—among them twenty officers who had studied at VMI—believing the next few hours might well determine the outcome of the war. He rode up and down the columns, urging his men with "Press on! Press on!" Speed and surprise were everything. By late afternoon his troops had completed the maneuver. Jackson stood atop a ridge in the woods, looking down on the unsuspecting Union front lines. "His eyes burned with a brilliant glow, lighting up a sad face," recalled General Fitzhugh Lee. "His expression was one of intense interest, his face was colored slightly with the paint of approaching battle, and radiant at the success of his flank movement . . . he did not reply once during the five minutes he was on the hill, and yet his lips were moving. . . . I know what he was doing then. Oh! Beware of rashness, General Hooker. Stonewall Jackson is praying in full view and in rear of your right flank!"

Shortly after five p.m. deer and rabbits came rushing out of the woods toward Hooker's 11th Corps—followed instantly by the chilling rebel yell as almost thirty thousand men came pouring out of the woods. "The bolt had descended like lightning from the sky," Abbott wrote. "The destruction of the whole army was menaced. . . . It was like a whirlwind's rush and roar, as it sweeps the desert. . . . In one half hour the whole aspect of the campaign was changed."

The Yankees fought back desperately. Union artillery opened up on the attackers, temporarily halting the advancing rebels. But Hooker's flank had collapsed and the rout began. His men abandoned their weapons and raced for their lives, many of them swimming across the river to relative safety. The rebels pursued them until the sun set.

No one settled comfortably; the armies continued to move in the moonlight. Once Jackson held the strategic ground between the Yankees and the river, Lee would attack to finish the destruction of Hooker's army. In the darkness Stonewall Jackson and several officers mounted their horses and began riding along the front lines, between the two armies, laying out their plans for the fight.

It was a very dangerous place to be, but Jackson paid little heed, knowing he was protected by the Lord's grace. He certainly had substantial evidence of that. A cannonball had shot between his legs, causing no damage in the Mexican campaign! At Sharpsburg he had been riding with General Lafayette McLaws when an artillery shell passed right between them, striking a courier, but it did not explode. Jackson had said to McLaws, "The enemy, it seems, is getting our range," then rode away quickly. "Much to my gratification," McLaws admitted, then added that several times during the day Jackson had reminded him that "God has been very kind to us today."

God was less kind on the night of May 2, 1863. As Jackson reconnoitered the battlefield he heard gunshots and artillery firing. Bullets struck nearby. Union troops were testing rebel lines.

Jackson rode easily. An aide grabbed his reins and said anxiously, "General, don't you think this is the wrong place for you?"

"The danger is all over," Jackson replied. "The enemy is routed. Go back and tell A. P. Hill to press forward." But this time Jackson was wrong. Hooker had launched a night movement, desperate to recover some of the ground he had lost. As Union troops rode out of the Wilderness, Jackson and his men turned their horses and galloped back toward their own lines. Before departing on this dangerous tour, Jackson had given orders that his troops were to fire on any soldiers coming up the road.

In the darkness Jackson's small party was indistinguishable from Union soldiers. Men of the 18th North Carolina, on edge waiting for the Union attack, saw several men racing toward them—and opened fire. Several of the men riding with Jackson were killed instantly. Jackson was hit three times, twice in his left arm and once in his right hand. He slipped from his saddle onto the ground as the firing finally stopped. A. P. Hill, informed that Jackson had been wounded, ran to assist him. "General, are you very much hurt?" he asked.

Jackson was alert and replied, "Yes, General, I think I am; and all of my wounds were from my own men." He then asked Hill to fetch a skillful surgeon. As Union skirmishers fought closer to rebel lines he had to be moved. In fact, two Union soldiers actually wandered past only a few feet away and were taken prisoner, without ever learning how close they had been to the Confederate hero. Litter bearers carried him for several hundred yards before one of them was struck in the arm by shrapnel from a Union shell and fell, dropping Jackson hard onto the ground. He suffered an additional painful shoulder injury and started bleeding again. His wound again was tied off and, with the assistance of several men, he stumbled toward safety. The general commanding the North Carolina brigade, William Dorsey Pender, recognized him, although he did not appreciate the severity of his wounds. His men were

This 1888 chromolithograph portrays the shooting of Stonewall Jackson. Jackson's
death not only deprived Lee of his most able and daring officer but plunged the entire
South into mourning. Jackson simply was irreplaceable.

being decimated by the shelling, Pender said, and he feared they could not hold the position. Witnesses reported that Jackson's eyes flashed with fire as he ordered, "You must hold your ground, General Pender. You must hold your ground, sir." That was the last battle order he ever gave.

Dr. Hunter McGuire gave him whisky and morphine and rode with him the four miles to the hospital at Wilderness Run. He nearly had died from blood loss, but surgeons were able to stanch the bleeding and save his life. His left arm was shattered, though, and Jackson concurred with the decision to amputate it. He recovered well and within a day, according to witnesses, was cheerful and talking about the battle.

It had been another great Confederate victory. The news that Stonewall Jackson had been gravely wounded enraged the rebels, who attacked again early the next morning, screaming, "Remember Jackson." As a Northern newspaper reported, "Never on battle-field did men face death with more recklessness than did the troops of Jackson, inspired by their fanatic, unflinching leader." General Hooker seemingly had lost his will to fight, failing to send as many as thirty-five thousand waiting troops into action. No one has ever been able to explain his decision. At about nine that morning, as he stood on the veranda of his headquarters, a Confederate cannonball shattered a pillar and knocked him unconscious. By the end of the day Lee was occupying Union headquarters and Hooker and his army were executing another "strategic withdrawal."

Hooker's generals wanted to launch another assault, confident that their superior numbers eventually would wear down the Southern army. They still had more soldiers ready to fight and continued to occupy several of the strategically most important positions on the battlefield. On the eve of the battle, an anxious Lee had admitted in a letter to President Davis, "As far as I can judge, the advantage of numbers and position is greatly in favor of the enemy," and even after days of fighting the balance of power had not changed significantly. But Hooker was disoriented and confused, and instead of fighting, ordered a withdrawal.

One threat remained: at Fredericksburg General Sedgwick had finally successfully crossed the river and driven the rebels from the infamous stone wall. But Lee, having defeated Hooker, raced reinforcements six miles to the city to drive back Sedgwick's attack. The brilliant strategy devised by Lee and Jackson had enabled the smaller rebel force to destroy Hooker's larger army. More troops had been in the fight than in any battle of the entire war and the casualties were enormous: Hooker's Army of the Potomac suffered 1,694 men killed, 9,672 wounded, and 5,938 missing, while Lee lost 1,724 killed, 9,233 wounded, and 2,503 unaccounted for.

As a student in Thomas Jackson's class at the
Virginia Military Institute, James Walker was
dismissed only weeks before his graduation
for challenging Jackson to a duel. The men
reconciled and became so close that on his
deathbed Jackson requested that Walker take
command of his brigade. Walker's gallantry
at Gettysburg caused his men to pay him the
greatest honor, nicknaming him "Stonewall Jim."

But the greatest cost was the loss of Stonewall Jackson. Upon being informed that Jackson
had been wounded, Lee said, "Jackson has lost his left arm . . . and now I have lost my right."
For a few days, though, it appeared that Jackson might survive. He was awake and alert,
jubilant over the great victory. With great satisfaction he handed over control of the Stonewall
Brigade to Colonel James Walker, who had been his student at VMI and had served bravely
with him for much of the fighting. The healing process had begun. His amputated left arm
was given a proper Christian funeral and buried not far from the hospital. When people
visited him to commiserate about his wounds, he dismissed them, explaining, "I consider
these wounds a blessing; they were given me for some good and wise purpose, and I would
not part with them if I could." As the battle raged around him, Lee feared Union troops would
reach the hospital; he ordered Jackson moved twenty-seven miles farther to the rear.

But three days after being wounded, Jackson's condition suddenly worsened. In the
middle of the night he became nauseous and complained of terrible pain on his right side.
Doctors examined him and found no wound, so they attributed it to his fall from the litter.
Jackson asked Jim Lewis to lay a wet towel on his side. Although doctors were not yet aware
of it, pneumonia, then a fatal condition, had set in, possibly caused by the fall.

A day later his wife arrived with his child. "I know you would gladly give your life for me,
but I am perfectly resigned," he told her. "Do not be sad. I hope I shall recover. Pray for me,
but always remember in your prayers to use the petition, Thy will be done." She took charge
as his nurse and within a day his pain had disappeared; his surgeons tried to fight the disease

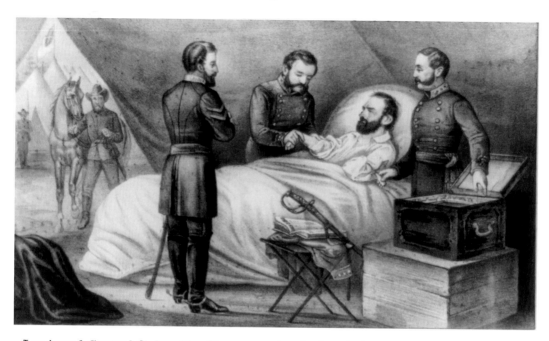

Lee issued General Orders No. 61, announcing Jackson's death and proclaiming, "We feel that his spirit still lives, and will inspire the whole army with his indomitable courage and unshaken confidence in God as our hope and our strength." This Currier and Ives print depicting his deathbed was published after the war.

but there was no effective treatment. They prayed and sang hymns. He was able to play with his daughter, whom he called his "Little Comforter." A day later Mary Anna Jackson was honest with her husband, telling him he was dying. Jackson replied, "It will be infinite gain, to be translated to heaven and be with Jesus."

For a time on his last day he became deluded, giving nonsensical military orders, but he suddenly had a last rational moment, when he said quietly, "Let us cross over the river, and rest under the shade of the trees." On the afternoon of May 10, Stonewall Jackson died. He was glad of the day, having reminded his caretakers only hours earlier, "It is the Lord's Day. . . . I have always desired to die on Sunday."

As Lincoln was learning, to his great distress, and as Lee knew, there are few great generals and only a handful of them might be considered military geniuses. Whatever combination of talent, skill, luck, and fortitude it requires to become that type of historic leader, Thomas

"Stonewall" Jackson possessed it. The day he died the Confederacy was holding its own in the war; Northern morale was at a low point and many people were questioning the continuation of the war. A Union soldier wrote to his father weeks after Jackson's death, "I should be exceedingly sorry to see our country divided and I do not think there is many more willing to do more for their country than I am, but I am almost inclined to think that we shall have to acknowledge their independence."

The Confederacy was stunned by Stonewall Jackson's death. That he had been killed by his own guns made accepting it even more difficult. The city of Richmond turned out for his funeral. It was reported that as the long line of mourners walked slowly past his coffin to pay their respects, one elderly gentleman reminded them, "Weep not; all is for the best. Though Jackson has been taken from the head of his corps, his spirit is now pleading our cause at the bar of God."

"You will have heard of the death of General Jackson," Robert E. Lee lamented. "It is a terrible loss. I do not know how to replace him." The answer, he was to find, was that replacing Jackson was impossible. And on that fact the war turned.

In the early years of the war, both sides used observation balloons to conduct aerial surveillance. Although the Union had a far more extensive program, and Lincoln was a supporter of these tethered balloons, which reached heights of one thousand feet or more, the program essentially was abandoned after 1863. But in that time it had proven its value.

The first observation balloons had been flown in wartime by the French more than half a century earlier. During the Civil War, Professor Thaddeus Lowe was selected to be the chief aeronaut for the Union army, building seven gas-filled balloons of different sizes. These balloons carried between one and five men and communicated with the ground by semaphore flags or, in the case of the larger balloons, by telegraph. The balloons were colorfully decorated; the side of the *Intrepid* bore a likeness of General McClellan being carried by an eagle.

Confederate attempts to create their own balloon corps were hampered by a lack of material, so they requested that women hand over their silk dresses, which were woven into a balloon and covered by varnish. Unfortunately, the ship carrying this first attempt went aground and was captured by Federal troops. But rebel balloons were employed near Richmond during the Seven Days' Battle.

Balloons were used successfully in several engagements, including the Peninsula Campaign, at Fredericksburg and Chancellorsville, in the attack on Island No. 10, and, seen here, the 1862 Battle of Seven Pines. In the Brady photograph the *Intrepid* is being filled and the illustration shows how balloons were used to report troop movements and direct artillery fire.

Because of their position well behind the line, as well as the heights they reached, no balloon was struck by fire or shell. The most dangerous episode took place in April 1862, when a balloon carrying General Fitz John Porter broke loose from its moorings and floated over enemy lines at Yorktown. Fortunately the winds carried the general back behind his own lines, where he landed safely. "The General was master of his position in the air," the *New York Times* reported, "as he generally is of that on land."

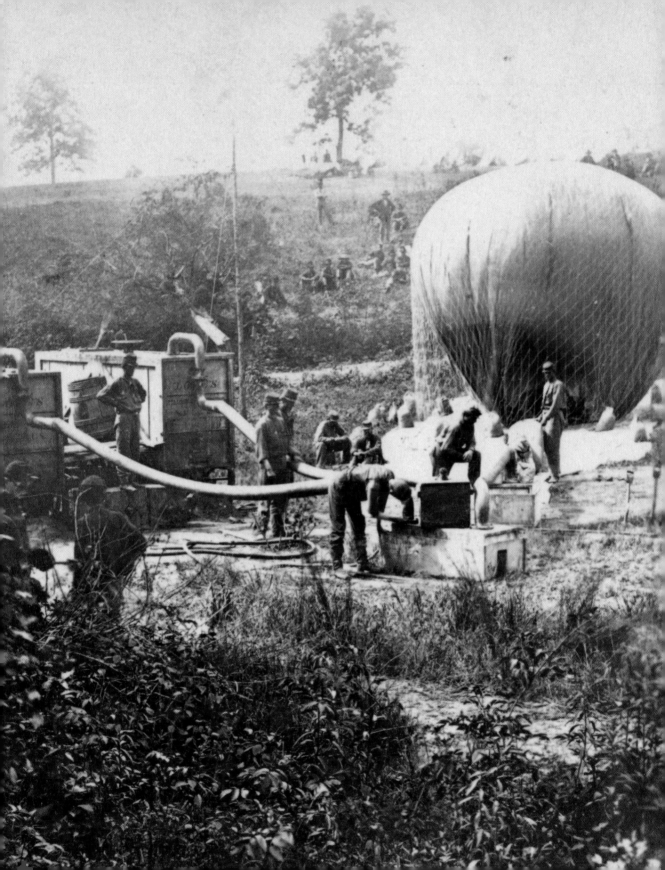

# BLOODIED
## BROTHERS
### The Battle of Gettysburg

Shoes.

According to legend, the Battle of Gettysburg began because Confederate soldiers had worn out their shoes and had been reduced to fighting barefoot. When, in the summer of 1863, General A. P. Hill was informed that shoes were available for his men in the nearby Pennsylvania town of Gettysburg, he permitted General Henry Heth to send in a party "and get those shoes." A rebel patrol walked casually toward the quiet town, but as they mounted a rise in the road, they spotted several Union soldiers walking slowly toward them. Both sides were stunned. They raced back to their lines and spread the word that the enemy was at Gettysburg. Within hours commanders on both sides had called for reinforcements and tens of thousands of troops marched to the battlefield. The bloodiest battle of the Civil War was about to begin.

◻ The printmaking firm Currier and Ives referred to itself as the "Grand Central Depot for Cheap and Popular Prints" that produced "colored engravings for the people." Historical accuracy was less important than marketing. This detail from the Battle of Gettysburg was produced within weeks of the fighting.

General Ambrose Powell Hill led rebel
troops throughout most of the major battles
of the war. At Chancellorsville he replaced
the wounded Jackson. He was criticized
after Gettysburg for moving before Lee's
army was in place, but Lee greatly
respected Hill's abilities.

It is an often-told tale, but it isn't quite true. While the Battle of Gettysburg did begin unexpectedly when the Yanks and the Rebs stumbled into each other, shoes had nothing to do with it. This was a battle for which each side had been preparing for weeks.

Lee's great victory at Chancellorsville had emboldened the Confederacy. Now he was under pressure to march his undersupplied army into the fertile farmlands of Pennsylvania for replenishment, then continue to Washington or even Philadelphia. Southern newspapers, glowing with optimism, practically demanded that he bring the war into the North, to inflict on the Yankees some of the pain the Confederacy had suffered. Robert E. Lee allowed himself to be swayed; looking north he saw a weakened Army of the Potomac commanded by an indecisive general he had already humiliated. He was well aware that the antiwar Copperheads had gained strength in the last election and more and more Northerners were wondering if continuing the war was worth it. One more victory could turn them and force Lincoln to find a compromise. As he wrote to Jeff Davis, his army would "give all the encouragement we can, consistently with the truth, to the rising peace party of the North."

Lee's optimism gradually grew into overconfidence, which then moved toward arrogance. "There never were such men in an army before," he told his generals. "They will go anywhere and do anything if properly led." Robert E. Lee was about to make his greatest mistake. He ignored several important facts: that his army was still outnumbered, that he lacked sufficient supplies, and that the war had created an economic boom in the industrial North rather than inflicting the hardships that had become part of daily life in the South. But most of all he overlooked completely the reality that Stonewall Jackson was no longer at his side.

Lee's intention to drive north was not a secret. The only question was where and when he would strike. For several weeks the two armies had skirmished along the Rappahannock, neither side able to gain an advantage. At Brandy Station, the largest cavalry battle of the entire war, bluecoats obtained General Jeb Stuart's private papers, among them Lee's orders for a rapid advance into Pennsylvania. Hooker sent some troops to that state's border, while leaving sufficient troops in place to protect Washington.

But once again Lee's army seemed to have vanished. No one could figure out where he was going. "The week was one of terror, confusion and doubt," Abbott wrote. "The vast army of Lee, like a giant monster preparing to spring . . . making deceptive dashes then retiring stealthily into concealment, was working its way . . . to what precise point no one could dare predict. Philadelphia and Washington were equally in panic."

By 1863, antiwar and anti-Lincoln sentiment was growing as Northerners began wondering if the huge number of casualties was worth it. This cartoon, published in Boston, attacks Lincoln's mismanagement of the war.

The reputations of both Confederate general Henry Heth (left) and Union general George Meade (right) were soiled at Gettysburg. Heth was blamed for sending troops into the town before the rebel army was prepared to fight, while Meade was criticized for not pursuing and destroying the retreating rebels.

But when Lee got to Pennsylvania, it would not be Hooker waiting for him. As the rebel army created havoc in Pennsylvania, ransacking towns and farms, sending any black man suspected of being a fugitive back south, Hooker bickered with the War Department. Lincoln had to replace him but had no obvious choice—one newspaper even suggested seriously that the president himself was best equipped to lead the army in the field. When Hooker finally resigned in June 1863, Lincoln offered command to the competent but generally undistinguished general George Meade. Meade apparently was stunned by the directive and initially believed the officer who arrived with Lincoln's message had come to relieve or arrest him, not give him command of the army. It was not a promotion Meade had sought, and he accepted it reluctantly, admitting, "I've been tried and condemned without a hearing, and I suppose I shall have to go to execution."

Meade was in no position to advocate clever plans or complex strategies. "I'm going straight at them," he wrote his wife, "and will settle this thing one way or the other." His strategy, he informed Lincoln, was "to find and fight the enemy."

While Union commanders searched for Lee, the Confederates were equally blind. While history credits Jeb Stuart's cavalry as being the eyes and ears of the Southern army, historians like Dr. Allen Guelzo, the Henry Luce Professor of the Civil War Era at Gettysburg College, describe that as one of the greatest myths of the war, pointing out that the cavalry rarely provided useful intelligence. Stuart set out on June 22 to circle behind the Yankees' right flank in order to harass them, turn their attention from the main thrust, and meanwhile assess their true strength. But to his consternation, the Union army was spread out over a much greater landscape than he had assumed, forcing him to ride much farther east than intended, during which time he was completely out of touch with Lee, so Lee was forced to plan his strategy without any information.

By dividing his army into three corps, Lee had successfully created confusion, but as he became aware that the Union army was closer than he had believed, he moved rapidly to concentrate his forces, abandoning a planned attack on the capital of Harrisburg, and ordered his army to unite near the prosperous town of Gettysburg.

When Meade took command on June 28, it had already become apparent that Lee was massing his army nearby. On the night of June 29, Johnny Reb's campfires were visible from the town. The new commanding general immediately ordered his army to meet the threat, and on the eve of battle, as many as 150,000 soldiers slept uneasily within a few miles of Gettysburg.

On June 30, as Confederate general Heth would write only eight weeks after the battle, "I ordered Brigadier General Pettigrew to take his brigade to Gettysburg, search the town for army supplies (shoes especially), and return the same day." It was Pettigrew's scouts who spotted bluecoats in the street, and the myth that the Battle of Gettysburg was fought over shoes was born.

Reinforcements for both sides continued to pour into the area. The Yankees would be bolstered by volunteers. Two days earlier Governor Curtin had issued an appeal for sixty thousand Pennsylvanians to take up arms "to defend their soil, their families, and their firesides." Among the men who responded was sixty-nine-year-old John Burns of Bendersville, a hard-drinking veteran of the War of 1812 who made the dubious claim of being descended from Scottish poet Robert Burns. He had attempted on several occasions to volunteer but had been rejected because of his age. But now the call went out for any able-bodied man who could aim a rifle, and on the morning of July 1 he dressed in his fanciest clothes—a swallow-tailed blue coat with gilt buttons and a black silk hat—and fell into the ranks of the 150th Pennsylvania Volunteers.

Upon being informed that an unidentified number of Union soldiers were in the town, Hill decided to send a sizable contingent into Gettysburg to assess the situation. At seven thirty a.m., a Union soldier named Marcellus Jones fired the first shot. The battle began before either army was fully prepared. Lee would have much preferred to wait until Longstreet's corps and Stuart's cavalry had gotten there. Meade reported, "A battle at Gettysburg is now forced upon us," and then added later, "We may fight it out here just as well as anywhere else." The battle was much larger than either commander had anticipated, and when it became apparent to Meade that a decisive victory could bring an end to the war, he said, "Very well. I select this battlefield!"

"The old hero of Gettysburg," crusty John L. Burns, was photographed by Mathew Brady with his rifle and his crutches outside his home as his fame grew throughout the nation in the weeks following the Battle of Gettysburg. Burns became the subject of poems and short stories in Northern periodicals.

The fighting intensified throughout the first day. Union general John Reynolds rushed his Iron Brigade into the fight—and was killed by a sharpshooter. As the rebels drove Reynolds's troops back, the elderly civilian volunteer John Burns suffered several slight wounds. While painful, they were not life-threatening—but they prevented him from retreating with the brigade. That put him in a desperate position: the penalty for a civilian—a so-called bushwhacker—caught on a battlefield was summary execution. Burns discarded his weapon and ammunition and crawled onto a cellar door, where Confederate troops found him. As a rebel doctor treated his wounds, Burns claimed he was a noncombatant and had been out searching for his cow. He was allowed to return home, where his wife reportedly called him "an old fool . . . getting holes in his best clothes." But in General Abner Doubleday's post-battle report, he praised Burns, who became nationally known as "the Hero of Gettysburg." And poet Francis Bret Harte immortalized his deed in "John Burns of Gettysburg," writing:

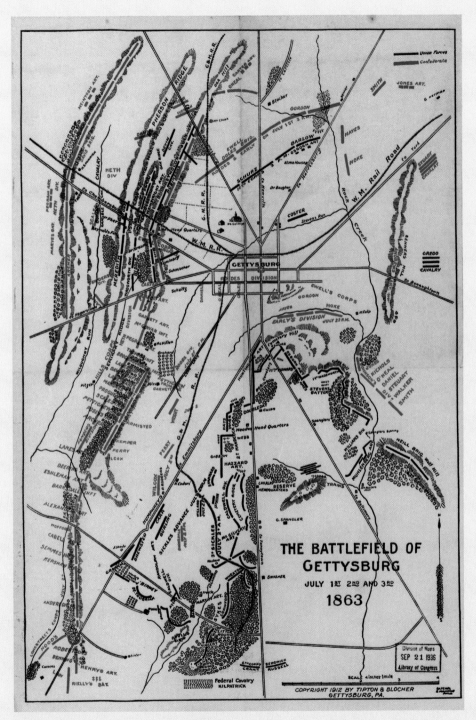

This map of the three days' fighting at Gettysburg illustrates the difficulty faced by the rebels (thick lines) in dislodging the Union troops from the hills outside the town.

While Burns, unmindful of jeer and scoff,
Stood there picking the rebels off,—
With his long brown rifle, and bell-crown hat,
And the swallow-tails they were laughing at.

But Burns was among the lucky ones, able to leave the battlefield with only minor wounds.
During the fighting that day the Yankees were driven back through the town, Meade's "troops

running along every available road" in retreat; at one point a brigade was caught between two rebel brigades who ran alongside them, firing as they ran, wiping out half the
Union troops. Thousands of bluecoats were captured. It was an inglorious retreat, and,
for a time, it appeared that Gettysburg was to be another rebel victory. But during this
scramble for safety, General Oliver Howard's men were able to seize and hold the high
ground atop Cemetery Hill, a vital strategic position just south of the town. For the next
three days, dug-in Union troops fought off repeated rebel attacks on their positions.

This is a misleadingly tranquil
view of Gettysburg taken from
Evergreen Cemetery gatehouse
on Cemetery Hill only days
after the end of the battle.

Probably more than on any other single day for the rest of the war, this was the time and place where Jackson could have made a difference. Lee urged Jackson's replacement, General Richard Ewell, to launch a frontal assault on Cemetery Hill, "if practical," before Union troops could fortify their defensive positions. But Ewell lacked the fortitude, electing not to risk that attack. Historians believe that Jackson would not have hesitated to accept that challenge and might well have turned the battle that day.

After finally arriving in the afternoon of the first day of fighting, Longstreet suggested that Lee try to maneuver around the Union left flank, to get behind Cemetery Hill and force Meade to leave the high ground to pursue him. But without sufficient intelligence, Lee had no idea what might be waiting for him on the other side of the ridge. He also lacked respect for Meade, believing his own army and his officers to be far superior, and so he remained quietly confident of victory. "The enemy is there," he told Longstreet, "and I am going to attack him." So as the first night fell, Union troops in the hills could look down upon the rebels occupying the town.

Throughout that night, newly arrived Union troops continued to reinforce the hills surrounding the town. With their stone walls, abundant trees and rocks, and a clear view of the fields below, they were an ideal defensive position. General Winfield Hancock called Gettysburg "the strongest position by nature upon which to fight a battle that I ever saw."

By noon on the second day, both armies were fully reinforced, each with about eighty thousand men in the field. Into the early afternoon Lee tried to dislodge the entrenched Union troops, pounding the hills with a massive artillery barrage. When Union soldiers tried to move to cover, sharpshooters hiding behind quickly constructed barricades in the town picked them off. The soldiers on the ridge dislodged tombstones and used them to provide protection. Finally, at four o'clock in the afternoon, Longstreet attacked the left flank with an estimated thirty thousand troops. As one Northern newspaper described the attack, "It was not an attack in line, it was not a charge, it was a melee, a carnival of death. Men hewed each other's faces; they grappled in close embrace, murder to both; and all through it rained shot and shell from one hundred pieces of artillery along the ridge." As rebel troops battled the Union defenders, several regiments successfully rounded the flank and got in position to roll up the Union lines. The next high ground—literally the last point of defense between the Confederates and the remainder of the Union army (now occupied with fending off a frontal assault)—was the 650-foot-high hill known as Little Round Top.

In the chaos, Little Round Top had been left unprotected for much of the day. Fortunately, Meade, perhaps sensing this weakness, had sent his chief of engineers, General Gouverneur Warren, to assess the situation. Warren was stunned to find this vital point undefended and

On the second day of the battle, Meade's chief engineer, General
Gouverneur K. Warren, discovered that a "rocky hill" south of
the town (which would become known as Little Round Top after
the battle) had been left undefended and would have given the
Confederates a perfect position to shell entrenched Union troops
on Cemetery Hill. Warren, seen here in an 1888 sketch,
managed to get reinforcements in place as the rebels were
climbing the hill and to defeat them.

moved rapidly to fortify it. Among several units moved into position in the woods on Little
Round Top was the 328-man 20th Maine, under the command of Lt. Colonel Joshua L.
Chamberlain. "This is the left of the Union line," he was told. "You are to hold this ground at
all costs." They got there and dug in just in time to save the Army of the Potomac.

The rebels began fighting their way up the hill. The outnumbered defenders raked them
with fire but still the enemy kept coming and coming. The fighting continued throughout the
afternoon until the enemy was less than thirty yards away—and those defenders who had
not been killed or wounded were down to their last few bullets. Lieutenant Holman Melcher
recalled, "The time had come when it must be decided whether we should fall back and give
up this key to the whole field of Gettysburg, or charge and try to throw off the foe."

If there truly was a moment on which the outcome of the war hinged, it occurred on July 2 on Little Round Top, when Maine professor Joshua Chamberlain organized a defense and defeated attacking Confederates in hand-to-hand fighting.

History has given credit for the heroics of the next few moments to Chamberlain, who indeed was in the thick of it, but there is ample evidence that what happened next was the result of confusion combined with the extraordinary bravery of the men of the 20th Maine. Some historians believe that Chamberlain and Melcher had agreed only to send several men into no-man's-land to try to assist the wounded. When Melcher fixed his bayonet, the rest of the troops heard the telltale snap and did the same. Seconds later Chamberlain gave the one word order, "Bayonet!" and Lieutenant Melcher drew his sword and sprang forward. The rest of the 20th Maine quivered for an instant, then with a great cheer followed, charging directly into enemy lines.

It was never determined what Chamberlain actually meant by that one word, though many people believed it was the first word of a longer order. The intention made no difference. Melcher flashed his sword and led the charge down the slope, screaming, "Come on, come on boys!" with Chamberlain only a few paces behind him. The charge down the hill stunned the rebels. As Chamberlain wrote in his after-action report, "The two lines met and broke and mingled in the shock. The crush of musketry gave way to cuts and thrusts, grapplings and wrestlings."

Although they could not have known it at the time, the extraordinary courage of Chamberlain's 20th Maine Infantry may not have been necessary: Confederate colonel William C. Oates, whose troops had been decimated by the withering fire from the hilltop, had made a decision: "To save my regiment from capture or destruction, I ordered a retreat."

When the fighting ended that day, the Union lines had staggered but held. Both armies had suffered tremendous casualties. "The dead literally covered the ground," Colonel Oates wrote. "The blood stood in puddles on the rocks. The ground was soaked with the blood of as brave men as ever fell on the red field of battle."

Later that night, *New York Times* correspondent Samuel Wilkeson made a dreadful discovery: he found the body of his son, nineteen-year-old Bayard Wilkeson. Wilkeson had been commanding an artillery battery on the first day of fighting. A Confederate shell had passed through his horse and shattered his own leg below the knee. Incredibly, he had cut off the remains of that leg, then was carried to a hospital where he lay bleeding to death for seven or more hours. Several days later his father's account of this family tragedy was published on the front page of the *Times* and roused the nation, serving as a symbol for the suffering of both North and South—and perhaps also serving as the model for the legendary speech that Lincoln gave on this battlefield several months later. "Oh, you dead, who at Gettysburg have baptized with your blood the second birth of Freedom in America, how you are to be envied!" Wilkeson wrote. He added, "Who can write the history of a battle whose eyes are immovably fastened upon . . . the dead body of an oldest born."

But even as he wrote those words, there remained one more day of fighting at Gettysburg. At the end of the second day of fighting, Meade gathered his commanders and discussed the possibility of withdrawing, but his officers insisted that they must hold their "immensely strong" position. At that meeting Meade warned General John Gibbon that Lee, having failed with attacks on both flanks, would likely come directly at him in the center of the line on the third day.

Lee believed that the Yankees were so demoralized that he could launch a frontal assault across almost a mile of broad and open field, directly into the heart of the Union guns. General

In the battle for Little Round Top, the Union suffered 565 casualties, including 134 killed, and the rebels lost 1,185 men, with 279 killed. Here two doctors examine fallen men only hours after the battle.

Longstreet tried desperately to dissuade him, telling him that "no fifteen thousand men ever arrayed for battle can take that position." But Lee insisted, believing the war could be won on that battlefield. "Never was I so depressed as upon that day," Longstreet wrote. "I felt that my men were to be sacrificed, and that I should have to order them to make a hopeless charge."

Lee tried one last gambit before ordering the charge. In an attempt to lure Meade into leaving his well-fortified position, he marched his troops out of the city, retreating to Seminary Ridge. "For some time the town had scarcely a soldier in it," reported *Harper's Weekly*. "Scores of dead and wounded men and horses, with broken wagons, bricks, stones, timber, torn clothing, and abandoned accoutrements, lay there. The frightened inhabitants peered out of their windows to see what the armies were doing to cause such a lull, and, almost afraid of their own shadows, they hastened away and crouched in corners and cellars at the sound of every shot or shell."

Meade refused to take the bait. Through the morning of July third the battlefield remained eerily silent, the lull before the coming storm. At one thirty, Lee began a great artillery barrage, hoping to soften Union defenses. An estimated 160 big guns rained explosives and iron on Cemetery Hill. Most of the shells, however, overshot their targets, landing well behind Union lines and destroying supplies but causing few casualties. To preserve ammunition, Meade allowed only some of his cannons to respond, and eventually he ordered them to stop firing, "as if silenced by the fire of the enemy," wrote Abbott, "while his gunners threw themselves flat upon the ground." Then, certain an attack on his center was coming, he positioned all of his big guns on either side of the field. And waited.

The Confederate barrage continued relentlessly for two hours. By then the Union artillery had ceased firing and whatever damage had been done was obscured completely by clouds of gun smoke. When the firing ended, General George Pickett, whose division was to lead the attack, asked Longstreet, "General, shall I advance?"

Longstreet could barely respond. Pickett remembered, "Presently, clasping his other hand over mine without speaking he bowed his head upon his breast. I shall never forget the look in his face nor the clasp of his hand when I said, 'Then, General, I shall lead my division on.'"

Three rebel divisions, comprised of almost fifteen thousand troops, came out of the woods on Seminary Ridge, assembling in plain view. It was time: They had been marching for days without sufficient rations and limited water. Three days of fighting had deprived them of sleep. And on this sweltering hot day, as temperatures approached 90 degrees, many of them were dressed in woolen uniforms. Whatever the result, this battle was going to end here.

Their line extended more than a mile across and a thousand yards deep. At two o'clock

General George Pickett commanded the three
Confederate brigades that led the doomed frontal
assault into the heart of Union lines on the last day
of the Battle of Gettysburg. Although several other
Confederate brigades also joined the attack, it is
Pickett's name that lives in history. Pickett's Charge
has become a metaphor for hopeless gallantry and
the waste of brave lives in a futile effort.

in the afternoon, with "a long, loud, unremitting, hideous screech, from thousands of voices,"
they began what has become honored in history as Pickett's Charge.

They ran with great daring and courage straight at Cemetery Hill, they ran as the men
around them fell, they ran for their lives, but there was no outrunning the guns that opened
fire on them. Federal artillery positioned on both sides began shelling the attackers, opening
up with shot and shell, blowing great holes in the ranks. As the Southerners got within four
hundred yards of the Union lines, the artillerymen began firing grapeshot and canister. Rebels
fell by the hundreds, by the thousands, and yet they kept coming. When one flag bearer fell,
another man picked up the colors and advanced them, and when he fell, still another replaced
him. When Pickett's men came out of the smoke at the base of the hill, the Yankees opened
up with small arms. "Volley after volley he [General Gibbons] poured into the surging mass,"
wrote Abbott, "and when the smoke cleared away, the brave charging lines were gone—not
broken, not retreating, but gone—gone like leaves before the wind."

Incredibly, a small number of men—about two hundred—under the command of Brigadier
General Lewis Addison Armistead managed to reach the stone wall on the south portion of
Cemetery Hill. Sticking his hat on his bayonet and raising it high as a beacon to guide his
troops, he screamed, "Come on boys, we must give them the cold steel! Who will follow me?"

His men followed him over the wall. They pushed back the federal troops and turned two
of their own cannons on them—only to discover there were no shells left. Within minutes
Armistead was hit multiple times and fell, to die two days later. Many historians regard this
brief success as the high point of the entire war for the Confederacy, the closest they came to

The Civil War was often fought employing traditional military strategies against new and powerful weapons. The result was massive casualties. Nowhere was that more apparent than at Gettysburg, during which acts of extraordinary courage became commonplace. The chaos, the death and destruction, and the confusion are all on display in this artwork.

an ultimate victory. But it lasted only minutes. When Meade learned of the only successful thrust into his lines he immediately dispatched reinforcements, who quickly and brutally repulsed the incursion.

The tattered remains of the three Confederate divisions retreated under fire to Seminary Ridge. Miraculously the town of Gettysburg had suffered very little damage. Union troops moved cautiously through the town, killing or capturing any Confederate stragglers. They pursued the rebels all the way to Seminary Ridge but didn't make much of a fight there. Pickett's glorious charge was over. More than half of the men who charged into the Union guns that morning were killed, wounded, or taken prisoner.

General Pickett's description of the aftermath is still haunting:

> No words can picture the anguish of that roll-call—the breathless waits between the responses. The "Here" of those who, by God's mercy, had miraculously escaped the awful rain of shot and shell was a sob—a gasp—a knell—for the unanswered name of his comrade. . . . Even now I can hear them cheering as I gave the order, "Forward!" I can feel the thrill of their joyous voices as they called out all along the line, "We'll follow you, Marse George. We'll follow you—we'll follow you." Oh, how faithfully they kept their word—following me on—on—to their death, and I, believing in the promised support, led them on—on—on—Oh, God!

The Army of the Potomac also had been mauled by three days of fighting. Meade, fearing that Lee would mount one more attack in desperation the following morning, collected his wounded from the battlefield but kept his defenses in position. But there was no fight left in the rebels. On the fourth, Lee sent a note to Meade requesting an exchange of prisoners. Meade refused, believing the four thousand Union prisoners held by the Confederates would be a heavy weight on Lee. As the exhausted Yankees held their positions, the rebels slipped away from the battlefield. They took their wounded with them, and their long line of retreat stretched for seventeen miles. As Alabama artilleryman Napier Bartlett recalled, during the forty-mile march "the whole of the army was dozing while marching and moved as if under enchantment or a spell—asleep and at the same time walking." Fearing another Union attack, Confederate commanders prohibited any stopping or resting.

Gettysburg proved to be the bloodiest battle of the entire war. The whole town of Gettysburg was transformed into a vast hospital, with casualties being treated in homes,

For the first time in history, cameras were able to record the brutality
of battle. In the aftermath of Gettysburg, one of the most difficult
problems was how to bury all the dead, among them these men killed in
a wheat field on the second day of fighting.

stores, even barns. Although precise numbers will never be known, officially in the three
days of fighting Union forces suffered 23,049 casualties, which included 3,155 killed, 14,529
wounded (an unknown number of whom would eventually die), and 5,365 missing. Lee lost
almost 40 percent of his army, reporting 28,063 casualties: 3,903 killed, 18,735 wounded, and
5,425 missing. Six Confederate generals died on the battlefield and five more suffered serious

wounds. In Pickett's command two generals were killed, as were seven colonels and three lieutenant colonels. "Only one field officer of my whole command . . . was unhurt, and the loss of my company officers was in proportion," he reported. Five thousand horses and mules were killed. After the battle a small mountain of amputated arms and legs grew on the fields and were buried in huge pits. Incredibly, only one civilian was killed—a woman named Ginnie Wade died when a stray bullet ripped into the house on the south side of the town and struck her while she was tending a sick relative. Elderly volunteer John Burns survived his wounds. Weeks later, when President Lincoln came to the town to honor the men of this battle with a brief speech, he invited John Burns to sit with him.

The dead by the hundreds were left bloating in the sun. The government hired Gettysburg residents to bury them, giving them hooks so they might grab the bodies by their belts and drag them into mass graves.

More than sixty Medals of Honor were awarded for gallantry on those three days, and among the recipients was Joshua Chamberlain.

Lee had suffered a devastating defeat. His aura of invincibility was gone forever. His officer corps was decimated. While the Union also suffered a great number of casualties, it had a much greater reservoir from which to eventually replenish its ranks. As one reporter noted, "Numbers might be restored, broken spirits never." In the North, there finally was a taste of great victory, and the fervor of the Copperhead Democrats was quieted. There were many battles still to be fought, but the Confederacy would never recover from the miscalculations of Gettysburg.

The North celebrated the victory. Within weeks, books about the great battle were being published. Stories of heroism, of survival, of simple human decency in the midst of incomprehensible horror riveted readers. In *What We Did at Gettysburg*, a woman told the story of refusing to leave her kitchen when the battle started because "we was all a baking bread round here for the soldiers, and had our dough a rising. The neighbors they ran into their cellars, but I couldn't leave my bread. . . . I stood working it till the third shell came

Along with Mathew Brady and the other Civil War photographers, artists like Edwin Forbes were able to capture the life and hardships of the soldiers. This 1870 oil painting, *Pursuit of Lee's Army. Scene on the Road Near Emmitsburg—Marching Through the Rain*, depicts Union troops on the march after the battle, but without any sense that a great victory has just been won.

through." She had refused to leave, she explained. "If I had, the rebels would a come in and daubed the dough all over the place."

The fallout from the battle shaped both armies for the remainder of the war. As the rebel army limped back toward the Potomac, Lincoln urged Meade to pursue Lee, attack him, and finish the war. Lee expected to make an orderly crossing of the Potomac, but heavy rains swelled the river and made it impossible for the Confederates to cross safely. As they paused on the northern bank, on the heights known as Marsh Run, Meade began planning an all-out attack. But his commanders were almost unanimous in their advice: The army was not ready to fight again. The attack should be delayed. Meade paused, giving Lee sufficient time to fashion a pontoon bridge of house and warehouse timbers, enabling his army to cross to the relative safety of Virginia. The crossing itself was perilous as many troops had to wade across an angry river with water to their armpits.

Meade continued his cautious pursuit, maintaining watch over all possible routes to Washington. But he failed to attack. In fact, many historians believe Meade had stumbled into the correct decision. Lee's army had regained its composure and was packed into a strong defensive position—and many of them, having tasted defeat, were craving another opportunity to fight the Yankees. Meade might well have ended the war on the banks of the Potomac, but the price would have been extraordinarily high.

Lincoln was furious that Meade had failed to press his advantage. "We had them within our grasp," he said later in despair. "We had only to stretch forth our hands and they were ours. And nothing I could say or do could make the army move." He had tried to prod Meade into ending the war there and then. At the president's behest, General Henry Halleck had telegraphed Meade, telling him, "The enemy should be pursued and cut up. . . . I need hardly say to you that the escape of Lee's army without another battle has created great dissatisfaction in the mind of the President."

Meade angrily offered to resign—but that offer was rejected. Lincoln instead wrote a long letter to him, explaining that it appeared to him that Meade was "not seeking a collision with the enemy, but were trying to get him across the river without another battle," adding, "I do not believe you appreciate the magnitude of the misfortune involved in Lee's escape—He was within your easy grasp, and to have closed upon him would, in connection with our other late successes, have ended the war—As it is, the war will be prolonged indefinitely. . . . Your golden opportunity is gone, and I am distressed immeasurably because of it."

Lincoln paused and considered the consequences of sending this letter, and never mailed it. Instead he wrote to General Howard several days later, after admitting that he had been "deeply mortified by the escape of Lee across the Potomac." He tempered his criticism, concluding, "A few days having passed, I am now profoundly grateful for what was done, without criticism for what was not done. Gen. Meade has my confidence as a brave and skillful officer, and a true man."

Lee also was in despair. He had been deeply shaken by the defeat. He took complete responsibility for the lives lost in Pickett's Charge on the third day, telling the survivors, "You men have done all that men could do. The fault is entirely mine." In his depression he offered his resignation to President Jefferson Davis. He wrote:

> We must expect reverses, even defeats. They are sent to teach us wisdom and prudence, to call forth greater energies, and to prevent our falling into greater disasters. . . . The general remedy for the want of success in a military commander is his removal. This is natural, and in many instances proper; for no matter what may be the ability of the officer, if he loses the confidence of his troops disaster must sooner or later ensue.
>
> I have been prompted by these reflections more than once since my return from Pennsylvania to propose to your Excellency the propriety of selecting another commander for this army.

Jefferson Davis rejected the offer, pointing out, "But suppose, my dear friend, that I were to admit, with all their implications, the points which you present, where am I to find that new commander who is to possess the greater ability which you believe to be required? . . . To ask me to substitute you by someone in my judgment more fit to command, or who would possess more of the confidence of the army, or of the reflecting men of the country, is to demand an impossibility."

Gettysburg would later be remembered as the most hallowed ground of the Civil War. But in its more immediate aftermath, both the North and South were stunned by the brutality. Even with the advent of telegraphy, it took weeks before accurate reports spread throughout the country; and for some weeks Southerners believed that Lee had won a great victory—with some newspapers even reporting that Lee's army was in Washington. It would be several more months before the entire story was known.

And then President Lincoln decided to go to Gettysburg to honor the men who had sacrificed there.

# SEVEN

# INTOXICATED BY WAR

## U. S. Grant Battles for Respect

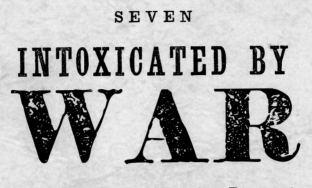

"My family is American, and has been for generations, in all its branches, direct and collateral," begin the memoirs of Ulysses S. Grant, the towering figure who left a deep and controversial imprint on American history. As general in chief he led the Union armies to victory, and then as twice-elected president he led the nation through the bitter and controversial Reconstruction. For decades he had spurned offers to write the story of the Civil War that only he could tell. But when his friend Mark Twain came to him in 1885 offering to pay handsomely to publish the book, Grant finally had good reason to accept—he was impoverished and dying of throat cancer and desperately needed the money to ensure his family's future.

Following his glorious public career, Grant had cofounded an investment bank with his friend Ferdinand Ward. Ward turned out to be a con man running an early version of a Ponzi scheme who ended up

◁ Artist George Cochran Lambdin, who was to become known for his paintings of flowers, spent the war distributing medicines and bandages, and capturing scenes of camp life with his brushes. He painted this portrait of Ulysses Grant in 1867.

bankrupting Grant as well as his investors. At about that same time Grant was diagnosed with the inoperable throat cancer that would kill him. Distraught at the possibility that he would leave his family in poverty, he accepted Twain's $10,000 advance and set to work. It required a Herculean effort for Grant to complete his work, spending six or seven hours a day to turn out three or four pages, while fighting the disease that made each spoken word painful. He finished the book only five days before he died.

The two-volume *Personal Memoirs of Ulysses S. Grant*, which sold an extraordinary 350,000 copies and left his family financially secure, tells the remarkable story of the man whose military and political genius helped mend the broken country. It is considered one of the finest presidential autobiographies ever written.

While Grant is often pictured with a cigar in his mouth and an open liquor bottle nearby, coolly dictating the strategy that defeated Lee, in fact he was a complex and sometimes troubled man—and at the beginning of the war perhaps the least likely man to be commanding the army at its end.

Hiram Ulysses Grant graduated from West Point in 1843 and joined other young officers making their mark in the Mexican-American War. Although officially he was a quartermaster, whose responsibilities were primarily coordinating logistics and providing materials, he led an infantry charge during the Battle of Resaca de la Palma. At Monterrey, the daring young officer carried a message on horseback through sniper-lined streets, dangling off his saddle to keep his mount between himself and the Mexican soldiers. He landed with General Winfield Scott at Veracruz and marched proudly with him into Mexico City to end the war. He gained respect and recognition during that final push into Mexico City when he managed to place a howitzer in a church belfry, a position from which he was able to deliver deadly fire on the entrenched enemy forces.

He was shaped by his experience in that war, coming to understand the complicated relationship between military necessity and politics. While he believed that war was unjust and unnecessary, his sworn duty to his country and his men was stronger.

In 1847, less than a year after returning to America, he married Julia Dent, the sister of a West Point classmate. He had to fight for her hand, as Mary Robinson, a slave belonging to the Dent family, recalled, and the match was made mostly because Julia's mother saw in him something others did not. "Old man Dent was opposed to him when he found he was courting his daughter," Robinson told a reporter, "and did everything he could to prevent the match, but Mrs. Dent took a great fancy to him in his venture. Mrs. Dent used to say to me:

'I like that young man. There is something noble in him. His air and the expression of his face convince me that he has a noble heart, and that he will be a great man someday.'"

Following the war, Grant's drinking, which was to plague him throughout his life, first became a problem. Alone in distant posts, he too often found solace in a bottle. "You do not know how forsaken I feel here," he wrote to Julia from Eureka, California. "I do nothing but sit in my room and read and occasionally take a short ride on one of the public horses." In 1851, while stationed in New York, he had joined the Sons of Temperance, a popular organization designed to fight alcoholism. It didn't help his problem, however, and he was soon accused of public intoxication and reporting drunk for duty. Rather than a court-martial, the army accepted his resignation in 1854. He was granted a discharge that stated, "Nothing stands against his good name."

Grant eventually would become a legendary military and political leader, but in fact as a civilian he was a dismal businessman and farmer. Providing an acceptable lifestyle for his family proved difficult for him. While contemplating his prospects outside the military, he wrote to his wife, "Whenever I get to thinking about the subject, however, poverty, poverty

Although Grant was against the Mexican-American War, writing, "I do not think there was ever a more wicked war. . . . I thought so at the time . . . only I had not moral courage enough to resign," he gained recognition because of his courage under fire. This hand-colored lithograph, *Grant at the Capture the City of Mexico*, was published after he achieved Civil War fame.

begins to stare me in the face, and then I think what would I do if you and our little ones want for the necessities of life." He eventually built a farm on sixty acres of family property near Saint Louis, Missouri, which he called Hardscrabble. He worked the land with a slave named William Jones, whom he had obtained from his father-in-law, a wealthy plantation owner. In addition to farming, he took whatever work became available, and at one point he was reduced to selling cordwood on Saint Louis street corners. It was there in 1857 that he supposedly encountered an acquaintance from West Point, William Tecumseh Sherman, who also had left the army and come upon hard times. The two men, who within a few years would become close friends and together help preserve the nation, commiserated on their sad state of affairs. At Grant's lowest point, he pawned his most valuable possession, a gold watch and chain, for $22 so that his family could afford to celebrate Christmas. The farm failed in 1857, and he freed William Jones, supposedly without payment. Having no other options, Grant finally accepted his father's long-standing offer to join the family tannery business, selling leather saddles and harnesses and buying hides from nearby farmers in Galena, Illinois. It was not a job he enjoyed, and when the war began he immediately responded to Lincoln's appeal

Ulysses and Julia Dent Grant and their children, in an 1868 painting by William F. Cogswell. This was one of several works of art showing Grant with his family as he began his presidential campaign.

for seventy-five thousand volunteers, remembering later with satisfaction, "I never went into our leather store again."

American history is replete with stories of men and women who rose from obscurity to extraordinary success, but very few were so completely unexpected or happened so rapidly as the ascension of U. S. Grant from alcoholic officer, failed farmer, and barely competent leather-goods merchant to the most celebrated and powerful man in the country.

When the war started men came forward and volunteered to fight for almost any reason imaginable; for Grant it was as much an escape from his mundane existence as it was to fight to keep the Union together. More important to him, it was an opportunity for redemption. He had been allowed to quietly leave the army with his reputation intact rather than face expulsion for drinking; still, it was not a noble end and this was a chance to repair that. In the beginning of the war, at least, he did not volunteer out of a desire to end slavery. Whatever his personal feelings—Mary Robinson recalled that "Grant was a very kind man to those who worked for him, and he always said that he wanted to give his wife's slaves their freedom as soon as he was able"—he did not join in public protest.

That changed quickly. Years later, Grant would explain to German chancellor Otto von Bismarck, "As soon as slavery fired upon the flag it was felt, we all felt, even those who did not object to slaves, that slavery must be destroyed. We felt that it was a stain to the Union that men should be bought and sold like cattle."

The Union army at the beginning of the war consisted primarily of volunteers created and trained by the states that were enrolled in the federal army. Grant's first attempts to enlist in Illinois were rejected by officers who were aware of his drinking problems, but finally he managed to convince Illinois governor Richard Yates to commission him a colonel in the state's 21st Infantry Regiment. In those early days of the war, officers with military training and battlefield experience could rise rapidly, and within months he had become a brigadier general in the state militia.

Grant eventually found the champion he needed in General John C. Frémont, who had explored the west with pioneer Kit Carson, and whom Lincoln had appointed commander of the army's Western Department. Both literally and figuratively, Frémont charted his own course. "The Pathfinder," as he was known, challenged the president by unilaterally declaring that anyone in the neutral state of Missouri who supported the rebellion would forfeit their property, a move that, in essence, freed the slaves. Lincoln overturned Frémont's emancipation

Explorer John C. Frémont became nationally renowned for his reports from the west, eventually winning the 1856 Republican nomination for president. At the beginning of the war Frémont provided the disgraced Grant with an opportunity to regain his reputation, putting him in command of a strategic base in Cairo, Illinois.

orders. But Frémont must have seen something of himself in Grant, whom he described as an officer with "dogged persistence" and "iron will," and he promoted him over more experienced officers to command troops in the west. Grant was given command of the troops gathered at Cairo, Illinois, a strategic point where the Ohio River connects to the Mississippi.

While the great battles in the east tend to dominate our history books, and names like Shiloh, Fredericksburg, Antietam, Chancellorsville, and Gettysburg will live forever in our national memory, the fight for control over the western states was vitally important. Jefferson Davis looked west, hoping to bring Missouri, Illinois, and Kentucky, with their factories, natural resources, and fighting men, into the Confederacy. Winning control of those states also meant controlling commerce on the great American rivers, the Upper Mississippi, the Missouri, and the Ohio, allowing the victor, as Frémont vividly described it, to "hold the country by the heart."

Newly promoted, General Grant had as his first mission to prevent the larger rebel forces from taking strategic ground. He occupied Paducah, Kentucky, gaining control of the mouths of both the Tennessee and Cumberland Rivers. While he was meant to maintain a mostly defensive posture, he instead took an offensive role, deciding to surprise Confederate general

Leonidas Polk's troops at the steamboat landing at Belmont, Missouri. Steamboats carried Grant's thirty-five-hundred-man force down the river, surprising the estimated seven-thousand-man garrison. The Yankees overwhelmed the rebel forces, capturing their supplies, horses and mules, and twelve pieces of artillery, as well as a substantial number of prisoners. But, after the battle, rather than withdrawing, the victors stayed and celebrated, thus giving "the Fighting Bishop"—as General Pope, an ordained Episcopal priest, was known—the opportunity to ferry troops across the river from Columbus and launch a counterattack. In the heavy fighting, Grant's horse was shot out from under him, almost killing him. He rallied his beleaguered troops, telling his officers, "We cut our way in and we can cut our way out." Grant's unnecessary invasion cost him six hundred casualties and he nearly lost his command. But at a time when many Union generals were criticized for keeping too much powder dry, an officer who took the fight into the enemy camp attracted interest.

Grant began restoring his reputation at the Battle of Belmont in November 1861, when his men defeated a substantially larger rebel force. When Confederate general Leonidas Polk (insert) counterattacked and surrounded the Union soldiers, Grant announced that "we had cut our way in and could cut our way out just as well," then led the fight to the safety of their boats.

This lithograph by Kurz and Allison, *Battle of Fort Donelson—Capture of Generals S. B. Buckner and His Army, February 16th 1862*—was published many years later, as Grant's reputation as a great and determined leader was firmly established. This victory opened up Tennessee and the west for the Union.

"I had been in all the engagements in Mexico which it was possible for one person to be in, but not in command," he wrote. Being in command had transformed him. After an undistinguished career as a peacetime soldier, after failing as a farmer and a businessman, Ulysses S. Grant had found his core strength. He was a battlefield leader. He was a man of courage with an innate ability to plan a campaign and inspire his men. And in the cauldron of the Civil War, those qualities enabled him to distinguish himself and rise rapidly through the ranks of command.

In February 1862, Grant proposed launching a combined attack by land troops and gunboats on Fort Henry, the gateway to the Tennessee River, and Fort Donelson, eleven miles away on the Cumberland River. Given permission by General Henry Halleck, who had replaced Frémont, a fleet of seven gunboats commanded by Rear Admiral Andrew Hull Foote rapidly battered Fort Henry into submission.

The assault on Fort Donelson began two days later. It was in this battle that U. S. Grant demonstrated the mettle that led eventually to the presidency. Fort Donelson was situated on high ground, a much stronger position than Fort Henry. The initial gunboat attack was repulsed, rendering those ships useless. Grant next ordered a land attack on the fort. Among those generals leading troops into battle was Lew Wallace, who almost three decades later would gain far greater fame with the publication of his novel *Ben-Hur: A Tale of the Christ*. The rebels understood that Fort Donelson could not withstand a prolonged siege and attempted to break out. Their surprise offensive staggered Grant's right flank. While other officers were shaken, Grant remained calm and resolute. By massing their troops for an attack on the right flank, he reasoned, the Confederates' left flank must have been weakened. He ordered General Charles F. Smith, his former commandant at West Point, to attack that flank. "Fill your cartridge-boxes quick, and get into line; the enemy is trying to escape and he must not be permitted to do so." Smith led the charge on the fort and captured the strategic positions surrounding it.

Rather than pressing their temporary advantage, the Confederates withdrew back into the fort. The outcome was clear; they were surrounded and could not survive a siege, and the rebels asked for terms. Grant replied by demanding unconditional surrender, and so became popularly known as "Unconditional Surrender" Grant.

As Northerners celebrated this new hero—and began mailing him cigars by the barrelful—rumors started spreading about him within the officers' ranks. There were unsubstantiated whispers that he was drinking again and may have been drunk at crucial points in the fighting. But he had won the first important Union victory of the war, so few people cared about these possible misdemeanors.

Mathew Brady said, "The camera is the eye of history," and both his posed studio portraits and photojournalism have kept the Civil War alive in our memory. This photo of William T. Sherman was taken in Brady's Washington studio sometime during the war. The determined look on Sherman's face became familiar to adoring Northerners.

The disorganized rebels were ordered to abandon Kentucky and West Tennessee and to rendezvous at Corinth, Mississippi, a vital railhead. General Albert Sidney Johnston eventually gathered forty-five thousand Confederate soldiers there. Grant pursued him, making camp with his forty-two thousand men about twenty miles away, planning to wait at Pittsburg Landing, near the Shiloh church, until General Don Carlos Buell got there with twenty thousand reinforcements.

The situation was clear to General Johnston. He could dig in and prepare to be attacked by a substantially larger Union force or he could seize the initiative. Grant simply ignored the latter possibility, perhaps believing that he had the measure of the man. He was so certain Johnston lacked fiber that he paid little attention to unmistakable signs that the rebels were moving. Even after ten Confederates captured by Sherman admitted they were the advance guard of a planned attack, he did nothing to prepare. This led to great criticism after the battle, although Grant continued to insist, "As to the talk of our being surprised, nothing could be more false. If the enemy had sent us word where and when they would attack, we could not have been better prepared." In fact, Grant had so little suspicion about Johnston's intentions that he sent a message to Buell stating that he did not believe there would be a fight at Pittsburg Landing—while the rebels' advance guard was within two miles.

The battle at Pittsburg Landing, or Shiloh, illustrates the many aspects of U. S. Grant; he could be inspiring and infuriating, he could show courage or be lackadaisical, he could be brilliant or dense. In this case, Grant was utterly surprised by the scale of Johnston's attack. It caught his army completely off guard. As Johnston's aide-de-camp reported, "The surprise was complete. . . . Colors, arms, stores, and ammunition were abandoned. The breakfasts of the men were on the table, the officers' baggage and apparel left in the tents." William Sherman, commanding a division of Grant's army, realized the danger when he "saw the glistening bayonets of heavy masses of infantry on our left front." The rebels drove forward fast and hard. The Union's raw and unprepared troops broke under the attack. Sherman displayed extraordinary courage leading his men into the battle; three horses were killed under him and he suffered two slight wounds. Johnston's strategy was to flank the Union lines and push them back against the swollen Tennessee River. And he almost succeeded. When the fighting ended on the first day, Confederate soldiers were sleeping in Union camps—but Johnston had been killed, bleeding to death after a minié ball severed an artery in his leg.

During the night almost twenty-five thousand fresh Union troops arrived; in the morning Grant committed them to the fight and throughout the day the rejuvenated Yankees drove the rebels back. By the end of the day the Confederates had withdrawn to Corinth. Buell and Wallace bore the brunt of the fighting, but it was Grant who got the credit for the victory while avoiding much of the blame. As the *Cincinnati Times* reported, "The decisive blow was given by General Grant, who headed a charge of six regiments in person, precipitating his whole body on the enemy's centre with such desperate force that they broke and ran. Retreat at once became general. Within half an hour the whole rebel army was falling back in dismay. Our rejoiced soldiers followed them, driving them through our camp in complete disorder. They were soon driven into broken country, where they would not form or fight."

Although publicly acclaimed, and despite the initial success of the rebel attack, Grant was blamed by his superiors for the fact that the attack led to massive casualties. Within weeks General Halleck assumed command of Grant's army. Rumors spread quickly that Grant was going to be put under arrest, supposedly for drinking before the attack, which would have led to his lack of preparation. But instead Halleck reduced Grant to little more than an observer. The two men had fundamentally different beliefs about the proper way to fight a war: Grant favored attack and destruction, to find the enemy and kill him, while the more cautious Halleck wanted to target strategic sites such as rail lines and ports and starve the enemy of supplies.

Grant had suffered enough embarrassment. After speaking to Halleck, he packed his papers and chests in preparation for resigning. This moment was the significant turning point in Grant's career. "You know that I am in the way here," Grant told his friend Sherman. "I have stood it as long as I can, and can endure it no longer."

Sherman urged him to stay, pointing out to Grant that even if he did resign, "events would go right along, and he would be left out; whereas, if he remained, some happy accident might restore him to favor and his true place." Sherman's advice proved prescient; in July Lincoln summoned Halleck east to become general in chief of the Union army, leaving Grant in charge of the forces in northern Mississippi and western Tennessee. He was once again in command and anxious to fight. He set his sights on the city of Vicksburg, the Confederate "Gibraltar of the West," considered one of the most important cities in the entire Confederacy.

"Vicksburg is the key," Lincoln wrote. "The war can never be brought to a close until the key is in our pocket."

Vicksburg, Mississippi, was a well-armed fortress, the Confederates' last defense in the Mississippi Valley. Four hundred miles from New Orleans, the city sat on a bluff two hundred feet high, looking down on a horseshoe bend in the Mississippi River. Its vantage point effectively granted control of the Mississippi to the army occupying the city. From there artillery could effectively cut off commerce, supplies, and communication. It was, as Jefferson Davis described it, "the nailhead that held the South's two halves together." The lifeblood of the Confederacy flowed on the river. If Union forces could take the city, they could lock hands with the troops who already had conquered New Orleans and effectively cut apart the Confederacy.

But the city occupied a position almost impregnable to any conventional military assault. As Abbott described the fortifications, "Forts and batteries, with connecting curtains, and armed with the heaviest ordnance, and garrisoned by thirty thousand rebel troops, crowned the bluff for miles." Confederate troops under the command of General John C. Pemberton looked down the river flowing below the city. There was little natural protection along its steep banks, leaving any man who tried to reach the summit from the river completely exposed.

The Union had already made several attempts to take Vicksburg. After capturing New Orleans, Admiral David Farragut had twice led naval expeditions up the Mississippi, bombarding the city and sending its terrified residents into shelters but inflicting very little damage. It was clear that the city could be not be taken from the river. "Our combined fleet lay there and gazed in wonder at the new forts that were constantly springing up on the hill tops," wrote the commander of the Union navy, David Dixon Porter, ". . . while water batteries seemed to grow on every salient point." A Confederate newspaper, the *Jackson Appeal,* boasted that "any further advance of the enemy against Vicksburg will be contested by greatly increased forces, derived from no matter where, and aided by all the artificial defenses that science can add to a naturally strong position." Making the situation even more difficult, torrential rains through much of the fall of 1862 had raised the river almost to flood stage; it surged through some levees, turning the hard ground throughout the basin into mud that bogged down men, horses, wagons, and caissons. "Marching across this country in the face of an enemy was impossible," Grant conceded.

While for Lincoln Vicksburg remained a seemingly invincible obstacle preventing the Union from securing complete control of the mighty Mississippi, for Grant it represented

After establishing his headquarters at Vicksburg in this wood-framed house, Grant was awakened one night by crashing sounds. His men, he discovered, were taking boards and timbers to construct scaling ladders and planks for a planned attack. He told them to continue and established his headquarters in a tent.

professional redemption, a final opportunity to win back the reputation he had lost at Shiloh. His future would be decided on the banks of the river at Vicksburg.

Grant's initial plan was sound; he intended to march forty thousand men to Mississippi's capital, Jackson, then turn west toward Vicksburg, while Sherman marched south from Memphis with thirty thousand troops. He believed that the rebel defenders would have to come out to meet one of these armies, leaving the city vulnerable to an attack by the other one. In theory the plan put General John C. Pemberton in a vise. If he moved against Grant, he could not stop Sherman; conversely, if he turned toward Sherman, there would be a path for Grant.

The offensive began in November, when Grant established his supply base in the town of Holly Springs. But the rebels had plans of their own; General Earl Van Dorn led a cavalry attack on that town, taking fifteen hundred prisoners and burning vast amounts of vital supplies. At the same time, rebel general Nathan Bedford Forrest, a daring and unusually brutal officer who became known as "the Wizard of the Saddle," staged a series of raids in western Tennessee, destroying railway tracks and telegraph lines. With his communications and supply lines gone, Grant halted his offensive—but he was unable to get word to Sherman, who proceeded down the river with thirty-two thousand men. On December 26, Sherman landed his army on the Yazoo River above Vicksburg and began slogging through the mud; three days later he reached the bluffs north of the city at Chickasaw Bayou.

Only days after Christmas, Sherman, still believing Grant was drawing attention away from his offensive, attacked.

Untroubled by Grant, Pemberton focused the full might of his forces on Sherman. The Yankees died in the mud long before reaching the cliff. Those brave men who got to the bluffs were shot before getting halfway up. Sherman finally withdrew, and heavy fog prevented him from renewing his futile attack. In the short battle the Union had suffered seventeen hundred casualties while two hundred rebels were killed or wounded. Sherman's official report was terse: "I reached Vicksburg at the time appointed, landed, assaulted and failed, re-embarked my command unopposed and turned it over to my successor."

When he bemoaned the staggering losses to Porter, the navy commander responded, "Only 1,700 men! That is nothing, simply an episode of the war. You'll lose 17,000 before the war is over. We'll have Vicksburg yet, before we die." Porter was wrong. Before the war was over, seventeen hundred would be considered a remarkably cheap price to pay for the victory.

Grant finally accepted the reality of his position. "Vicksburg is so strong by nature," he wrote to General Stephen Hurlbut in Memphis, "and so well fortified that sufficient force cannot be brought to bear against it to carry it by storm against the present Garrison. It must be taken by a regular siege or by starving out the Garrison. I have all the force necessary for this if my rear was not threatened."

The Union faced a perplexing situation: Somehow Grant had to transport his men to the eastern, more vulnerable, side of the city without steaming directly beneath the rebel artillery. The horseshoe bend in the river made that impossible. So he adopted an unorthodox solution: with the assistance of twelve hundred black contrabands, his men began digging a canal across the DeSoto Peninsula, the isthmus formed by the horseshoe. If he was able to accomplish that, the Mississippi would be opened to federal shipping—without fear of Vicksburg's guns. The strategic value of the city would be blunted.

Lincoln apparently supported this effort; he had worked there years earlier and knew the area, and took special interest in Grant's strategy. But to prevent him from succeeding, Pemberton moved a battery within range and began shelling the men as they worked. The

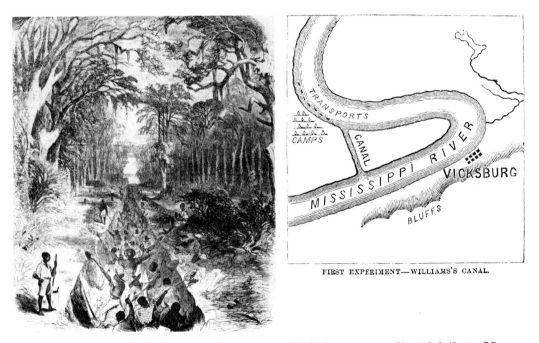

FIRST EXPERIMENT—WILLIAMS'S CANAL.

Grant's attempt to build a canal to bypass Vicksburg was a dismal failure. More than three thousand contraband and soldiers (seen in this illustration from *Harper's Weekly*) were reduced by sickness and exhaustion and occasional rebel snipers to fewer than seven hundred men. The dozens who died every day were often buried in the levees, the only ground high enough. Grant finally gave up the effort.

danger from this bombardment, combined with flooding rains and disease, proved too much. So Grant finally gave up on "his Big Ditch," as the effort was derided in Northern newspapers. But the lure of somehow bypassing Vicksburg was too tempting, and other engineering projects were begun. Seventy miles above the city a five-mile-long canal was cut into Lake Providence in hopes that a water route could be found through swamps, bayous, creeks, rivers, and small lakes to the Red River, which flowed into the Mississippi 150 miles below Vicksburg. Rebel sharpshooters appeared to make their presence known, then faded into the woods. Confederates sank ships, cut down trees, and even put up a makeshift fort—Fort Greenwood—to make passage almost impossible. Another effort was begun farther north, at a place called Moon Lake. In reality, Grant had little hope that any of these projects would succeed, but he knew that it would be impossible to mount a land offensive until the ground dried in the spring, and he wanted to keep his men occupied, noting, "Employment was better than idleness for the men."

The Northern newspapers were highly skeptical about his lack of progress. As one paper reported, "Grant is getting along at Vicksburg with such rapidity that in 15 or 20 years he will be ready to send a gunboat to find out if the enemy hasn't died of old age." When rumors surfaced that Grant was whiling away the winter months with the help of warming spirits, Lincoln dispatched several people to check up on him, among them noted journalist Charles Dana, Congressman Elihu Washburne, and General Lorenzo Thomas—in addition to a team of doctors. When Dana left his position as managing editor of the *New-York Tribune*, Secretary of War Stanton appointed him an investigating agent of the War Department and dispatched him on various important missions, ranging from checking up on cotton speculators to, in this case, determining if Grant was capable of commanding an army or, as rumor had it, was in his cups.

Grant was told Dana had been assigned to report on the pay service in the western armies, but both men knew his real mission. He and Grant actually became friends and Dana reported to Stanton that rather than a drunk, Grant was "modest, honest, and judicial . . . not an original or brilliant man, but sincere, thoughtful, deep, and gifted with a courage that never faltered. Although quiet and hard to know, he loved a humorous story and the company of his friends." On occasion Grant did give in to temptation. His chief of staff, Colonel John Rawlins, who had been at Grant's side since he had joined the Illinois militia, was as much his conscience as a military adviser. It was Rawlins who kept Grant's drinking in check, threatening to resign his commission if Grant relapsed.

By the time the high tides of spring had dropped and the swamps had drained, Lincoln

General Grant makes an observation in this 1888 bright and colorful Kurz and
Allison lithograph, *The Siege of Vicksburg*. Unlike many battles of the war, which
were fought and over before they could be reported, the siege continued for so long
that people could follow Grant's progress—or, as many Northerners pointed out, lack
of progress. So the victory had special meaning, as civilians had the opportunity to
become emotionally involved.

had signed the Emancipation Proclamation and Southern slaves and black Americans were being recruited for the army. "At last the waters began to recede," Grant wrote, relieved, "the roads crossing the peninsula behind the levees of the bayous, were emerging from the waters." With the areas surrounding Vicksburg now passable, Grant embarked on another bold plan: he intended to march his army downstream through seventy miles of concealing forests, circling the city on the far bank, on the Louisiana side of the river, while Porter's transports raced beneath the city's guns at night. Those boats would then ferry the army across the river below Vicksburg, enabling Grant to cut off Pemberton's lines of communication and supply and attack from the far more vulnerable eastern side.

It was an audacious plan. Grant did not know the disposition of other Confederate forces in that region and he would be completely cut off from his supplies. It would require his engineers to build makeshift roads through swamps and bayous. Sherman believed it was far too risky and tried to dissuade him, but the increasingly desperate Grant was determined to occupy Vicksburg.

The offensive began after dark on the sixteenth of April, when three transports laden with supplies got up full steam to run the gauntlet. The ships were shielded on either side by barges; a wall of hay and cotton bales had been piled high on the barge facing Vicksburg's

When Lincoln named General Henry Halleck general in chief of the armies in July 1862, Halleck picked Grant to replace him in command of the western army. As Grant began his march on Vicksburg, Halleck wrote, "The eyes and hopes of the whole country are now directed to your army. In my opinion, the opening of the Mississippi River will be to us of more advantage than the capture of forty Richmonds."

guns to offer protection, while on the far side additional bales of hay afforded cover for the captain and crew. As the ships began their race, a celebratory ball was in progress in the city—the town and its Confederate garrison had turned out in formal regalia to dance away the night. Then the big guns on the shore opened fire on the ships.

Two of the three transports sailed through the barrage to safety. The third was destroyed but its crew swam ashore. Within the week five additional transports survived the hazardous journey and sat waiting for Grant's thirty-three thousand men to arrive on the northern riverbank.

Fully aware of the dangers his men would be facing, Grant launched several diversionary attacks. Sherman feinted toward Chickasaw Bluffs, causing the panicked Confederate commander, General Carter Stevenson, to inform Pemberton that "the enemy are in front of me in force such as has never before been seen at Vicksburg." The diversion was a triumph; Pemberton responded to the plea by sending three thousand men who had been ordered south to march quickly to reinforce Stevenson instead.

Meanwhile, Union colonel Benjamin H. Grierson embarked on one of the most daring cavalry missions of the entire war. In civilian life Grierson had been a music man, traveling to Illinois towns to teach music and organize amateur bands. In 1860 he'd written several popular songs for Lincoln's campaign. He also harbored a strong dislike for horses, having been kicked in the head by a pony and temporarily blinded when he was eight years old. At the beginning of the war he had enlisted in the infantry, strongly preferring walking to riding, but as he wrote years later, "General Halleck jocularly remarked that I looked active and wiry enough to make a good cavalryman."

Grant dispatched Grierson on a daring sixteen-day raid through the Mississippi countryside; after crossing the Tallahatchie River his seventeen hundred men split up into smaller units and began striking suddenly, then withdrawing. They burned factories and bridges, train cars and water tanks; they tore up railroad tracks and telegraph lines; they took prisoners and destroyed supplies, fighting when necessary but avoiding it when possible—but mostly they succeeded in sowing confusion as to their numbers, their strength, and their location. They were an extraordinarily disruptive force, moving seemingly with impunity through places no Yankee had ever reached. They rode through forests and swamps, sometimes disguised in Confederate uniforms. They were reported here, then there, then miles and miles away. Pemberton sent more and then more men to find them and stop them, and eventually more than a battalion was scouring the countryside searching for some sign of Grierson's raiders. By the time the rebels finally picked up their trail, Colonel Grierson and his men had covered six hundred miles, suffering three men killed and seven wounded while keeping the attention of a large number of rebels. For his efforts Grierson was promoted to general and acclaimed as a Union hero. He had done his job, successfully diverting Pemberton's attention while Grant's army crossed the Mississippi.

Grant intended to make his crossing at Grand Gulf, twenty-five miles below Vicksburg, but a determined Confederate defense there forced him to ferry his troops across the Mississippi farther south. As he reported in early May, "I was on dry ground on the same side of the river with the enemy. All the campaigns, labors, hardships and exposures . . . that had been made and endured were for the accomplishment of this one object." Now on hard ground, Grant revived his initial plan, hoping to lure Pemberton out of Vicksburg by attacking Jackson. Marching rapidly, his men smashed through Confederate defenses. "This army is in the highest health and spirits," he reported to Halleck. ". . . They have marched as much by night as by day, through mud and rain, without tents or much other baggage and on irregular rations without a complaint." They lived off the land they crossed, taking what supplies they needed from farms and from homes; they ransacked towns and seized livestock. Near Port Gibson they came upon an extraordinary prize: fifty thousand pounds of bacon.

When the Yankees captured Jackson, Mississippi, and threatened to destroy Confederate general Joe Johnston's army, Pemberton had little choice but to send reinforcements to save him. Grant drove the rebels back into Vicksburg and prepared to mount a massive assault on the city. In only nineteen days General U. S. Grant had successfully crossed the Mississippi,

marched his men through 180 miles of rough country, won five different battles in which the rebels suffered almost nine thousand casualties, captured the state capital, destroyed countless munitions, and was camped only miles from the prize.

In the North, Grant's Mississippi offensive was front-page news; his accomplishments in so brief a period of time led to comparisons with the greatest military leaders in history, in particular Napoleon. "General Grant is a modest, unassuming man," reported the *New York Herald* in a laudatory account, ". . . a man of business, and very popular with the troops."

All that was left for him was to finally take the city. After two full-scale attacks were repulsed, Grant's army had taken a substantial number of casualties. The enemy was simply too strong and too well positioned to be defeated in battle. Grant set upon another course. "I now determined upon a regular siege—to 'out-camp the enemy,' as it were, and to incur no more losses. The experience of the 22nd convinced officers and men that this was best, and they went to work on the defenses and approaches with a will. With the navy holding the river, the investment of Vicksburg was complete. As long as we could hold our position the

For many months the siege of Vicksburg, as seen in this lithograph, was a long-distance fight, with artillery shelling enemy positions. This scene features the position of Union general Alvin P. Hovey, who commanded a ten-thousand-man division known as "Hovey's Babies" because he only accepted single men as volunteers.

enemy was limited in supplies of food, men and munitions of war to what they had on hand. These could not last always." And so the siege of Vicksburg began.

Siege! It is one of the oldest and most brutal forms of warfare. It requires starving the enemy, who is trapped in his own refuge—but it also inflicts that pain upon civilians caught in that trap. A siege requires digging, fortifying, sniping—and patience. Grant had the men, the shovels, the guns, and the gunboats. The question was whether he had the patience.

Both the Yankees and the rebels began digging. The Union troops dug trenches that moved inexorably closer—literally foot by foot—to the city; the Confederates dug caves to protect themselves from incessant shelling. Eventually Grant's men would dig fifteen miles of trench works, while inside the beleaguered city troops and residents and hired slaves burrowed more than five hundred shelters into hillsides, in which they hid—some of them large enough to hold five hundred people. The city moved underground; people brought furnishings, laid carpet, set up sitting rooms. Week after week, through the end of May and all of June, into early July, the Union continually bombarded the city, eventually firing more than sixteen thousand shells. Snipers on both sides remained steady in position, ready to take aim at anyone even briefly exposed. It was not so much the numbers of men and women who were killed or wounded but rather the constant fear under which they lived.

Inside Vicksburg the siege began to have effect. Food and fresh water were running out; after the pet and stray dogs and cats were eaten, the markets offered mule and rat meat— which, it was said, tasted surprisingly like squirrel. The occasional collapse of a cave added to the nightmares. Ammunition was so scarce that troops would pick up unexploded Yankee shells and salvage the gunpowder. Pemberton tried to send the slaves and civilians out of the city—but Grant refused to allow the civilians safe passage. Those caught inside the city held tightly to the hope that General Joe Johnston's army would rescue them.

Johnston did mount several attempts to relieve the city but was easily pushed back by Grant's growing army, which eventually numbered seventy-five thousand troops. Among the Union soldiers who took part in the fighting were newly recruited and barely trained black troops who distinguished themselves in battle. The first real fight in which black troops participated took place at Milliken's Bend, where barely trained soldiers who had gotten their muskets only a week earlier blocked the rebels. Confederate commander Henry McCulloch, anticipating that the raw troops would break when real fighting began, boasted, "I will take the n——r camp or wade in blood to my knees."

After several earlier skirmishes, the one thousand black troops of Herman Lieb's "African Brigade" waited hidden behind a levee as four regiments approached. And then, as Abbott wrote:

When they had arrived within a few feet of the breastwork, as if by magic a long line of black faces seem to emerge from the earth. Not a man flinched . . . the ground was soon covered with the slain and the rebel lines wavered and writhed in agony. . . .

The slaves and their masters were brought face to face in the death-grip, and the masters bit the dust . . . such a desperate prolonged hand-to-hand fight had not been witnessed during the war . . . two men were found dead side by side, one white, the other black, each with the other's bayonet through his body. One heroic freeman took his former master prisoner. The battle terminated in the utter rout of the rebels.

Two hundred Confederates were killed and 500 wounded; 127 Union troops died and 289 were wounded.

As Stanton reported to Lincoln, "Many persons believed, or pretended to believe, and confidently asserted, that freed slaves would not make good soldiers; that they would lack courage, and could not be subjected to military discipline. . . . The slave has proved his manhood, and his capacity as an infantry soldier, at Milliken's Bend, at the assault upon Port Hudson, and the storming of Fort Wagner."

President Davis previously had threatened to hang the white officers of black regiments and sell captured black soldiers into slavery, but in May 1863, Confederate secretary of war James Seddon announced a new policy, stating that the rebel army was "never to be inconvenienced with such prisoners" and instead "summary execution must therefore be inflicted on those taken." Interpreting this directive as orders, the Southern army in fact began murdering captured black soldiers. Before the war ended hundreds of black troops would be massacred after surrendering.

Lincoln responded by issuing his own order of retaliation at the end of July, proclaiming, "It is therefore ordered that for every soldier of the United States killed in violation of the laws of war, a rebel soldier shall be executed; and for every one enslaved by the enemy or sold into slavery, a rebel soldier shall be placed at hard labor on the public works and continued at such labor until the other shall be released and receive the treatment due to a prisoner of war."

While there is no record that any executions took place, there was retaliation. In June, the black 54th Massachusetts was taken by paddleboat down the Altamaha River to raid the riverside town of Darien, Georgia. They landed entirely unopposed as the residents of that small town fled to safety with as much as they could carry. The commander of the 2nd South Carolina Infantry, Colonel James Montgomery, who had once fought at the side of

# Haines Bluff evacuated by the Enemy—

movements on Port Hudson were carried out. Sherman marched rapidly down the river—and joined forces with Grant at Grand Gulf—The whole Army advanced On Jackson and Black River—7th May—Capturing that place and Raymond—&c as before described—(See Map page 1503.) The Rebel Gen'l Pemberton fell back with his whole forces into the entrenched works at Vicksburg—Haines Bluff was evacuated by his order as he could not defend so long a line with the men he had under him—the enemy carried away all the Stores and guns with him—A squadron of Cavalry of Gen Steeles Escort occupied the place soon after and a force from Admiral Porters fleet was landed and took possession and began to fortify it still more. The enemy's fortifications around Vicksburg were a series of strong redoubts. Connected at many places with rifle trenches. Capable of moving field artillery behind them—and arranged with great military skill.

This beautiful page from Robert Knox Sneden's sketchbook from mid-May 1863 indicates the terrain and enemy placements around Vicksburg while describing the withdrawal of General Pemberton from his forward entrenchments.

John Brown, ordered the town pillaged. His soldiers, wrote one witness, took "'sofas, pianos, chairs, mirrors, carpets, bedstands, carpenters' tools, coopers' tools, books, law books, account books . . . china sets, tin ware, earthen ware. . . .' Some men returned with chickens, pigs, cows and even a few liberated slaves." And when they had taken it all, Montgomery then ordered the town burned to the ground to serve as "an example to the rest of the South" that "they are to be swept away by the hand of God."

The flames, supposedly, were visible fifteen miles away. The 54th's commander, Colonel Robert Gould Shaw, was horrified, responding, "When it comes to being made the instrument of the Lord's vengeance, I myself don't like it," but he was unable to prevent it from happening. Although he filed a formal protest about his commander's actions, his death in battle a month later ended any official inquiry. Certainly no one could have known it on that June day in 1863, but as they watched Darien burn, they were looking at the future.

Grant had little to do as his troops made slow progress toward Vicksburg, and unfilled hours are always dangerous for those who drink. In early June, he invited Charles Dana to join him for a brief trip up the Yazoo River by small steamer to Satartia. As they came within two miles of the small port town, they were greeted by a gunboat officer, who warned that it was still occupied by rebel troops and urged them to turn back. Dana awakened Grant for instructions; the woozy Grant claimed to be ill and told Dana to make the decision. As Grant was "too sick to decide," Dana wrote later, "I immediately said we would go back to Haynes's Bluff, which we did."

The general's furious aide, John Rawlins, wrote a note to him: "Tonight I find you where the wine bottle has just been emptied," and warned, "Your only salvation depends upon your strict adherence to that pledge [that he would not drink]." Then, fearing for "the safety of this army," he searched Grant's tent for liquor, smashing every bottle he found on a tree stump.

As the Union army battled Lee at Chancellorsville and Gettysburg, Grant moved steadily closer to the fortifications. Soldiers on the front lines were so close, they would yell at one another and trade supplies. By the end of June tunnels had reached the outer defenses, packed with thousands of pounds of powder. On June 25, one mine was detonated. "The effect was to blow off the top of the hill," Grant wrote in his memoirs. Men were thrown into the air, "some of them coming down on our side, still alive. I remember one colored man, who had been under ground at work when the explosion took place, who was thrown to our side. He was not much hurt, but terribly frightened. Someone asked him how high he had gone up. 'Dunno, massa, but I think 'bout three mile,' was his reply."

Inside Vicksburg conditions had continued to deteriorate. It was said that people had been reduced to eating shoe leather. The Yankees began preparing for the final assault. Rumors spread that Grant intended to launch that attack on Independence Day, the Fourth of July. No one any longer doubted the outcome. The unanswered question was how many people would die reaching that inevitable conclusion.

Pemberton, who had long been accused of secretly harboring Northern sympathies, recognized that his loyalties would be questioned if he decided by himself to surrender the city. So he consulted his staff, who concurred with him. On July 3, Pemberton asked for an armistice to discuss "terms of capitulation."

The Confederate proposition was carried across the lines by General John Bowen, who had been friends with Grant in Saint Louis. In it, Pemberton claimed an ability to hold out for a prolonged period but wanted to avoid a "further effusion of blood." Grant had gained recognition for his toughness and responded, "The useless effusion of blood you propose stopping by this course can be ended at any time you may choose, by an unconditional surrender of the city and garrison." But he did tell Bowen, "I can assure you will be treated with all the respect due to prisoners of war."

Grant and Pemberton personally met at three o'clock that afternoon. Grant acknowledged the rebel leader as "an old acquaintance" but reiterated that he would accept nothing less than unconditional surrender. The two men talked under the shade of an oak, as their armies stood openly on the embankments watching their own fates being negotiated. Grant insisted on unconditional surrender. Pemberton bristled, responding, "Never. So long as I have a man left me. I will fight rather."

"Then, sir, you can continue the defense. My army has never been in better condition to prosecute the siege," Grant replied.

Negotiations stretched through much of the next day. Horses grew tired as couriers exchanged notes and responses. Grant finally agreed to several concessions, the most important one the granting of parole to Pemberton's estimated thirty thousand soldiers. That meant rather than being taken prisoner and marched north, these men would not fight until they were exchanged for captured Northern prisoners. This European custom had the effect of taking these men temporarily out of the war without the expense of maintaining them in a prisoner-of-war camp. On the morning of the Fourth of July, the Stars and Stripes was raised over Vicksburg and, as the *Herald* reported, "each regiment stacked arms in front of the position they had held so gallantly during the siege, the works extending for nearly nine miles."

It was an extraordinary victory. As General Halleck later wrote, "When we consider the nature of the country in which this army operated, the formidable obstacles to be overcome, the number of forces. . . . No more brilliant exploit can be found in military history."

INTERVIEW BETWEEN GRANT AND PEMBERTON.

An amazing scene from *Harper's Weekly*: After months of siege commanders U. S. Grant and Confederate general John C. Pemberton sat calmly together in sight of their troops, negotiating the terms of surrender. There were no terms: Unconditional Surrender Grant burst into fame.

No one greeted the surrender of Vicksburg with more enthusiasm than President Lincoln. The entire length of the Mississippi River was once again in Union hands. As Lincoln said two months later, after the first steamboat from Saint Louis reached New Orleans, "The Father of Waters again goes unvexed to the sea."

Although Lincoln and Grant had yet to meet personally, the president realized that finally he had found a general who wanted to fight. Weeks later, when Grant was criticized for his drinking, Lincoln supposedly asked, "Can you tell me where he gets his whiskey?"

The critic responded, "We cannot, Mr. President. But why do you desire to know?"

"Because," Lincoln said in all seriousness, "if I can only find out, I will send a barrel of this wonderful whiskey to every general in the army."

It is estimated that roughly three million men fought in the Civil War—although the fact is that a very small number of those men were women. As many as 750 women disguised as men fought on both sides. Their reasons were personal. Some of them, like Frances Louisa Clayton (at left), went to war as a man named Jack Williams (right) to be with her husband until his death at the Battle of Stones River. While the details of her military career are sketchy, Clayton fought with the 4th Missouri Artillery in several major battles and supposedly was wounded three times, including while fighting under General Grant in the Battle of Fort Donelson. Sarah Edmonds Seelye, who served as Franklin Flint Thompson in the 2nd Michigan Infantry, explained, "I could only thank God that I was free and could go forward and work, and I was not obliged to stay at home and weep."

While the contributions of women as spies, nurses, and patriotic supporters have long been recognized, the role played by these fighting women is much less known. Nevertheless, Dr. Mary Walker earned the Medal of Honor, and Sally Ann Tompkins was actually commissioned as a major in the Confederate army.

Maria Lewis of the 8th New York Cavalry was more than duplicitous; she was a black woman who fought disguised as a white man.

While many women served in the Civil War and returned home without being unmasked, some of them did become known publicly. Albert Cashier of the 95th Illinois Infantry fought in more than forty battles—and was actually Jennie Hodgers. Mary Galloway was "unmasked" by Clara Barton, who was treating her for a neck wound suffered at Antietam.

At least one woman was hiding more than her gender. At Fredericksburg "a real soldierly, thoroughly military fellow" distinguished himself, according to Colonel Elijah H. C. Cavins of the 14th Indiana, and after the battle was promoted to sergeant. A month later she gave birth, causing the colonel to write to his wife, "What use have we for women, if soldiers in the army can give birth to children?"

It was easy for a woman to enlist. At that time physical examinations were perfunctory, many of the soldiers were so young it wasn't at all unusual to see a fresh-faced person, few of them had any sort of formal training, and soldiers generally slept in their clothing and rarely bathed. In fact, the secret wasn't a

complete secret. Stories suggesting the presence of women in soldier's clothing ran in the *New York Times*, the *Richmond Examiner*, and various Chicago papers. Supposedly, even Lincoln had to confront this reality when a woman named Mary Ellen Wise, who had been wounded at Lookout Mountain, appeared in Washington to demand her back pay. An angry Lincoln made sure she got her the money she was owed.

# EIGHT

# THE STATES OF WAR

## The War Comes Home

Throughout the summer and fall of 1863 the men of the Union and the Confederacy fought valiantly and sang boastfully, but mostly they suffered and died.

They marched to the same tunes. The Yankees sang: "The Union forever! Hurrah, boys, hurrah! / Down with the traitors, up with the stars; / While we rally 'round the flag, boys, we rally once again, / Shouting the battle cry of freedom!" And the rebels responded with their own version, "Our Dixie forever! She's never at a loss! / Down with the eagle and up with the cross, / We'll rally 'round the bonny flag, we'll rally once again, / Shout, shout the battle cry of Freedom!"

And they died in increasingly large numbers: In September, during the Battle of Chickamauga, rebel troops managed to fight their way into a

Eastman Johnson was one of many American artists who traveled with the army, finding inspiration in small deeds of heroism. The oil painting *The Wounded Drummer Boy* is based on an incident at Antietam, when a wounded young drummer asked a soldier to carry him so he could continue performing his job.

After withdrawing from Chattanooga, General Braxton Bragg laid a trap, allowing his scouts to be captured in order to spread false information that he was retreating. Instead, he stood and fought Union general William S. Rosecrans's Army of the Cumberland at Chickamauga, resulting in the second-highest number of casualties of the war.

deep ditch held by Colonel John T. Wilder's Lightning Brigade. Wilder's Indiana boys were equipped with new Spencer repeating rifles, a gun that fired fourteen rounds a minute, and four ten-pound cannons. The Union troops positioned two of their cannons to shoot straight down the length of the ditch, directly into the charging Confederates. And then they opened fire with canister. "At this point," said Wilder, ". . . it actually seemed a pity to kill men so. They fell in heaps, and I had it in my heart to order the firing to cease to end the awful sight. . . . When the firing ceased, one could have walked for two hundred yards down that ditch on dead rebels without touching the ground." In the three-day battle the Union had suffered 16,170 casualties, while the victorious rebels took 18,454 killed, wounded, or missing.

As the soldiers died by the thousands, Lincoln in Washington and Jefferson Davis in

Richmond dithered, seemingly helpless to do anything more than commit more and more troops to the grinders. Legend has it the two men had met once, years before. In April 1832, the Sauk and Fox Indians led by Black Hawk were on the warpath, returning to their ancestral homeland in northern Illinois. According to the *Farm Journal*, "Tales of pillage and massacre spread like wildfire," and a militia was raised. Among the volunteers was twenty-three-year-old Abraham Lincoln, who was described as "a tall, homely young man dressed in a suit of blue jeans." He was elected captain of the 4th Regiment, Whiteside's brigade, mounted volunteers, Illinois militia. The *Journal* wrote that Lincoln was sworn in by "a very fascinating young man of easy manners and affable disposition," a young lieutenant named Jefferson Davis. Their paths may have crossed again years later while both men were in Washington, Davis serving in the Senate, Lincoln in the House of Representatives.

They were very different men. Lincoln was rough-hewn and had grown up working the land; Davis was the son of a relatively prosperous family and grew up on a cotton plantation. Lincoln was self-educated; Davis attended private schools and colleges and graduated from West Point. In the Black Hawk War, Lincoln had volunteered for the Illinois militia and was elected captain by his men; upon graduation from the military academy Davis had become a commissioned officer in the regular army. By nature Lincoln was an inspiring orator and through experience had become a master politician; Davis lacked both those inspirational qualities and political skills. But perhaps more than anything else, it was their unshakable beliefs about slavery that made them implacable enemies: Lincoln said flatly, "I think that if anything can be proved by natural theology, it is that slavery is morally wrong," and "Those who deny freedom to others, deserve it not for themselves; and, under the rule of a just God, can not long retain it." Davis believed the opposite just as passionately: "[Slavery] was established by decree of Almighty God. . . . It is sanctioned in the Bible, in both Testaments, from Genesis to Revelation. . . . Slavery existed then in the earliest ages, and among the chosen people of God; and in Revelation we are told that it shall exist till the end of time shall come."

While Lincoln had come to power as a politician, Davis's career had been built on his military success at the Battle of Buena Vista in Mexico. In February 1847, General Zachary Taylor's forty-five hundred troops were at Buena Vista Pass, outnumbered more than four to one by Santa Anna's army. Among the Americans were Colonel Jefferson Davis and his 1st Mississippi Rifles. Taylor was said to despise Davis. A decade earlier the young soldier had wooed and won the hand of Taylor's daughter, and against his wishes they had married. Three months later she had died of malaria and the two men had never reconciled. Now they found themselves fighting shoulder to shoulder for survival on a Mexican plain.

Suddenly, two thousand Mexican infantry cavalrymen, armed with long lances, galloped at Colonel Jeff Davis's Mississippi Rifles and charged, determined to ride through the Americans and into Taylor's lines. Davis remained calm as the cavalry raced toward him; he drew his saber and ordered his men to form an inverted V formation, with the open end enticing the Mexicans inside. Davis's men held fire as the Mexicans rode into the gap. The Mexican troops stopped their charge, puzzled by the lack of musket fire. For an instant time seemed to pause. Then Davis lowered his sword and the first line of the Mexican cavalry disappeared in obscuring gun smoke.

Within minutes the Mexicans had turned and fled the cross fire, securing Jefferson Davis's reputation. In his official report General Taylor noted, "The Mississippi riflemen, under Colonel Davis, were highly conspicuous for their gallantry and steadiness. . . . Brought into action against an immensely superior force, they maintained themselves for a long time unsupported and with heavy loss, and held an important part of the field until reinforced. Colonel Davis, though severely wounded, remained in the saddle until the close of the action."

But the story that cemented Davis's celebrity was what Taylor had admitted to his former son-in-law after the battle: "My daughter, sir, was a better judge of men than I was."

Davis returned from the war as a hero and was rewarded with an appointment to the United States Senate by Mississippi's governor. In the Senate Davis became a forceful advocate for the extension of slavery into new states and territories. In 1853, after losing an election for governor of Mississippi, he was named secretary of war by President Franklin Pierce. Four years later he returned to the Senate, and when secession began he was chosen by acclamation the first—and only—president of the Confederate States of America.

During the war, he and Lincoln showed little respect for each other. Lincoln steadfastly refused to refer to Davis by name or position, calling him only "the leader of the insurgents." Lincoln's feelings about the Confederate government were evident when he finally agreed to meet with Davis's representatives, whom he would only acknowledge as "influential persons," at Hampton Roads in February 1865. During that conference, he later said, one of those "influential persons" pointed out, "Well, according to your view of the case we are all guilty of treason, and liable to be hanged."

Lincoln hesitated, then responded, "You have stated the proposition better than I did."

Jefferson Davis had no better opinion of his enemy. In his response to the Emancipation Proclamation, he did acknowledge Lincoln as the "President of the United States," although he referred to the United States as "a foreign power."

Whatever their differences, Lincoln and Davis both had to deal with difficult problems on the home front. In the South, the war had crippled the economy and caused vast shortages of many goods. The Union naval blockade instituted soon after the attack on Fort Sumter gradually had become effective: the inability to trade cotton and tobacco devastated the economy. The relentless Union attacks on the railroads prevented even those crops that were grown in abundance in the South from reaching the regions that needed them. At one time, for example, a bushel of corn selling for $1 in parts of Georgia cost $12 in Virginia.

The shortage of natural salt, necessary to preserve beef for the troops, was so acute that by 1862 the governor of Alabama wrote, "The salt famine in our land is most lamentable. . . . The earthen floors of smokehouses, saturated by the dripping of bacon, were dug up and

SOWING AND REAPING.

SOUTHERN WOMEN HOUNDING THEIR MEN ON TO REBELLION.        SOUTHERN WOMEN FEELING THE EFFECTS OF REBELLION, AND CREATING BREAD RIOTS.

This cartoon, illustrating how the fortunes of war had transformed Southern women from swooning supporters to angry rioters, was published in May 1863 by *Frank Leslie's Illustrated Newspaper* after Richmond women revolted against shortages.

boiled." Newspapers were reduced in size and even printed on the back of wallpaper stock due to a shortage of printing paper. To alleviate a shortage of metals, South Carolinians offered their lead window weights and water pipes to be smelted into ammunition. But while Southerners learned to live with these inconveniences, they could not live without bread and meat. "Such is the scarcity of provisions," wrote one Southerner, "that rats and mice have mostly disappeared, and the cats can hardly be kept off the table."

"Living is hard," wrote Alabamian John Forsyth to a relative. "If you could smuggle us something to eat or to wear it would be a sublime charity." But then he added, "Still, we have no idea of giving up." Others believed differently. By November 1862, the situation had become so dire that a Mississippi planter warned the governor, "Men cannot be expected to fight for the Government that permits their wives and children to starve."

In Richmond, speculators had driven up the cost of scarce staples like bread and bacon ten times higher than normal. In April 1863, the women of Richmond had suffered enough. "We are starving," said one desperate woman as a crowd began gathering. "As soon as enough of us get together we are going to the bakeries and each of us will take a loaf of bread. That is little enough for the government to give us after it has taken all our men." Hundreds of housewives and boys, many of them armed with axes, rioted. Screaming "Bread or blood!" they ransacked shops and carts and broke into storage lockers and sealed cases, looting everything from food to jewelry.

Finally, President Davis appeared. Standing on a wagon, he appealed for understanding, even offering the rioters his last loaf of bread. "You are hungry and have no money," he said, then emptied his pockets and threw his few coins to the crowd, adding, "Here is all I have." When that failed to calm the mob, he warned them that if they did not disperse in five minutes he would order the local militia to fire on them. When troops blocking Main Street from sidewalk to sidewalk began loading their weapons, the crowd dispersed. But the shortages and the anger did not end, and a different cry, "Bread or peace," arose, growing louder as despair spread.

Lincoln faced different problems in the North. The war had been a boon to the region's economy. The government was buying everything farmers and textile mills could produce to feed and uniform the army. Jobs were plentiful and the stores were busy. Imported goods were readily available. There remained only one significant shortage: the military machine needed more and more soldiers. States began drafting men between twenty and forty-five in the summer of 1862, and a year later Congress passed a nationwide draft, setting quotas for each Congressional district. Included in that legislation was a provision that allowed men to buy their way out of conscription for $300 or pay someone else to serve in their place—meaning that the wealthy could avoid service. Although Lincoln himself was too old to be drafted, as a patriotic gesture he paid a "representative recruit," nineteen-year-old Pennsylvanian J. Summerfield Staples, to take his place in the army.

Northerners' growing resentment over forcing the poor to serve while offering the wealthy a legal means to avoid the draft, and exempting blacks because they were not citizens, finally exploded in New York City in July 1863. The *New York News* had been campaigning against conscription, writing that instead of compelling "white men to serve the blacks," the government should be trying to end the war. The paper warned that black laborers were waiting to take white men's jobs by working for lower wages. That message resonated strongly among the city's large Irish immigrant community, which already had sent thousands of men to the war—at Antietam alone more than five hundred Irish immigrants had been killed or wounded. On July 13, as the names of the first draftees were published, thousands of men gathered outside the provost marshal's office on Third Avenue and Forty-Sixth Street. The rioting began at midmorning as the mob attacked draft headquarters. Fire Engine Company No. 33 arrived—and set the building on fire. More fires were set; the Colored Orphan Asylum on Fifth Avenue began burning, but fortunately the children inside managed to escape. Telegraph lines were cut. Trolley and train tracks were ripped up. Wagon traffic was blocked. Stores were looted. The mob took control of parts of the city. Police began firing at the rioters, first with blanks, then with live ammunition, but were overwhelmed and beaten, their weapons taken from them.

Lincoln personally met his "replacement," John Summerfield Staples, telling him, "I hope you will be one of the fortunate ones." Staples was paid a $500 bounty for his service and his father received $50 for his consent. Staples survived the war, mostly guarding prisoners and working in hospitals, and died of a heart attack when he was forty-three.

As the casualties mounted, men in both the North and the South resisted conscription. *The Incident in Second Avenue During the New York Draft Riots, July 1863* (top) saw one rioter shot to death during a mob attack on an armory, while the 1862 Currier and Ives lithograph (bottom) probably was published soon after the Confederate Congress approved a draft and shows unwilling men being forced to fight for "King Cotton."

That night, wrote an eyewitness named Martha Perry, "the city was illuminated by [fire]. I counted from the roof of our house five fires just about us." The next day, "Men, both colored and white, were murdered within two blocks of us, some being hung to the nearest lamp-post, and others shot. An army officer was walking in the street near our house; when a rioter was seen to kneel on the sidewalk, take aim, fire, and kill him, then coolly start on his way unmolested. I saw the Third Avenue street car rails torn up by the mob." The chaos continued for almost three days, until the draft was suspended. In the mayhem, at least 300 people were seriously injured, including 119 killed—most of them rioters, but at least 12 innocent black men were hanged. About fifty buildings were destroyed, and damage was estimated at several million dollars.

Several thousand troops, some of them coming from the fight at Gettysburg, were dispatched to the city to restore order. They began patrolling the streets, shooting to kill. The riots were over. Less violent protests took place in Boston and other cities. Six weeks later the draft resumed, and eventually a total of twenty-four hundred New Yorkers answered the call.

While in the South the Confederate Conscription Act was equally despised, Davis faced a far greater danger from the growing number of rebel deserters. Many soldiers who had fought hard for two years or more had been through enough and simply walked away from their units. They risked their lives to do so, as the penalty for desertion was death. It was not an idle threat: in western North Carolina fifteen deserters were captured and executed by a firing squad, among them a thirteen-year-old boy. In some places deserters banded together for self-protection and survival. In Jones County, Mississippi, Jasper Collins deserted after the passing of the "Twenty-Negro Law," which exempted men owning twenty or more slaves from fighting. "This law," Collins complained, "makes it a rich man's war and a poor man's fight." He joined Newton Knight, who supposedly had been tortured and forced to watch as all of his family's possessions were destroyed after he refused to rejoin the 7th Mississippi Battalion at Vicksburg. Knight and Collins eventually led a 125-man band of deserters and draft dodgers who lived off the land, declaring themselves Southern Yankees and vowing to forcibly resist any effort to confront them. They raided plantations, shot tax collectors, and at times fought it out with Confederate troops. When threatened, they would disappear into swamp hideouts known as the Devil's Den and Panther Creek.

When the *Natchez Courier* reported that Jones County had seceded from the Confederacy, Jefferson Davis had no choice but to send battle-hardened troops to put down the rebellion. Using bloodhounds, Colonel Robert Lowry's two hundred men tracked Knight's band into the swamps, capturing and hanging ten of them while others were mauled by the dogs. But most of those men, including Knight and Collins, escaped and survived the war.

In most cases, if deserters hadn't committed crimes, Jefferson Davis commuted their sentences. But there was little he could do to combat the food shortages and desertions, and he lacked the personal charisma to rally Southerners around the cause. Morale throughout the Confederacy continued to decline.

As the substantial Union advantages in men and supplies began to wear down the will of the Confederacy, Southerners found solace in the daring exploits of guerrilla fighters such as John Singleton Mosby and his Rangers. In the tradition of the Revolutionary War's legendary Swamp Fox, Francis Marion, Mosby, known as the Gray Ghost, brought his men together for lightning-quick raids, after which they dispersed and returned to homes in northern Virginia, becoming known as "citizens by day and soldiers by night."

Before the war Mosby had been a Virginia lawyer, but when the fighting started he enlisted—although he had been outspoken against secession. He began his military career riding with Jeb Stuart's cavalry, serving as a scout and courier. After distinguishing himself at Fredericksburg, he was given command of Company A, 43rd Virginia Battalion, a small unit that operated behind Union lines, staging hit-and-run attacks to disrupt communications and raid supply trains, steal horses, attack lightly guarded outposts, and take prisoners. Mosby's Rangers, or Raiders, as they also were known, burst into Confederate lore on a cold, rainy night in March 1863, when about two dozen men slipped silently into the town of Fairfax Court House, about ten miles from Washington. While the garrison there was sleeping off a raucous party, Mosby sneaked into the quarters of the commander, Brigadier General Edwin Stoughton, the youngest general officer in the Union army. He lifted the covers and smacked Stoughton on his behind. The general sat up and demanded angrily, "What is the meaning of this? Do you know who I am?"

"I reckon I do, General," responded the intruder. "Did you ever hear of Mosby?"

Stoughton brightened. "Have you got that rascal?"

"Nope," the stranger said, "but he has got you." The Rangers withdrew as silently as they had entered, taking with them Stoughton, two captains, thirty enlisted men, and fifty-eight horses—without firing a single shot.

When Lincoln was informed of this raid he was predictably furious, but not about the loss of Stoughton. "I can make a better brigadier in five minutes," he said. "But those horses cost one hundred and twenty-five dollars apiece!" At some point, perhaps after this, Mosby sent Lincoln a lock of his hair, which reportedly amused the president.

While each side put guerrilla bands into the field, none of them operated as successfully as Mosby's Rangers—although he insisted his men were enlisted soldiers entitled to all legal

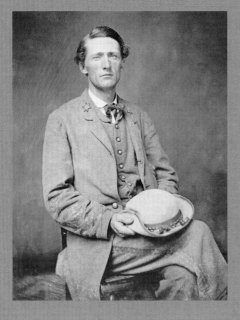

Peacetime attorney John Mosby (at left) and his guerrilla outfit (below) successfully conducted one of the most audacious raids of the war, kidnapping General Stoughton and thirty-two of his men without firing a single shot. When he safely reached Confederate lines, he wrote, "I knew I had drawn a prize in the lottery of life and my emotion was natural and should be pardoned."

protections of war. They controlled the area of the Shenandoah Valley between the Blue Ridge and Bull Run Mountains so completely that it became known as "Mosby's Confederacy." His feats of derring-do continued to thrill beleaguered Southerners. As Abbott described a typical raid, "Mosby, the most redoubtable of rebel guerillas, with his hardy band, made a plunge through Snicker's Gap . . . and completely surprised our supply-train. The small guard, overpowered, fled in all directions. Mosby captured and destroyed seventy-five wagons, took two hundred prisoners, nearly six hundred horses, two hundred beef cattle and quite a quantity of valuable stores."

Mosby's Rangers, continued to successfully harass the Yankees throughout the war. They destroyed railroad tracks and telegraph lines and kept hundreds of Yankees busy searching unsuccessfully for them.

When General U. S. Grant assumed command of the Union army he mistakenly believed Mosby's Rangers were "unlawful combatants," not official members of the Confederate army. He ordered General Phil Sheridan, "Where any of Mosby's men are caught, hang them without trial." Although reluctant, Sheridan carried out these orders; at least six raiders were executed at Front Royal, Virginia.

John Mosby believed that these executions had been carried out by General George Armstrong Custer's brigade, and in return he requested and received permission from the government in Richmond to hang an equal number of Custer's men. Seven prisoners were selected by lottery and three of them eventually were executed. Mosby then sent a message to Sheridan warning that this retaliation would continue as long as the Union persisted in this policy. The executions stopped immediately.

At the end of the war, Mosby's men faded back into the community, but John Mosby was personally paroled by Grant; the two men actually became close friends and Mosby served as a campaign manager when Grant ran for president. Later, President Rutherford B. Hayes appointed the remarkable Mosby as consul to Hong Kong and he eventually served the government as an assistant attorney general and in the Department of the Interior. When asked about his wartime service, rather than boasting, he said simply, "It is a classical maxim that it is sweet and becoming to die for one's country; but whoever has seen the horrors of a battlefield feels that it is far sweeter to live for it."

Mosby's disgust with the romanticized notion of warfare proved tragically accurate for Colonel Robert Gould Shaw, the well-bred Bostonian given the controversial honor of leading the black 54th Massachusetts into battle. Even after Lincoln had issued the Emancipation Proclamation, many people—on both sides of the conflict—remained strongly against letting free blacks and freed slaves fight. Even those people who supported allowing blacks into the army wondered how they would perform under fire. On July 11, 1863, only weeks after Gettysburg, while New York City was racked by the draft riots, they found out. Shaw's 54th Massachusetts was ordered to attack strategically important Fort Wagner, or Battery Wagner. Sitting on an island in Charleston Harbor, the stronghold had thirteen siege guns and eighteen hundred troops to protect the southern entrance to the city. The only access to the fort was a small strip of beach less than sixty yards wide that offered no protection. It was, essentially, a killing zone. The First Battle of Fort Wagner, which had taken place only a week earlier, had resulted in 339 Union casualties and just 11 rebel casualties.

At Shaw's request, the 54th Massachusetts was assigned to launch this second attack. After a daylong bombardment by ironclad gunboats, the 54th led five other regiments in a desperate frontal assault. They marched, reported the *New York Herald*, "half a mile over smooth, hard beach in direct view of the enemy, and exposed every step to the murderous fire of his guns. . . . There has been no conflict during the war in which Union troops displayed more heroism."

Among the men who made that charge was a former slave named William Carney. When the 54th's flag bearer was fatally wounded, Sergeant Carney grabbed the US flag before it hit the ground and proudly carried it forward. Although wounded several times, he managed to hold on to the flag. As he proudly told his men, "Boys, I only did my duty; the old flag never touched the ground." The five thousand Yankee troops stormed the ramparts, capturing a corner of the fort and holding it for about an hour. But they were overwhelmed

Sergeant William Carney's Medal of Honor citation reads: "When the color sergeant was shot down, this soldier grasped the flag, led the way to the parapet, and planted the colors thereon. When the troops fell back he brought off the flag, under a fierce fire in which he was twice severely wounded." After being discharged from the army because of his wounds, Carney spent more than three decades as a mailman. He died in an elevator accident in the Massachusetts State House in 1908.

When this Kurz and Allison print was published in1890, the text below the image summarized the cost of the attack on Fort Wagner: "Union losses: Gen. Strong, Cols. Shaw, Chatfield, Putnam, Gen. Seymore, 1,200 soldiers; Confederate losses: 16 officers and 300 soldiers." The attack proved the courage of black soldiers, who would make an enormous contribution to the Union victory.

In the attack on Fort Wagner, wrote black soldier James Henry Gooding, "The 54th rushed to within twenty yards of the ditches, and, as might be expected of raw recruits, wavered—but at the second advance they gained the parapet. The color bearer of the State colors was killed on the parapet. Colonel Shaw seized the staff when the standard bearer fell, and in less than a minute after, the Colonel fell himself. When the men saw their gallant leader fall, they made a desperate effort to get him out, but they were either shot down, or reeled in the ditch below."

by the defenders and withdrew under fire. The attackers suffered sixteen hundred casualties, the rebels only two hundred. The bravery of black soldiers thrilled the North. Sergeant Major Lewis Douglass, Frederick Douglass's son, reported in awe, "This regiment has established its reputation as a fighting regiment. Not a man flinched, though it was a trying time. . . . I wish we had a hundred thousand colored troops—we would put an end to this war." For his courage, although it took almost forty years, William Carney was awarded the Medal of Honor, the first black American to receive that honor.

Among those soldiers killed in the attack was Colonel Shaw, who was shot through the heart while leading the charge. The Confederate commander, General Johnson Hagood, had known Shaw before the war. In a show of contempt for a white man who would betray his race by leading black troops into battle, Hagood not only refused to return Shaw's body to the North, he ordered his men to throw it into a mass grave with black soldiers who had fallen in the fighting. "We have buried him with his n———s," he said defiantly. That comment actually became a rallying cry for Union troops. They may not have felt entirely comfortable with the concept of fighting alongside black soldiers, but they certainly admired their grit and courage. Rather than being insulted, Shaw's abolitionist parents later told reporters, "We would not have his body removed from where it lies surrounded by his brave and devoted soldiers. . . . We can imagine no holier place than that in which he lies, among his brave and devoted followers, nor wish for him better company—what a body-guard he has!"

For Jefferson Davis, the addition of as many as 150,000 brave black soldiers to his enemy's ranks was simply the latest in a continuing series of setbacks. Among the few advantages he enjoyed over Lincoln was the quality of his military leaders. Lincoln had long been searching for generals like Lee, Longstreet, and Stonewall Jackson to lead his army. And in August 1863 even that slight advantage was threatened when Robert E. Lee offered Davis his resignation.

Lee had been worn down by the war; he was exhausted and sick—and had suffered several small heart attacks. The defeat at Gettysburg, the lack of supplies and reinforcements, and the relentless criticism he was beginning to receive in Southern newspapers had finally proved too much for him to endure. "I have not yet recovered from the attack I experienced the past spring," he wrote to Jefferson Davis from his camp in Orange County, Virginia. "I am becoming more and more incapable of exertion, and am thus prevented from making the personal examinations and giving the personal supervision to the operations in the field which I feel to be necessary. . . . I am so dull that in making use of the eyes of others I am frequently misled. . . . I therefore, in all sincerity, request Your Excellency to take measures to supply my place. I do this with the more earnestness because no one is more aware than myself of my inability for the duties of my position."

President Davis was shocked by Lee's letter. For personal, political, and military reasons, he could not possibly accept Lee's resignation. Many people were questioning Davis's leadership. Too many men were dying or coming home maimed with too few victories to show for it. Slaves were walking off plantations and shortages were affecting everyone. He was accused of favoring certain generals, such as the greatly disliked and seemingly ineffective Braxton Bragg, above those who had proved themselves in the field. Lee, meanwhile, retained the respect of both the troops and the civilian population. Clearly Davis believed that Robert E. Lee at less than his peak was far superior to any other Confederate general. And so he rejected Lee's resignation.

After accepting this vote of confidence Lee turned his attention to the west, where the armies were converging around Chattanooga, an important railway hub and the gateway to the rich agricultural farmlands of Georgia and Alabama—and to the great city of Atlanta. Davis, too, knew its importance, sending troops who had fought at Gettysburg and Vicksburg to reinforce General Bragg's force holding the city.

The Union forces were led by General William Rosecrans. The key to his success would be to get his sixty-thousand-man Army of the Cumberland safely across the Tennessee River. To disguise his intentions, Rosecrans sent a small force of four thousand men slightly north of the city. These troops spent nearly three weeks creating a diversion, shelling the city,

General Braxton Bragg's (left) Army of Tennessee met General William
Rosecrans's Army of the Cumberland for the first of a series of battles at
Stones River on December 31, 1862. Although Bragg would defeat Rosecrans
several times, he was severely criticized for not pressing his advantage.
Rosecrans (right) eventually was relieved of command, but his reputation
survived and years later he was elected to Congress.

placing pontoon bridges at strategic points along the riverbank, even making feints to cross
the Tennessee at several points. The deception was a success and the Yankees crossed the river
without opposition thirty miles west of the city, then proceeded to outflank Bragg's men.

Like McClellan in the North, Braxton Bragg had long been criticized for his indecision.
"Old Rosy" had gotten around him and placed his Army of Tennessee in a precarious position.
He had no choice but to abandon the city. The Union troops marched into Chattanooga, having
lost only six men—four by accident—in taking the city. It was an extraordinary victory. "If we
can hold Chattanooga and East Tennessee," Lincoln said, "I think the rebellion must dwindle
and die."

Jefferson Davis was outraged. Allowing the Yankees to maintain control of Chattanooga
essentially meant surrendering Tennessee and Georgia. He wanted Lee to march west and
join forces with Bragg to recapture the city. Lee refused, instead sending James Longstreet to
support Bragg.

Rosecrans had been emboldened by his bloodless victory and cautiously pursued the
retreating rebels, looking for an opportunity to catch Bragg's army and finish him. In fact, he

The war seemed to consist of long periods of waiting and marching, punctuated by a day or two of bloody battle. The Battle of Chattanooga stretched from September through November 1863. This photograph of Union soldiers relaxing in camp was taken during that period along the Tennessee River.

had made a disastrous miscalculation; he assumed the overcautious Bragg would continue his retreat. Instead, Bragg had made camp to await Longstreet and the promised reinforcements at LaFayette, Georgia, about twenty-five miles from Atlanta.

General George Thomas urged Rosecrans to strengthen Chattanooga before setting out to overtake Bragg, but Rosecrans was confident he knew what Bragg would do. In his pursuit Rosecrans allowed his three corps to become widely separated as they moved through the mountain passes. Bragg's reinforced army and Rosecrans's hastily reassembled forces clashed on the banks of Chickamauga Creek.

Chickamauga is a Cherokee name meaning, appropriately, river of death. In two days of fighting in the thickets, each side lost about a third of its men. The battle was so chaotic that at one point the only order Bragg could give his generals was "Be governed by circumstances." For a time Bragg sensed complete victory: the Union troops had been routed, and he was about to crush them. But General Thomas formed a defensive position on a high point called Horseshoe Ridge and his division held the line there against waves of attackers throughout the day. At one point Thomas's men were on the edge of defeat, fearful that they lacked

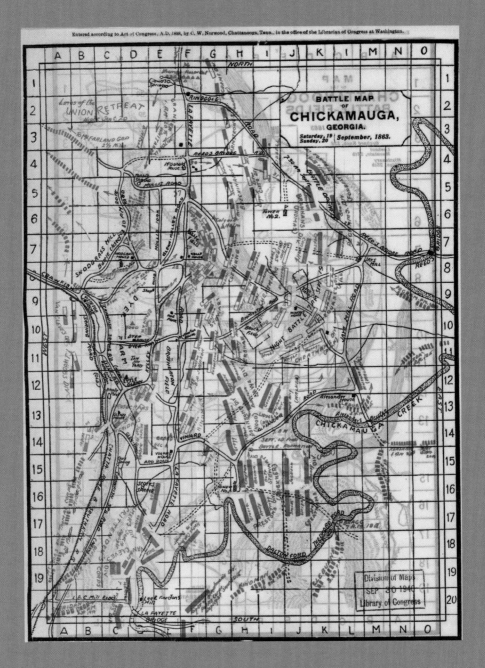

As this battle map illustrates, two massive forces clashed at Chickamauga, and after two days of fighting Union forces retreated back to Chattanooga; thirty-four thousand men were wounded in the battle, which was "won" by the Confederates, but it ended with the Union still in possession of the city.

enough ammunition to beat back another ferocious attack. Thomas saw a cloud of dust about a mile away moving toward him, but he could not discern which side was raising it. If it was reinforcements, he could hold out; if it was the enemy, there would be no escape. He waited there patiently, watching. The *New York Herald* would write, "In the dust that emerged, thick as the clouds that precede the storm, nothing could be distinguished but a moving mass of men." Thomas sent a man to find out "who and what that force is. . . . In a few moments he again emerged from this timber, and following him came the red, white, and blue crescent-shaped battle-flag."

When the battle ended at dark, Thomas led an orderly withdrawal back to Chattanooga. He was credited with saving the army and preventing the Confederates from gaining access to the west, and from that day forward he would be known as the Rock of Chickamauga.

Rosecrans's badly wounded army occupied the city and began fortifying it against the expected attack. "We have met with a serious disaster," he reported to General Halleck. "Enemy overwhelmed us." But Bragg also had taken monumental casualties and lost the confidence of his officers. A dozen generals in his command appealed to Davis to replace him. As Longstreet reported to Richmond, "I am convinced that nothing but the hand of God can save us or help us as long as we have our present commander. . . . Can't you send us General Lee?"

But it was not Robert E. Lee who traveled to Tennessee; instead it was President Davis, who wanted to personally assess the situation and, if necessary, quell this brewing mutiny. After listening to Bragg's complaints, Davis decided to leave him in charge. There was little else he could do; Lee was needed to defend Richmond.

Bragg's men formed a vast semicircle around Chattanooga, stretching from a point upstream on the Tennessee River to a point below the city just west of Lookout Mountain. The only open route into the city was a narrow path over Walden's Ridge, which was little more than a sixty-mile-long mud trail. The siege line had been set. Few supplies could get into the city. Eventually Rosecrans's men would be starved into submission. Just like at Vicksburg, it was only a matter of time. The Yankee troops were put on half rations, the animals less. Within weeks, twenty horses and mules were dying each day.

Once again Lincoln faced a similar situation. He had completely lost confidence in Old Rosy, believing he had been befuddled by events during the Battle of Chickamauga, and had been left "confused and stunned, like a duck hit on the head." Lincoln dispatched U. S. Grant west to take charge of the newly formed Military Division of the Mississippi, which consisted of all Union forces from the Appalachian Mountains to the Mississippi. Among Grant's first

As a Virginia teenager, George Thomas was whisked to safety by his family's slaves during Nat Turner's rebellion. Thomas then broke the law by teaching those slaves to read. "Old Slow Trot," as he was briefly nicknamed, was Sherman's roommate at West Point. He pulled an arrow out of his own chest while fighting Indians and turned down an offer to fight for Virginia when the war began. Because of the care and caution with which he managed his commands, he became known to his men as "Old Pap Thomas." He "looked upon the lives of his soldiers as a sacred trust, not to be carelessly imperiled," wrote one of his men, engendering a deep loyalty that served him well at Chickamauga.

actions was to relieve Rosecrans of his command, replacing him with George Thomas. But his most important objective was to relieve Chattanooga. He telegraphed to Thomas to hold the city at any price, to which the general replied, "We will hold the town till we starve."

Grant struggled to get into the city. After making his way by train to the town of Bridgeport, forty miles from Chattanooga, Grant was forced to travel the rest of the way over Walden's Ridge on horseback. It was, as his aide John Rawlins wrote, a hazardous journey, especially as Grant had recently been injured: "The roughest and steepest of ascent and descent ever crossed by army wagons and mules. Over washouts and gullies, Grant had to be lifted from his horse and carried over the obstacles. Once, his horse slipped, and he came crashing down, reinjuring his already wounded leg."

Grant had been hardened at Vicksburg. He immediately began searching for a way to get desperately needed supplies into the city. The Army of the Cumberland's chief engineer, General William "Baldy" Smith, had devised a plan to build a pontoon bridge across the Tennessee at Brown's Ferry, a crossing ten miles downstream from Chattanooga that led to an open road through Lookout Valley. A sawmill was already at work cutting lumber for the bridge and a handmade steamboat for transporting supplies. Grant supported the plan and at three a.m. on the morning of October 27, Union troops boarded makeshift boats and floated silently through the night, directly under Confederate guns. After a brief firefight, they captured Brown's Ferry, then fought off a determined counterattack. Just as Smith had envisioned, the "Cracker Line" had been opened to supply the city (the nickname referred to the hard biscuits—hardtack—that were carried into the city). The first boatload of supplies was brought upriver by the steamer *Chattanooga*, which had been hastily built by attaching a stern-wheeler, powered by an old engine, to a scow made from lumber cut at the mill. The supply route was eventually plied by steamboats and barges, while mules, horses, and wagons crossed the pontoon bridge, bringing sufficient rations and other necessities into the city. His army's survival assured, Grant began planning to break out.

At about the same time in the east, residents of Gettysburg were preparing to dedicate a national cemetery. The fierce fighting in those first days of July had left the town with the job of burying thirty-five hundred Union soldiers from at least ten states, as many as a thousand of them lacking any proof of identity. It was decided to bury them on the battlefield, including seventeen acres atop Cemetery Hill where fighting had taken place. The official dedication ceremony was scheduled for November 19, 1863. The featured speaker that day was noted orator and politician Edward Everett, but President Lincoln had also accepted an invitation to add "a few appropriate remarks." The nation had been shocked by and was still mourning the vast number of casualties. Lincoln's speech was intended to be only a few words to pay his respects, and those of the entire Union, to the thousands of courageous men who had fought there, been wounded there, and died there.

The brief speech he gave that day, the Gettysburg Address, has secured a place in American history. His words, beginning with the familiar "Four score and seven years ago our fathers brought forth upon this continent a new nation, conceived in liberty, and dedicated to the proposition that all men are created equal," have been memorized and recited by children for more than a century, and have come to help define our national character. But as with so many landmark events in history, the stories that are told about it aren't all accurate. Supposedly Lincoln scribbled the speech on the back of an envelope while on the train to Gettysburg. Andrew Carnegie later claimed that not only had he seen Lincoln writing his speech on the train, he'd handed him the pencil to do so. In fact, Lincoln wrote the first page of his speech, which was in ink, in the White House, and then added the final version of the second page, in pencil, after arriving at the Gettysburg home of Judge David Wills.

Lincoln rode on horseback to the cemetery, part of a procession that included more than twelve hundred soldiers. Among the marchers was Henry Cochrane, who reported, "As he went along his trousers gradually worked up, revealing the tops of his home-made gray socks, of which he was entirely unconscious." The new burial ground adjoined the town's old cemetery, and a sign that predated the battle read, ironically, "All persons found using firearms on these grounds will be prosecuted with the utmost rigor of the law."

While most of the bodies had already been buried, the battlefield was still littered with the wounds of the war. Cochrane described the desolation: "Rifle pits, cut and scarred trees, broken fences, pieces of artillery wagons and harness, scraps of blue and gray clothing, bent canteens, abandoned knapsacks, belts, cartridge boxes, shoes and caps, were still to be seen."

The crowd, estimated at between ten and twenty thousand, stood and listened politely as Everett delivered his carefully rehearsed, two-hour oration. Cochrane noted, "His periods were

Only three photos of Lincoln at Gettysburg exist. In this image, he can be seen on the left of the crowd. To his right is his friend and bodyguard, Ward Hill Lamon. The photo at right (top) was taken about a week earlier. Edward Everett (above, bottom) concluded his two-hour speech by admitting, "I must leave to others, who can do it from personal observation, to describe the mournful spectacle presented by these hillsides and plains at the close of the terrible conflict. . . . The horrors of the battle-field, after the contest is over, the sights and sounds of woe . . ."

polished, his diction graceful, and his language classical, but his great effort is long forgotten."

Lincoln spoke next. The 272-word dedication took him less than four minutes to deliver, surprising the audience, which had anticipated hearing one of Lincoln's long recitations. While many history books claim the speech was greeted with thunderous applause, there remains considerable debate about its reception. Major William Lambert remembered, "The brevity of the speech, the absence of rhetorical effort, and its very simplicity prevented its full appreciation." Clark Carr, a member of the Cemetery Commission, wrote with disappointment, "His expressions were so plain and homely, without any attempt at rhetorical periods, and his statements were so axiomatic . . . and so simple, that I had no idea that, as an address, it was anything more than ordinary."

Ward Hill Lamon, marshal of the District of Columbia, who was on the platform, overheard William Seward telling Everett after Lincoln's speech, "He has made a failure, and I am sorry for it. His speech is not equal to him." Everett seemed to agree, saying, "It is not what I expected from him. I am disappointed." Lamon himself admitted that he agreed with Seward, telling him, "I am sorry to say that it does not impress me as one of his great speeches." The audience, he wrote, also seemed to agree. Rather than the reported cheering, "the silence during the delivery of the speech, and the lack of hearty demonstrations of approval immediately after its close, were taken by Mr. Lincoln as certain proof that it was not well received."

Others judged it a success. One of the planners of the event, Benjamin French, wrote, "Anyone who saw and heard as I did, the hurricane of applause that met his every movement at Gettysburg would know that he lived in every heart. It was no cold, faint, shadow of a kind reception—it was a tumultuous outpouring of exultation."

Opinions on the address in fact seem to have been consistent with political leanings. Those people and journals who did not support Lincoln did not like his speech and reported it was poorly received. Conversely, Lincoln's supporters marveled at its beauty. But as the speech was published throughout the entire country, its simple power captured the attention of the public. Several weeks later *Harper's Weekly* noted, "The few words of the president were from the heart to the heart. They cannot be read without kindling emotion. . . . It was as simple and felicitous and earnest a word as was ever spoken." The *Chicago Tribune* agreed, reporting, "The dedicatory remarks by President Lincoln will live among the annals of the war."

Lamon later reported that Lincoln's own assessment was that his speech was a failure. But there is little evidence to support that. In fact, the president loaned his copy of the speech to the Associated Press so that it could be widely published and he was known to handwrite copies for charities and friends. But it wasn't until after the war, and after his assassination, that the grace and power of his few words became so widely recognized and appreciated, and grew to become a lasting tribute to those people who fight for freedom.

In addition to taking more than sixty-six hundred casualties in the Battle of Chattanooga, the rebels lost forty cannons and sixty-nine limbers and caissons, seen lined up neatly outside General Bragg's former headquarters.

While Lincoln's stirring words at Gettysburg spread throughout the nation, in Chattanooga there was hard fighting to be done. Grant was determined to smash through the lines of rebel troops in the hills surrounding the city. Reinforced by the men and supplies that flowed through the Cracker Line, he began his offensive on November 23. The Confederate forces already had been weakened by the more than twelve thousand troops General Bragg had dispatched to assist Longstreet.

On the first day of fighting, the Yankees quickly overwhelmed a small rebel force at Orchard Knob, which retreated after firing a single volley. On the second day, Grant's men attacked the Confederates on the slopes of Lookout Mountain. Much of the fighting in this "Battle Above the Clouds" was obscured by fog, but eventually the defenders broke and retreated toward the summit—making it impossible for Confederate guns on the mountain to fire without hitting their own men. The sun rose on the morning of the twenty-fifth to reveal a huge American flag flying proudly on top of Lookout Mountain—the highest point from which the Stars and Stripes would wave in the entire war.

On the third day, when Sherman's flanking attack on Missionary Ridge stalled, Grant ordered General Thomas's twenty-four-thousand-man Army of the Cumberland to assist Sherman by launching an assault on the rifle pits at the base of Missionary Ridge. They were to capture those positions and wait there for further commands, but this was the opportunity Thomas's men had been waiting for since their humiliation weeks earlier at Chickamauga. When the signal gun was fired, they charged into the heart of the Confederate defense, screaming their battle cry, "Chickamauga!" Within minutes they had taken the rifle pits— and then kept going, scrambling up the ridge. Grant watched in awe from his headquarters on Orchard Knob, wondering aloud, "Who ordered these men up the ridge?" Thomas's men fought their way up the steep slope, routing the nine thousand Confederate defenders. In less than an hour they took Missionary Ridge. The rebels were in full retreat, burning the supplies they couldn't carry and bridges to prevent pursuit. The west was won. And the road into Georgia was open.

The day after the victory at Chattanooga, the United States celebrated its first official Thanksgiving. George Washington had declared the new nation's first Thanksgiving, and since that time each state had set aside its own day of observance. Lincoln, at least partially in gratitude for the victory at Gettysburg, had declared that from this day forward the entire nation would give thanks for all its blessings on the same day, the fourth Thursday of November. "In the midst of a civil war of unequalled magnitude and severity," he had proclaimed weeks earlier, he had taken steps to "implore the interposition of the Almighty

Hand to heal the wounds of this nation and to restore it as soon as may be consistent with the Divine purposes to the full enjoyment of peace, harmony, tranquillity and Union."

As the civil war moved into its fourth year, the outcome seemed more certain. The great advantage in men and supplies enjoyed by the North had finally begun to wear down the Confederacy. The command superiority and the fervor that had led the South to great victories were no longer apparent. In Washington, the now confident Lincoln placed the victorious U. S. Grant in command of the entire army, while in Richmond the increasingly despairing Jefferson Davis searched for some spark that might renew the passion that had so recently burned so brightly.

Lincoln is known to have personally written five copies of the Gettysburg Address. This one supposedly was written on the back on an envelope while he was en route to Gettysburg.

In fact that never happened. This is believed to be a facsimile of a copy of the address written by Lincoln and given to Alexander Bliss to raise money for the Baltimore Sanitary Fair.

President Lincoln spent most of his time during the First Battle of Bull Run sitting in the War Department's new telegraph office, learning details of the battle in almost real time. For the first time an American leader had direct contact with the battlefield. Months earlier, Lincoln had directed a Pennsylvania Railroad supervisor named Andrew Carnegie to extend telegraph communications into Northern Virginia, and by the end of the war, Carnegie's US Military Telegraph Corps had strung more than four thousand miles of wire, trained twelve hundred operators, and carried almost a million messages.

Lincoln used this technology to exercise his control as commander in chief directly over the Union armies. In 1863, for example, when General Hooker proposed taking Richmond, Lincoln wired, IF LEFT TO ME, I WOULD NOT GO SOUTH OF THE RAPPAHANNOCK, UPON LEE'S MOVING NORTH OF IT. . . . I THINK LEE'S ARMY, AND NOT RICHMOND, IS YOUR TRUE OBJECTIVE POINT.

The Confederacy never developed this technology enough to be useful. The ability of the Union to repair cut wires to maintain communications gave the North a decided advantage. A Union soldier (right) repairs a wire. From the top left, a telegraph key, a battery carriage of a field telegraph station, soldiers laying wire during a battle, and a field telegraph station.

# NINE

# THE LEADING MAN

## Abraham Lincoln Runs into History

Abraham Lincoln was always strong enough to fight for peace—but he also was smart enough to avoid a brawl whenever possible. He demonstrated that noble combination of courage and wisdom early in his political career, when he was challenged to a duel to the death. While serving in the Illinois state legislature in 1842, Lincoln had quarreled with state auditor James Shields over banking policy. The Illinois State Bank had gone bankrupt and, with Shields's approval, was refusing to accept the paper money it had issued in payment for debts, effectively wiping out the savings of working people.

In a tradition that dated back to the founding fathers, both Lincoln and his betrothed, Mary Todd, attacked Shields in a series of anonymous letters published in the *Sangamo Journal*. Writing as "Aunt Rebecca," Lincoln and Todd derided Shields's decision, calling him "a fool as well as a liar," adding, "With him truth is out of the question." They continued to attack him personally, ridiculing the extraordinarily vain Shields as someone who might say, "It is not my fault that I am so handsome and so interesting."

⌐ Lincoln sat for artist George Peter Alexander Healy in August 1864, but the painting was not completed until 1869. Although it was intended to be an official portrait, President Grant selected a different portrait, by William Cogswell, to hang in the White House.

The earliest known photograph of Lincoln, taken when he was a
thirty-seven-year-old lawyer and congressman-elect from Illinois
by Nicholas H. Shepherd. The daguerreotype of Mary Todd Lincoln
also was taken by Shepherd, in 1846.

Shields uncovered their true identity and twice insisted that Lincoln retract his "slander, vituperation and personal abuse." When Lincoln refused, Shields demanded satisfaction, challenging him to a duel. With his honor at stake, Lincoln accepted.

Under the Code Duello, the accepted rules of dueling, Lincoln was permitted to set the conditions. Rather than pistols, he decided they would fight with "cavalry broadswords of the largest size." His reason, he later explained, was, "I did not want to kill Shields, and felt sure I could disarm him," adding later, "I didn't want the d——d fellow to kill me, which I rather think he would have done if we had selected pistols." In addition, he cleverly added that the combatants must be separated by "a plank ten feet long, and from nine to twelve inches abroad, to be firmly fixed on edge, on the ground, as the line between us, which neither is to pass his foot over upon forfeit of his life," which would give the six-foot-four-inch Lincoln a decided advantage in reach over the five-foot-eight-inch Shields.

Dueling had been outlawed in Illinois, so they met on Bloody Island, a towhead opposite Saint Louis, not part of Missouri or Illinois. According to legend, as the two combatants prepared to engage, Lincoln swirled his great sword in the air and sliced a branch off a tree. Some stories claim that the falling branch almost hit Shields. Most of these tales agree that Shields was so intimidated by Lincoln's clever demonstration that he accepted a truce and they retired from the field with their honor, though it has also has been reported that the men were talked out of their foolishness by mutual friends who got to the field before the duelists took their positions.

Lincoln and Shields eventually made peace with each other, and Shields later distinguished himself as a leader during the Mexican-American War and the Civil War. At the Battle of Kernstown in 1862, Brigadier General Shields earned his place in history as the only Union officer to defeat Stonewall Jackson. As a reward, Lincoln promoted his former adversary to the rank of major general.

Lincoln never spoke about the duel; years later, when asked if he really had agreed to duel to defend Mary Todd's honor, he responded crossly, "I do not deny it, but if you desire my friendship, you will never mention it again."

But the grit and wit Lincoln demonstrated to defuse this situation without harm or shame coming to either man proved vital throughout his presidency. He constantly faced not just military problems but also political challenges. By 1864 the country had wearied of the war; the easy victory that once had been promised was long forgotten and as the presidential election approached, there was considerable doubt that Lincoln would be reelected. He was

After his duel against Abraham Lincoln was settled without harm to either participant, James Shields went on to enjoy a remarkable career. He fought in both the Mexican-American War and the Civil War, earning recognition as the only federal general to tactically defeat Stonewall Jackson, and later became the only person in our history to be elected a senator from three different states.

under political attack from almost every side: opposition members of his own Republican Party openly spoke of challenging his nomination with a staunch abolitionist candidate, while Democrats searched for a peace candidate—someone who would make peace with the Confederacy, even if it meant allowing slavery to continue in certain Southern states.

Not only could Abraham Lincoln bend with the political winds; when necessary he could find a way to make them change direction.

To ensure strong support from his own Republican Party while draining support away from the abolitionists, he firmly embraced emancipation. When Congressman James Ashley introduced a thirteenth constitutional amendment to permanently abolish slavery everywhere in the country, Lincoln made its passage a cornerstone of his campaign.

The election of 1864 was shaping up to be a referendum on slavery. What price would Northerners be willing to pay to end this war?

The best way to answer that question, the president knew, was to end the war before the election. But as that hardly was probable, he needed to at least make it clear that victory was in sight. As he told the National Union League during the campaign, "It is not best to swap horses while crossing the river," or, as it became better known in history, "Don't change horses in midstream."

Among the men being pressured to run against Lincoln were Secretary of the Treasury Salmon P. Chase and the nation's newest hero, Ulysses S. Grant. Grant undoubtedly was the most popular man in the United States and would be difficult to defeat. Lincoln responded brilliantly to that possibility: he placed Grant in command of all Union forces, making him the nation's first lieutenant general since George Washington. While the increased national visibility undoubtedly would raise Grant's popularity even higher, Lincoln cleverly had tied their fates together: if Grant was victorious, Lincoln would be acclaimed for picking him; if Grant failed, only Grant would be blamed.

Grant himself expressed little interest in running against Lincoln. Instead, he proposed an audacious plan to end the war: he intended to launch simultaneous attacks on the rebel strongholds of Mobile, Richmond, and Atlanta.

But in early 1864, President Lincoln faced a challenge outside his daily military and political struggles, although at the time he may not have realized its dangerous implications: a plot to assassinate Confederate president Jefferson Davis.

In late February, Union cavalry general Judson Kilpatrick launched a daring raid on Richmond. Its objective was to demonstrate that the Confederate capital was vulnerable, to circulate copies of the Emancipation Proclamation, and, most important, to free an estimated five thousand starving Union soldiers from the Libby and Belle Isle Confederate prisons. Approved by Secretary of War Stanton, the plan was simple: while more than three thousand men circled Robert E. Lee's flank and raised a ruckus, a smaller force of five hundred men under the command of twenty-one-year-old colonel Ulric Dahlgren would slip into the city and liberate the prisoners.

The raid quickly collapsed. "Kill-Cavalry," as Kilpatrick was known, encountered resistance from local militias whom he mistook for Confederate soldiers. Thinking that the advantage of surprise had been lost, he withdrew. Dahlgren, completely unaware that the main force had retreated, fought to within three miles of the city center before he was killed and most of the men riding with him were wounded or captured.

That night, a thirteen-year-old boy searching Dahlgren's body supposedly found a cigar case, a notebook, and a copy of what appeared to be his official orders. Among these "Special Orders and Instructions," which Dahlgren apparently had written, was a startling command:

Extraordinarily vain but admittedly clever, Judson Kilpatrick
(left) once caused a larger rebel force to withdraw by shouting
orders to nonexistent reinforcements. To restore a once-promising
reputation hurt by a poor performance at Gettysburg, he proposed
the surprise raid into Richmond that led to the death of twenty-
one-year-old Ulric Dahlgren (right). Kilpatrick successfully guarded
Sherman's flank on his march through the South, his men setting
many of the fires that have burned through history.

"The bridges once secured, and the prisoners loose and over the river, the bridges will be secured and the city destroyed. The men must keep together and well in hand, and once in the city it must be destroyed and Jeff. Davis and Cabinet killed."

Was Dahlgren's real mission to assassinate Confederate president Jefferson Davis and burn Richmond?

The publication of the so-called Dahlgren Papers in the Richmond newspapers created an uproar throughout the Confederacy. Assassinate the president! Burn the city! The outrage at this barbaric act spread across the ocean to Europe. Some claimed that Lincoln had approved of this nefarious plot.

But the publication of these orders created almost as much surprise in the North as in Dixie. Government officials immediately denounced them as a forgery intended to weaken Union resolve and create renewed sympathy in Europe for the Southern cause. Robert E. Lee sent a photographed copy of these orders to Union general George Meade, whom he had known from their days together at West Point, to determine their authenticity. Meade conferred with Kilpatrick, who acknowledged that the orders were genuine—with the exception of the final few words, ordering the burning of the city and the assassinations. Meade responded to Lee, writing, "Neither the United States Government, myself, nor General Kilpatrick authorized, sanctioned, or approved the burning of the city of Richmond and the killing of Mr. Davis and cabinet." It appeared that the federal government was claiming Dahlgren himself had written the damning addition.

The Dahlgren Affair was never resolved. There were further twists and turns; the fact that the young colonel's name appeared to be misspelled was cited as evidence that he did not write those orders. The men riding with him said they were given no such orders. At the end of the war the actual papers were delivered to Secretary of War Stanton and disappeared. Only copies exist. Historians differ in their conclusions: many experts believe they were real orders and might possibly be traced directly to Lincoln, while others blame Dahlgren. Most important, though, it appears that Jefferson Davis accepted them as real and, in response, sent agents to Canada, where the Confederate Secret Service had established a base, with orders to retaliate against Lincoln. Various plans were formulated, from sending yellow fever–infected clothing to Lincoln to kidnapping him and putting him on trial for war crimes. While none of them ever came to fruition, there are those who suggest that this was the beginning of a long chain that ended with John Wilkes Booth pulling the trigger at Ford's Theatre.

Whatever Lincoln's thoughts on the matter, his focus remained firmly on the war and reelection. In April 1864, the Senate passed the Thirteenth Amendment and sent it to the

House. And while that was happening, the two great generals of the Civil War, U. S. Grant and Robert E. Lee, were preparing to collide at Richmond. Grant finally had abandoned the Union strategy of capturing key cities and places; he intended to destroy Lee's army and march into Richmond. Under Grant's command, General Butler's thirty thousand troops were positioned south of Richmond; if the defenders in that city left to reinforce Lee, Butler would attack. Grant's advantage in manpower was his greatest weapon: he would suffer as many casualties as necessary, but by striking relentlessly he eventually would wear down and kill the rebel armies.

General William Sherman was ordered to march his hundred thousand men toward Atlanta, but his real objective, he knew, "was to go for Joe Johnston." Like Grant, he vowed to "make this war as severe as possible and show no signs of tiring till the South begs for mercy."

In early May 1864, Grant's army crossed the Rapidan River and moved anxiously into the nearly impassable tangle of forest and swamps known as the Wilderness. It was in this seventy-square-mile jungle a year earlier that Joe Hooker's men had been mauled by Stonewall Jackson; the muddy ground was still littered with their bones. Grant did not intend to repeat that mistake.

Lee watched with satisfaction, offering no resistance as the Army of the Potomac crossed the river. Unlike the Yankees, his men knew those woods; they lived there and had learned all its secrets. Once again, what he lacked in numbers he would make up for in cunning. Lee waited until Grant's army was caught completely in the Wilderness, and then he attacked.

Lee had underestimated Grant, expecting him to respond to the offensive as previous Union generals had done and withdraw rather than continuing to take heavy casualties. But Grant was different, as General Longstreet had warned Lee. Grant and Longstreet had been close friends before the war—in fact, Longstreet had been Grant's groomsman at his wedding—and he knew well that when Grant set his mind to something, he didn't waver and he didn't quit. As Longstreet told his fellow officers, Grant "will fight us every day and every hour until the end of the war."

The fighting in the Wilderness raged for two long days, two great armies led by two great generals going toe to toe, slugging it out. At times it was impossible to even see the enemy, but the firing never ceased, never slowed. Artillery was useless, unit movements were difficult; this was one man against another. As Longstreet had predicted, the Union took substantial casualties, but Grant never hesitated. His strategy remained straightforward: he was going to bludgeon the rebels into submission. When Grant's commanders urged him to respond artfully to Lee's tactics, he disdainfully replied, "Oh, I am heartily tired of hearing about what Lee is

Courage, confusion, chaos, and death are apparent in this highly dramatized 1887
lithograph, *Battle of the Wilderness*. This was the first confrontation of the historic
struggle between two of America's greatest generals, Grant and Lee. Both sides
suffered heavy casualties in this first battle of Grant's Virginia Overland Campaign,
although there was no decisive victor.

going to do. Some of you always seem to think he is suddenly going to turn a double somersault, and land in our rear and on both of our flanks at the same time. Go back to your command, and try to think what we are going to do ourselves, instead of what Lee is going to do."

By the end of the second day both armies had been badly bloodied, yet neither had gained any advantage. "The battle had been a series of impetuous assaults by the rebels and by the patriots," Abbott reported. "The carnage on both sides was dreadful. . . . The rebels had been thwarted in all their plans to break our lines. We had been bloodily driven back from every endeavor. . . . The battle closed on a disputed field. Both parties claimed the victory; for each could state with truth that he 'had repelled the fierce attack of the enemy.'"

The toll in the Wilderness was horrendous: the Union took eighteen thousand casualties, 18 percent of the army—but the rebels lost an equally large part of their army. Grant could absorb those losses and replace those men, especially with black troops being allowed to fight; Lee could not. In another blow to the Confederates, Longstreet was shot by his own men in an incident eerily similar to the death of Stonewall Jackson. While Longstreet survived, Lee had lost another great leader on whom he depended at a time when he was most needed.

As the fighting died down, Union soldiers assumed they were going to withdraw as usual; this time, though, things were different. As Lincoln had said of Grant, "Once [Grant] gets possession of a place, he holds on to it as if he had inherited it." When the Union army reached the key crossroads, rather than turning right toward the Rapidan River, they were ordered to turn left—south, to Richmond. Great cheers arose from the troops as the men realized the significance of that order. Regimental bands started to play. A dispirited retreat had turned quickly into a triumphant march. These men wanted to finish the fight.

The roads converged near the village of Spotsylvania Court House. The rebels got there first and occupied the high ground. They constructed extensive breastworks and dug in. The fighting resumed, this time out of the woods. Day after day and into the night, the two sides pummeled each other. Both armies brought artillery into the battle, adding to the carnage. Grant continually hammered at Lee's right flank, trying to force the rebels to abandon their well-defended positions. The battle raged through much of May. Grant made still another feint but this time attacked on the weakened left flank. The Confederates were driven back—until the Yankees practically walked into batteries that Lee had prepared. The assault was blunted.

Lee sent a rebel division through a dense forest into the Union rear, where they attacked a supply train coming from Fredericksburg. Yankee troops descended on them, driving them back into the woods, but not before hundreds more men had been killed and wounded.

Grant and Lee continued to push and probe, leaving piles of corpses, searching for that one error, that one advantage, that might cause the entire enemy army to collapse. Neither side could find that weakness, but Grant's willingness to commit his men to the battle gradually took its toll. The Confederates were slowly driven back toward Richmond. After weeks of engagement, which consisted of daily skirmishes punctuated on occasion by several hours of heavy fighting, Lee's army was securely entrenched behind a six-mile-long earthworks barrier at a crossroads known as Old Cold Harbor. Their backs were only ten miles outside Richmond.

Grant determined to smash through the rebel lines, whatever the price he had to pay in blood. There would be no surprises, no maneuvering; he intended to strike Lee with all the subtlety of a fist in the face. He ordered a frontal assault directly into the center of the Confederate defense. His motive for such an ill-fated effort has long been questioned. While he certainly believed that it could succeed, there also might have been a political reality: the Republican Party convention, which would renominate Abraham Lincoln, was to take place in less than a week. A great victory outside Richmond would be an added reason to celebrate—and would remind voters that the war was coming to an end.

A delay in Union preparations gave the rebels an additional full day to prepare for the assault. They had taken advantage of the rolling terrain to hide their fortifications from Union observers, and in some places their rifle pits and trenches were two and three levels deep. There was almost no intelligence about the enemy's positions, and there was no battle plan beyond attack, gain a foothold, and exploit it.

Grant's troops, and their officers, were aware that they would be marching straight into hellfire. The night before the assault, Lieutenant Colonel Horace Porter walked among the quiet campfires and was surprised, he wrote, to see "that many soldiers had taken off their coats, and seemed to be engaged in sewing up rents in them. This exhibition of tailoring seemed rather peculiar at such a moment, but upon closer examination it was found that the men were calmly writing their names and home addresses on slips of paper, and pinning them on the backs of their coats, so that their dead bodies might be recognized upon the field, and their fate made known to their families at home."

These rudimentary dog tags, which ensured they would not be buried as "Unknown," proved necessary. At four thirty in the morning the signal gun sounded and fifty thousand men—in an unbroken line seven miles long—charged into the mist and thick fog. They didn't need to see the field; their only direction was forward. Attacking the entire length of the line, Grant believed, would prevent Lee from reinforcing his weakest points during the fighting.

The battle was over within minutes; the horror would linger for days. In the first hour as

For 130 years, Robert Knox Sneden's incredible five-thousand-page memoir was hidden away in a bank vault and a storage bin. The memoir included more than a thousand sketches and drawings, like this map of the fighting at Spotsylvania. Except for three dozen sketches that had been printed in an 1880s book series, none of the drawings had been seen before.

In this 1865 photograph, African Americans, either soldiers or contraband employed by the Union army, collect the remains of the estimated eighteen hundred troops killed more than a year earlier in the Battle of Cold Harbor. Contraband performed many of the unpleasant duties, although prisoners of war and even unwelcome civilian relic-hunters were often put to the task at gunpoint, freeing white soldiers to fight, another advantage enjoyed by the North. Captain James Moore, in charge of this effort, reported its difficulty. "The bones of these men were gathered from the ground where they fell, having never been interred," he admitted, "and by exposure to the weather, all traces of their identity were entirely obliterated."

many as a thousand Union troops were killed or wounded. The fighting continued through much of the day; Grant's men lay pinned down in the open field, often shielding themselves behind the bodies of their fallen comrades. The few attackers who somehow managed to reach Southern lines were quickly and brutally beaten back. When it was possible, soldiers used bayonets, water cups, and hands and feet to build an earthen barrier between them and the rebel guns. Grant seemed utterly unaware of the slaughter and continued to push his commanders to renew the attack, but they flatly refused. General "Baldy" Smith ignored a direct order to make another assault—and his refusal was never punished. Brigadier General Emory Upton also disobeyed, informing his superiors, "Our men are brave, but cannot accomplish impossibilities." Troops simply refused orders to move; they had marched too far; they had seen too much. It was on this battlefield that the common soldier finally stood his ground. As one Union soldier wrote, "The army to a man refused to obey the order, presumably from General Grant. . . . I heard the order given, and I saw it disobeyed."

That night Grant admitted to his staff, "I regret this assault more than any one I have ever ordered. I regarded it as a stern necessity, and believed that it would bring compensating results; but, as it has proved, no advantages have been gained sufficient to justify the heavy losses suffered." But earlier in the day he had reported to Washington, "Our loss was not severe, nor do I suppose the enemy to have lost heavily. We captured over 300 prisoners." For some time, in fact, the magnitude of the defeat was hidden from the public. Even weeks later the number of casualties reported was less than half the actual toll of 7,000 men killed or wounded in the Battle of Cold Harbor. Whether that was done for political reasons or to boost morale was never determined.

But much worse was what took place on the battlefield. During the next four days countless wounded soldiers lay dying in the heat, while rebel sharpshooters prevented anyone from rescuing them. At first their cries for help were loud and desperate, but gradually those cries faded away. While military tradition allowed for the dead to be collected and the wounded to be offered help, Grant's refusal to admit defeat delayed the imposition of a truce for four days. By that time precious few wounded soldiers were still alive. "The stench of the dead men became unbearable," wrote Union private Frank Wilkeson. When he finally went safely into no-man's-land, "Every corpse I saw was black as coal. . . . They were buried where they fell. I saw no live man lying on this ground. The wounded must have suffered horribly before death relieved them, lying there exposed to the blazing southern sun o' days, and being eaten alive by beetles o' night."

Grant would not be dissuaded by a single defeat, no matter how painful. He was a soldier,

Popular illustrators, far behind the lines, had little knowledge on which to base
a realistic view of combat, nor would such realism have necessarily been all that
welcome. The slaughter at Cold Harbor was hidden from the public, probably to
prevent more antiwar sentiment. Even Currier and Ives misnamed this print *Battle of
Coal Harbor* and reported beneath the image, "Union troops advanced under a heavy
fire of grape and canister, driving the rebels before them and taking the position,
which was firmly held in spite of the enemy's desperate efforts to regain it." In fact, as
Grant later wrote, "At Cold Harbor no advantage whatever was gained to compensate
for the heavy loss we sustained."

a leader, and he understood that the path to a final victory includes bitter losses. Rather than wallowing at Cold Harbor, or withdrawing, he completely surprised Lee by successfully executing a daring maneuver around Lee's flank: covered by a series of distractions that convinced Lee that his target was Richmond, Grant's army slipped away from Cold Harbor, crossed the Chickahominy, James, and Appomattox Rivers unseen, and marched south to the city of Petersburg before Lee could respond. Grant was aware of the danger; while crossing the rivers his army was divided and exposed and had Lee caught him, the damage could have been disastrous.

But the risk was worth it. Petersburg was the key rail link to Richmond, and capturing it would cut off the flow of supplies into the Confederate capital. Lee understood its strategic importance and had previously admitted, "If he gets there, then it will be a siege, and then it will be a mere question of time."

Grant's operation was an "astonishing feat," reported Abbott. "This rapid and successful movement of an army of one hundred and fifty thousand men, in the presence of so formidable an enemy, is one of the marvels of war. This vast army, infantry, artillery, cavalry and baggage-train . . . would fill any one road . . . for a distance of nearly one hundred miles. . . . Through swamps, and dust, and blazing sunlight, and midnight darkness, they pressed on till the enterprise was triumphantly achieved."

While Abbott greatly overestimated Grant's strength, his breathless description of this deception was accurate. More than seventy thousand Union troops were ready to attack the twenty thousand Confederates in Petersburg. His first foray against the rebel defenses pushed them back to within two miles of the city. Two miles of rail linking Petersburg and Richmond were destroyed. But rather than pressing his advantage, Grant hesitated, perhaps to give his men needed rest or to await further reinforcements. That brief pause gave Lee sufficient time to meet the threat. By the time Grant launched a full-scale assault, the city had been fortified. The Battle of Petersburg raged for almost four days; the Southern troops under General Beauregard blunted every attack. Grant tried his entire arsenal—from artillery barrages to hand-to-hand fighting, from skirmishing to charges. The result was the loss of another ten thousand men without much gain. The city remained securely in rebel hands.

Grant finally had to change his tune: he ordered his men to dig in outside the city and the siege of Petersburg began. As at Vicksburg, he intended to either starve the rebels into surrender, force them to leave their defensive positions and attack, or abandon the city and retreat south, leaving Richmond to be taken. The Overland Campaign was over. Grant's attempt to batter the Confederacy into surrender had cost him fifty thousand dead and wounded in only a few months, with little to show for it. Now his army settled in, ready to stay as long as necessary, ready to stop burying more dead.

The disastrous campaign had political ramifications. In the North the antiwar Democratic Copperheads gained strength as the casualty lists grew longer and longer and the end of the war seemed further away. Once again people wondered aloud how many Americans would die for "the Negro cause," then questioned whether it was worth it. On the floor of the House of Representatives Maryland Democrat Benjamin Harris spoke for a growing movement when he announced, "I am a peace man, a radical peace man; and I am for peace by the recognition of the South, for the recognition of the southern confederacy."

Those antiwar voices were heard throughout Dixie and strengthened Confederate resolve. Many people believed if the rebel army could hold out till after the November election, the slave states might well be able to negotiate a peace agreement that satisfied their grievances.

As Grant's popularity declined, Lincoln's conduct of the war became more difficult to defend. Grant was assailed as "a butcher," a man who too easily spent American lives, a man who lacked the vision of "Bobby Lee." Lincoln's hopes to have the war won or over before the

Legendary American painter Winslow Homer went to the front lines as an artist-correspondent for *Harper's Weekly* magazine and spent four years on and off recording the war. This image, *Defiance: Inviting a Shot Before Petersburg, 1864*, shows a Confederate soldier daring sharpshooters to take aim. The damage done to the terrain also is evident, as the horizon is replete with destroyed trees.

HOMER 1864

country voted for president in November had been dashed in the Wilderness, at Spotsylvania, and at Cold Harbor. The presidential election of 1864 was going to be a mandate on the war.

The Democrats responded to the rising anger by nominating General George McClellan as their candidate. The rivalry between Lincoln and the general he had replaced for his lack of aggression was well known, but McClellan never embraced his party's peace platform, which called for a cease-fire and a negotiated settlement, promising only to fight the war more effectively than Lincoln.

Meanwhile, the Republican Party temporarily changed its name to the National Union Party in an attempt to attract the votes of pro-war Democrats. It seemed like a futile effort; McClellan remained tremendously popular while Lincoln was seen as weak and ineffective. Not one of the previous nine American presidents had been reelected to a second term and there was no reason to believe that Lincoln would be different. In fact, in late August he wrote on a sheet of paper, "This morning, as for some days past, it seems exceedingly probable that this Administration will not be re-elected. Then it will by my duty to so cooperate with the Government President elect, as to save the Union between the Election and the inauguration;

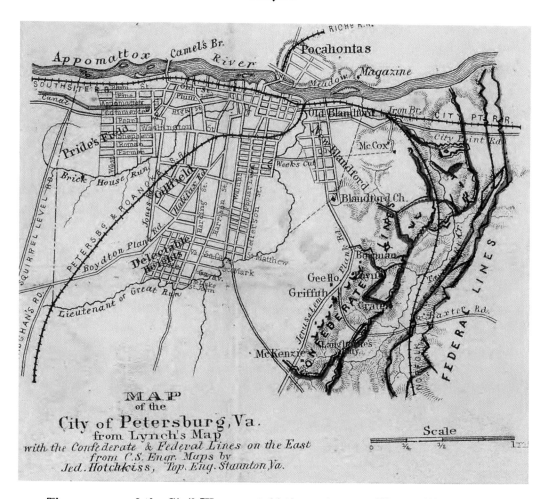

MAP
of the
City of Petersburg, Va.
from Lynch's Map
with the Confederate & Federal Lines on the East
from C.S. Engr. Maps by
Jed. Hotchkiss, Top. Eng. Staunton, Va.

Scale

The progress of the Civil War was told through maps. The proliferation of newspapers and illustrated weekly magazines allowed civilians to follow the movement of the armies. Maps also were published and sold by printers. Boston's Prang and Company offered a "War Telegram Marking Map," which came with colored pencils allowing people to plot the events themselves. It was advertised as "a companion to every person interested in the pending struggle of our nation."

as he will have secured his election on such ground that he cannot possibly save it afterwards." He then folded the paper and asked the members of his cabinet to sign the back of it— without allowing them to read it. It was an odd request but they did so, although it would be several months before he explained his purpose.

The Confederates strategized about how best to take advantage of the approaching election. General Longstreet proposed an offensive into Kentucky, suggesting that if it were successful, "The enemy will be more or less demoralized and disheartened by the great loss of territory which he will sustain, and he will find great difficulty in getting men enough to operate with before the elections in the fall, when in all probability Lincoln will be defeated and peace will follow in the spring."

Robert E. Lee favored a far different strategy. He believed Grant had made too large an investment in the capture of Petersburg and had neglected to leave sufficient troops in position to protect Washington. While Grant was focused on Petersburg and then Richmond, Lee decided to send balding, bearded General Jubal Early, then commanding Stonewall Jackson's ten-thousand-strong "foot cavalry," to take control of the Shenandoah Valley and then march north to threaten Washington City.

Lee's plan made sense. Only months earlier a virtually impregnable force of forty thousand artillerymen equipped with nine hundred guns and abundant munitions had guarded the city's thirty-seven miles of fortifications. The sixty-eight forts ringing the city were connected by trenches and rifle pits. But Grant had ordered those men to Petersburg and had left Washington protected by only twenty-five thousand untested heavy artillery units. They were no match for Early's veteran army. If Early could threaten Washington, Grant would be forced to react, either weakening his siege lines around Petersburg by rushing troops north to protect the capital or by attacking Lee's well-prepared and deeply dug in army.

Incredibly, among the men riding with Jubal Early was the former vice president of the United States and Lincoln's opponent in the 1860 presidential election, John Breckinridge. It was impossible to imagine what onetime senator Breckinridge was feeling as he sat on his horse only five miles away from the White House, close enough to see the familiar Capitol dome—but not quite close enough to see the panic spreading through the city. Rumors claimed that as many as fifty thousand rebel troops were preparing to attack. Communications with Northern cities had been cut. Pretty much any man who could fire a gun was rushed to the front. The hospitals were emptied of wounded soldiers capable of fighting. Clerks from the Quartermaster Corps, the army's paper pushers, were issued weapons and joined the front lines. As a captured Union soldier told Early, Washington was being defended by a ragged collection of "counter jumpers . . . hospital rats and stragglers."

There was considerable confusion about who was in charge of the defense. Several generals seemed to be vying for command. Finally, army chief of staff Henry Halleck exploded in fury, warning in a note to his staff, "We have five times as many Generals here as we want, but are greatly in need of some privates. Anyone volunteering in that capacity will be thankfully received."

The Union capital, with all of its riches, was for all intents and purposes open to Early's army. "We could have marched into Washington," Confederate general John B. Gordon later wrote. "I myself rode to a point on those breastworks at which there was no force whatsoever. The unprotected space was broad enough for the easy passage of Early's army without resistance." The main fortification that had to be taken was lightly defended Fort Stevens, which guarded the Seventh Street Pike leading into the heart of the city. It could have been quickly and easily taken. But "Old Jube" paused on the outskirts of the city.

No one really knows why. Some historians suggest he had received poor intelligence, that he believed Grant's reinforcements had already arrived and were ready to fight. But others contend it was simply that his army was exhausted. His men could go no farther

Fort Stevens, seen here, was part of the ring of fortifications protecting Washington, DC. It was the major line of defense standing between Jubal Early and the capital, and the rebels came within several hundred yards of its walls. It was on these ramparts that President Lincoln stood tall, practically taunting rebel sharpshooters.

This *Harper's Weekly* illustration depicts soldiers protecting President Lincoln at Fort Stevens. As was reported at the time, "He made a bee line for Fort Stevens, about as fast as the old coach horses could take him, and arrived before the whole of the Sixth Corps got there. On arriving at the Fort, the President left his carriage and took his position behind the earthworks of the Fort." Supposedly, when Lincoln refused to take cover, Secretary of War Stanton warned he would have him removed by force, causing the president to reply, "I thought I was the commander-in-chief."

without relief. In only three weeks, they had marched 250 miles and fought several battles in unrelenting and unusually oppressive summer heat. They were worn out; the burning sun, the humidity, and the sleepless nights had sucked the energy out of them.

By the time they had gathered sufficient strength, Union reinforcements were pouring into the city. Veteran troops now occupied Fort Stevens. General Early knew he had missed his chance to make history. He put up a fight: he sent out skirmishers to test the defenses, his artillery shelled the fort, and his sharpshooters took aim at every target, but, as he admitted, "I had . . . reluctantly to give up all hopes of capturing Washington, after I had arrived in sight of the dome of the Capitol." His intention was to make enough noise to discourage any Union attacks, then safely slip back across the Potomac that night.

At the height of the danger an escape route for the president had been planned, and a steamer lay waiting if necessary, but the president was determined to stay. He personally greeted the reinforcements and led them through Washington's streets to the fort. There is some debate about what happened there, and whether the president made one or two visits. But there is no doubt about his bravery—or his foolhardiness. General Horatio Wright invited the president to observe the action. It was a terrible mistake. Standing exposed on the parapets, the instantly recognizable bearded figure in a stovepipe hat must have made the most inviting target to rebel snipers. A nearby Union soldier watched in awe as Lincoln stood tall and unshaken while bullets started raising "little spurts and puffs of dust as they thudded into the embankment on which he stood."

According to legend, a young Massachusetts captain named Oliver Wendell Holmes saw the danger and shouted, "Get down, you damn fool, before you get shot!" Only when Lincoln turned around did the future Supreme Court chief justice—or whoever it was—realize he was screaming at the president of the United States. Lincoln's secretary John Hay confirmed this incident, writing, "A soldier roughly ordered him to get down or he would have his head knocked off."

Lincoln again was watching with "a remarkable coolness and disregard of danger," according to General Horatio Wright, as about two thousand Yankees prepared to make a surprise charge on a rebel position. The president was standing with Wright and army surgeon C. C. V. Crawford when Crawford suddenly fell, gravely wounded in his thigh by a Confederate bullet. Wright suggested strongly to the president that he take cover, but Lincoln ignored him. The president finally stepped down after Wright insisted, warning him that he would have him forcibly removed for his own safety.

Lincoln clearly was enjoying himself. The war had come to him. Every few minutes he would stand and peer over the parapet and watch the distant action. This marked the only time in American history that a president has been under enemy fire.

The rebels suffered more than one hundred casualties in that surprise attack. That night, as his foot cavalry began withdrawing, General Early said ruefully, "We haven't taken Washington, but we've scared Abe Lincoln like hell!"

The real damage that Early had done was to Lincoln's reelection chances. It seemed incredible that after years of fighting, after suffering tens of thousands of casualties, the federal army had made such little progress that the outnumbered enemy was still capable of threatening the Union capital.

The campaign was nasty. Abraham Lincoln was a realist. While he rejected suggestions from his own party that he withdraw and allow a candidate with better prospects to be

In the bitterly contested election of 1864, Lincoln campaigned on slogans such as "Don't change horses in Mid-stream," and "Peace, Amnesty and Emancipation," while McClellan promised "Fidelity to the Union under the Constitution as the only solid foundation for our Strength" and "McClellan: The Hero of Western Virginia! South Mountain! and Antietam."

nominated, he did admit to a friend, "You think I don't know I am going to be beaten, but I do, and unless some great change takes place, beaten badly." It was more than pride or vanity that kept him in the race; Lincoln believed deeply in the cause. The negotiated peace favored by the Peace Democrats might end the fighting and bring the country back together, he knew, but it would not end slavery. And that was a condition to which he could never agree. "[Slavery] is an issue which can only be tried by war," he said, "and decided by victory."

By the summer of 1864, more than 150,000 free black Americans were fighting—and dying—or working for the Union army. Their freedom was not negotiable, Lincoln said, telling visitors to the White House, "There have been men who have proposed to me to return to slavery the black warriors of Port Hudson and Olustee to their masters to conciliate the South. I should be damned in time and in eternity for so doing."

Lincoln found some hope in the fact that the Democratic Party was badly divided. Their candidate, McClellan, refused to support the main plank of the party platform, which promised "a cessation of hostilities, with a view to an ultimate convention of the States, or other peaceable means, to the end that at the earliest practicable moment peace may be restored on the basis of the Federal Union of the States." In accepting their nomination

McClellan made it clear that he would not face the gallant men he had commanded and tell them that "we had abandoned that Union for which we had so often periled our lives."

In contrast to Lincoln's support for the Thirteenth Amendment, which would end slavery in the United States forever, the Democrats exploited racial fears during the campaign, warning that freed black men would run off with white women and take good-paying jobs away from white men. It appeared that even McClellan was willing to reach a compromise with the Southern states over slavery as the price of ending the war.

It was generally believed that only a miracle could save Lincoln from a crushing defeat. And then, unexpectedly, the miracle occurred. On August 5, Rear Admiral David Farragut led a flotilla of federal warships into Mobile Bay, closing that vital supply port to blockade runners. And on Friday, September 2, Secretary Stanton received an urgent telegram from General Henry Slocum announcing, "General Sherman has taken Atlanta. The Twentieth Corps occupies the city."

Newspapers were on the streets within hours, special editions blaring the incredible news. The celebrations started just as quickly. The capture of Atlanta was greeted throughout the North with laughter and tears and prayers. For the first time it was possible to believe the war might soon be over. The *New York Herald* called the news "cyclopean!"

The prospects for the outcome of the election were instantly changed. Secretary Stanton boasted, "Sherman and [Admiral] Farragut have knocked the bottom out of the [Democrats'] Chicago platform." The *Richmond Examiner* reported the impact even more bluntly, criticizing Jefferson Davis for removing Joe Johnston from command. "The result is disaster at Atlanta in the very nick of time when a victory alone could save the party of Lincoln from irretrievable ruin. . . . It will obscure the prospect of peace, late so bright. It will also diffuse gloom over the South."

As the election approached, Lincoln made a daring decision: this was the first general election to take place during wartime and the president made sure that soldiers got to vote. They were either given furloughs to go home or handed a ballot in the field. It was a move that seemed certain to aid McClellan, who had retained the respect and loyalty of the troops. As historian James McPherson wrote, "No other society had tried the experiment of letting its fighting men vote in an election that might decide whether they were to continue fighting." The Democrats were offering them the greatest prize of all: the chance to go home alive.

It was the soldiers' vote that swung the election in at least six states. These men had fought too long, they had lost too many, they had sacrificed too much to accept anything but total victory. Abraham Lincoln was reelected in a landslide, with support from almost

80 percent of the troops. It was a complete affirmation of his winning-at-whatever-the-cost strategy. As McPherson pointed out, "The men who would have to do the fighting had voted by a far larger majority than the folks at home to finish the job."

After celebrating his reelection, the president met with his cabinet and, for the first time, allowed them to read the memorandum they had willingly signed. This was what he had intended to tell president-elect McClellan, he said, then explained that it meant, "You raise as many troops as you possibly can for this final trial, and I will devote all my energies to assist and finish the war." Even if he had been turned out of office, his dedication to the cause would never have wavered. It had proven to be unnecessary; the nation that had barely elected him four years earlier, that had often criticized his conduct of the war, had come to respect and even love him. To reward that confidence, he had to finish the war. But to do that the Confederacy had to be completely destroyed.

Among the historic events during the Civil War that changed the face of warfare forever was the first successful use of a submarine to sink an enemy ship. On February 17, 1864, the Confederate submarine *Hunley*, seen in dry dock in this 1863 oil painting, sank the Union navy warship *USS Housatonic* (insert, right). The *Hunley's* eight-man crew hand-powered the forty-foot-long ironclad ship by turning a crank connected to the propeller (insert, far right). The submarine carried a single torpedo containing 135 pounds of gunpowder at the end of a sixteen-foot-long rod. The torpedo struck *Housatonic's* powder magazine, causing the ship to explode. Five Union sailors were killed in the attack. For some never-determined reason, the *Hunley* subsequently sank and its crew perished.

The sub was raised in 2000 with its crew still at their stations. They were given a proper burial. Researchers have endeavored to discover what caused the demise of the *Hunley*.

U.S.S. HOUSATONIC. CIVIL WAR SLOOP BLOWN UP BY MINE NEAR CHARLESTON.

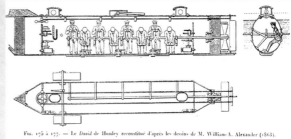

Fig. 175 à 177. — Le *David* de Hunley reconstitué d'après les dessins de M. William-A. Alexander (1863).

# TEN

# BURNING MAN

## General Sherman Marches Through Georgia

"War is hell," Union general William Tecumseh Sherman supposedly said.

And to the Confederacy, Sherman was the Devil who brought with him the fires of damnation.

Although Sherman probably never said those precise words, there is no doubt that he believed them. When Grant moved on Richmond, he ordered Sherman to strike into the deep South, "to move against Johnston's army, to break it up, and to go into the interior of the enemy's country as far as he could, inflicting all the damage he could upon their war resources."

Grant did not issue more specific written orders, he explained, because he and Sherman had spoken at length and both men knew the terrible things that had to be done. Jefferson Davis, Robert E. Lee, and the Confederate army had made clear there would be no negotiated settlement, no compromise, that they intended to fight to the end of their capabilities. Accomplishing that, both Grant and Sherman realized, required inflicting great pain upon the South, a strategy that began with ripping up the fragile railway systems that held the South together.

When ordering the residents of Atlanta to evacuate their city, Sherman

⌐◻ **William Tecumseh Sherman, seen in this 1866 portrait by George Peter Alexander Healy, believed, "It is only those who have never heard a shot, never heard the shriek and groans of the wounded and lacerated . . . that cry aloud for more blood, more vengeance, more desolation."**

wrote to Mayor James Calhoun and the city council, "War is cruelty, and you cannot refine it; and those who brought war into our country deserve all the curses and maledictions a people can pour out. . . . You might as well appeal against the thunder-storm as against these terrible hardships of war. They are inevitable."

While Richmond was the political center of the Confederacy, the magnificent city of Atlanta was its economic heart. It was the commercial center that kept the Confederate army supplied. Four major rail lines converged there; the munitions factories, the foundries, the factories, and the warehouses were located there. The matériel that poured out of the city kept the rebels fighting, while Georgia's plantations kept them fed. But even more than that, Atlanta was the symbolic capital of the Southern way of life. It was the gracious place later romanticized by Margaret Mitchell in her epic *Gone with the Wind*: a land of sparkling white mansions tended by obedient slaves, of perfect fields and beautiful carriages, and genteel gentlemen and ladies. A place where men greeted women with a brush of their lips on a white-gloved hand.

And Sherman intended to destroy it.

In May 1864, his 110,000 men left Chattanooga, Tennessee, and marched south, initially following the railway lines. Joe Johnston's 55,000 rebel troops were waiting for them. The outmanned and outgunned Johnston intended to block Sherman's path by taking well-fortified defensive positions and letting the Yankees crash into them. But Sherman refused to take the bait, instead continually flanking Johnston's army, never letting him throw a telling punch. Over and over, while a sizable force flirted with the rebel lines to hold them in position, other units would maneuver around Johnston's flank and threaten his supply lines, forcing the Confederates to withdraw. It was an exquisite military dance, with both sides moving deftly in response to enemy jabs.

There were daily skirmishes and several pitched battles, and casualties continued to mount, but neither Sherman nor Johnston could maneuver his opponent into a compromised position. In late June Johnston made a stand at Kennesaw Mountain and an exasperated Sherman elected to fight him there. The bluecoats lost three thousand men as they vainly attempted to fight their way uphill against entrenched defenders. It was an expensive lesson that Sherman would not repeat.

Sherman faced his own problems getting supplies. The farther south he marched, the more difficult it became to protect the railway tracks on which he depended. As Johnston retreated, he destroyed bridges and tracks, but somehow Union engineers managed to repair them quickly.

In mid-July, on the same day that Union troops crossed the Chattahoochee River and took dead aim at Atlanta, a panicked Jefferson Davis sacked Johnston. "You have failed to arrest the advance of the enemy to the vicinity of Atlanta," the orders read, "and I . . . express no confidence that you can defeat or repel him." Johnston was furious, convinced that he had forced Sherman to stretch his thin supply line too far and that the North already was becoming frustrated at his lack of real progress and would elect McClellan. All he had to do was hold him outside Atlanta. Davis felt very differently; he wanted victories, and he wanted the Union to bleed.

To the great delight of Sherman and his staff, Johnston was replaced by General John Bell Hood, an able leader respected for his bravery and his aggressiveness. Hood had been badly wounded at Gettysburg and had lost a leg at Chickamauga—he had to be strapped into his saddle—and yet he continued to attack. Unlike Johnston, Sherman believed, J. B. Hood was sufficiently reckless to come out of his defensive positions and fight—even against a larger army.

The Union army moved to within eight miles of Atlanta. Rather than risking an assault, Sherman decided to cut the four railroad lines into the city, forcing the rebels to either retreat or leave their fortifications and fight in the open. Hood answered on July 20. Finding a gap several

General Joe Johnston (left) was, according to General Longstreet, "the ablest and most accomplished man that the Confederate armies ever produced." But President Davis, declaring "no confidence that you can defeat or repel [Sherman]," replaced him with the more aggressive John Bell Hood (right), who attacked and was beaten three times, essentially destroying his army's offensive capabilities.

miles wide between Union forces, he attacked at Peachtree Creek, hoping to make the Yankees pay a bloody price before their reinforcements arrived. The attempt was beaten back by General Thomas. Once again, the Rock of Chickamauga stood firm; five hundred rebels were killed, more than a thousand were severely wounded, and a substantial number of prisoners were taken.

Two days later, the resilient Hood made a second attempt. Leaving a sizable force in position, he marched thirty thousand men fifteen miles in the night and launched a surprise attack in the early morning light. It almost succeeded. The Battle of Atlanta was fought through the day, and the rebels made substantial gains. But the grueling night march had made coordination impossible, and before Hood's troops could strike the Union rear to relieve the pressure, federal reserves had been sent forward to fill the gap.

During the fighting, Sherman's subordinate and close friend, General James Birdseye McPherson, was inspecting his lines when he encountered a rebel patrol. He turned and tried to escape but was shot in the back and killed, becoming the highest-ranking federal officer to die in battle. Confederate captain Richard Beard asked a captured Union officer, Colonel R. K. Scott, to identify the slain man. "Sir, it is General McPherson," Scott replied. "You have killed the best man in our army."

Shouting, "Come on boys, McPherson and revenge!" the Yankees fought back. Sherman ordered his artillery to shell rebel positions, decimating their ranks. Sherman's superiority in men and guns proved too much and Hood retreated behind his defenses, as Sherman had predicted.

Hood still had some fight left in him. On the twenty-eighth of July, as Union troops

It was reported that Sherman wept openly when he learned that one of his most respected young commanders, the thirty-five-year-old general James B. McPherson (above), had been killed.

This is a detail from the cyclorama *The Battle of Atlanta*. The entire painting-in-the-round, which created an experience of being at the scene, was 42 feet high and 358 feet in circumference, the largest painting in the country. It depicts a cavalry fight at Decatur on July 22, in which rebel troops have broken through Union lines and are resisting counterattacking troops. This cyclorama was introduced in Detroit in 1887 before being installed in Atlanta.

circled the city to cut off the last remaining rail link, the Macon and Western coming from Savannah, the rebels attacked one last time at Ezra Church. It was a hopeless effort, and the Yankees poured murderous fire into the Confederate lines. "This battle discouraged our men badly," wrote a Confederate officer, "as they could never understand why they should have been sent in to such a death trap to be butchered up with no hope of gaining anything."

In less than a week Hood had taken more casualties than Johnston had suffered throughout his entire campaign. Hood had given the Confederacy the fight it had wanted, and his army had lost an estimated sixteen thousand men. Sherman's army had been badly wounded, too, but he had the ability to replace those men and arms.

When Sherman departed Chattanooga, Atlanta had been a bustling city of about twenty thousand residents, more than a quarter of them working in military-related jobs. But as his army approached, thousands of civilians fled the city, reducing its population by more than half. So when Union artillery blasted the city for thirty-seven consecutive days, there were fewer civilian casualties than might be imagined.

After taking the beating at Ezra Church, Hood had hunkered down inside the city, his army manning the more than twelve miles of defensive earthworks that encircled Atlanta. The network of redoubts, rifle pits, dugouts, and twisting barricades had taken a year to construct, much of the labor done by slaves hired from their owners. To Sherman's great disappointment, Hood had finally accepted the wisdom of Johnston's defensive strategy.

Sherman understood that a direct attack on those fortifications was hopeless, that "an assault would cost more lives than we can spare." Instead he set out to sever the last supply lines into the city, intending to choke the city into submission. But his own supply lines were already stretched too far; moving around the city to attack those rail lines would force him to operate deep in enemy territory without sufficient food and munitions. That was not a risk he was willing to take. Yet.

To force the issue, Sherman increased the daily bombardment. At times more than five thousand shells a day landed inside the city. His objective, he wrote to one of his commanders, was simple: "make the inside of Atlanta too hot to be endured. . . . One thing is certain, whether we get inside of Atlanta or not, it will be a used-up community by the time we are done with it," adding later, "Let us destroy Atlanta and make it a desolation."

As the presidential election came closer, and with it the likelihood that Lincoln would be defeated, both Grant and Sherman were stalled. The fighting continued sporadically; men died or were wounded every day in skirmishes. Those people remaining in Altlanta burrowed shelters in their backyards and railroad embankments or hid inside steel bank vaults. During lulls in the shelling they kept up a pretense of normal life. Newspapers were published daily. For minutes at a time everything appeared normal—and then the whine of an incoming shell would trigger a mad scramble for the safety of the earth.

The residents in Richmond also created an illusion of normal life. Men and women promenaded in Capitol Square and attended "starvation parties," which were little different from prewar parties except that no food or beverages were served. At these parties they savored "the feast of reason and the flow of soul." As the *Richmond Daily Dispatch* would later report, "Richmond laughed while it cried, and sang while it endured, and suffered and bled." Incredibly, even in the most challenging moments their confidence in Uncle Bob, as they referred to Lee, never wavered.

In late August, Sherman's patience ran out. The dangers of waiting with his supply lines exposed continued to grow. He finally decided to take the gamble. The artillery barrage stopped suddenly on August 26. Scouts sent out by Hood reported that the Yankees were gone. Their camps were abandoned. For a full day the Confederates believed that Sherman had fallen back across the Chattahoochee. People cautiously ventured out of their shelters; military bands played in celebration. Hood's staff reportedly was "gleeful."

But rather than withdrawing, sixty thousand Union troops had marched west, far beyond

After occupying Atlanta in September 1864, Sherman collected sufficient supplies for his march across Georgia to Savannah. When he departed in early November, he ordered anything that might aid the rebels when they reoccupied the city to be destroyed. This is what was left of the railroad depot.

the rebel fortifications, then turned south fifteen miles outside the city. Even before Hood fully appreciated the threat, the Yankees had successfully cut off the Atlanta and West Point Railroad. To make certain that the railroad tracks could not be reused, Union soldiers heated them until they were malleable; then they twisted them, sometimes bending them around trees. These steel loops eventually became known as "Sherman's neckties." Atlanta's last lifeline was the Macon and Western Railroad, which ran near the small towns of Rough and Ready and Jonesborough. The rebels raced to protect it.

Sherman had beat them there and built log parapets. Hood did not know the size of the Union forces or that his troops were so greatly outnumbered. The rebels fought valiantly, throwing themselves in waves into the Union guns, and they had some success. But after two days of hard fighting, the Battle of Jonesborough ended.

Atlanta was completely cut off.

In the middle of the night of September 1, the city was rocked by massive explosions. A giant fireball rose into the air. Then another, and another. The thunderous blasts were heard by Union troops fifteen miles away in Jonesborough. As a witness later wrote, "The very earth trembled as if in the throes of a mighty earthquake. The houses rocked like cradles, and on every hand was heard the shattering of window glass and the fall of plastering and loose bricks." Every building within several hundred yards was leveled, and fires began spreading.

It took some time for Sherman to confirm his hopes: Hood was destroying his supplies, including eighty-one railroad boxcars crammed with food, medical supplies, and eighteen tons of ammunition, enough to have sustained a fight for weeks. Sherman's officers pleaded

As General Hood prepared to abandon Atlanta, he discovered that an officer "too much addicted to drink of late to attend to his duties" had failed to remove vast stores of supplies and ammunition. Rather than leave them for Sherman, he ordered them destroyed. It took more than five hours to blow them up. Seen here is what was left of the munitions train and a rolling mill.

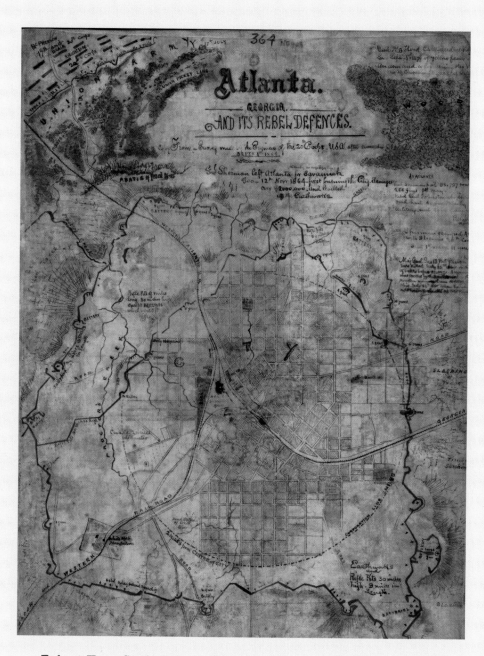

Robert Knox Sneden's beautifully hand-drawn map shows the rebel
fortifications that completely ringed Atlanta.

with him to press his advantage and crush Hood's army, but Sherman refused, believing that destroying the railroad tracks had greater long-term strategic value.

Hood's army successfully slipped out of Atlanta. A day later Sherman's troops entered the city. They were greeted jubilantly by the black population that had remained behind. While certainly a significant military victory, perhaps more important was the fact that the capture of Atlanta is credited with saving Lincoln's presidency. With the Confederacy reeling, there was little McClellan could offer voters that Lincoln was not poised to deliver.

Three days after taking control of the city, Sherman ordered the remaining residents to leave: "I have deemed it to the interest of the United States that the citizens now residing in Atlanta should remove," he wrote, "those who prefer it to go south and the rest north." This first order barely gave a hint of the cold, efficient, and brutal way Sherman was to fight throughout the South.

This illustration, *Exodus of Confederates from Atlanta*, first appeared in the 836-page *Harper's Pictorial History of the Civil War: Contemporary Accounts and Illustrations*, published in 1866.

Sherman was aware that his stay in Atlanta would be brief. The longer he remained in one place, he knew, the more difficult it would be to protect his lines of supply and communications. As many as half of his troops were necessary to keep those lines open. So he did not want the additional responsibility of feeding the civilian residents of the city. As a gentleman and an officer, he actually appealed to General John Bell Hood, whose army was regaining its strength south of the city, to assist the few thousand men and women who would be forced to leave the city. Hood grudgingly complied, responding that this order to evacuate "transcends, in . . . ingenious cruelty, all acts ever brought to my attention in the dark history of war." After several other bitter exchanges, Hood warned defiantly, "We will fight you to the death. Better die a thousand deaths than submit to live under you or your Government and your negro allies."

When the city leaders appealed, pointing out that the lives of children, the elderly, and even pregnant women would be at stake, Sherman was unmoved. He fully understood the "distress that will be occasioned" but responded that the only avenue to peace was surrender and reunion. "We don't want your Negroes or your horses, or your houses or your land, or anything you have," he wrote, "but we do want and will have a just obedience to the laws of the United States. That we will have, and if it involves the destruction of your improvements, we cannot help it."

The Union army transported those civilians out of the city, leaving them near Hood's encampment. One of these people, a young woman named Mary Gay, wrote that they "were dumped out upon the cold ground without shelter and without any of the comforts of home."

William T. Sherman had embarked on a path that was to make him one of the most beloved, controversial, and reviled men in American history.

"Cump," as he was known to friends, was one of eleven children of Ohio lawyer and state supreme court justice Charles Sherman. He was eleven years when his father died, leaving his family in financial ruin, and he went to live with the family of Ohio senator Thomas Ewing. Senator Ewing obtained a place for him at West Point and he graduated sixth in the class of 1840. His military career was undistinguished; he fought against the Seminoles in Florida but missed the career-making opportunity to fight in the Mexican-American War enjoyed by many of his classmates. In 1850, he married Senator Ewing's daughter in a lavish wedding attended by President Zachary Taylor, Henry Clay, and Daniel Webster. While stationed in San Francisco in 1848, he was present when vast gold deposits were discovered along the

Sacramento River—he even helped write the official letter confirming the find—and yet was unable to profit from it. With such prominent connections, his prospects seemed bright, so he resigned his commission in 1853 and became a gentleman banker in San Francisco. Many of his friends from West Point and the military entrusted him with their investments, but when the gold rush bubble burst in 1857, his bank collapsed and those funds were lost. He cashed in much of his own fortune to reimburse men like Braxton Bragg and George Thomas, both of whom would join him as celebrated Civil War generals.

But like Grant, who was to become his close friend, there was little about Cump Sherman's early life that would predict the way his tactical skills and tenacity, his courage, and his determination would enable him to rise and succeed under the most challenging circumstances. Nor that he would be both idolized as a war hero and vilified as a war criminal.

Sherman was serving as the first superintendent of the Louisiana State Seminary of Learning and Military Academy, later to become Louisiana State University, when civil war threatened. While the Southerners around him boasted of their loyalty to the South and predicted that the North would not fight for the slaves, he tried to warn them that a civil war would be long and costly. For him the argument was not about slavery but rather about the cost of secession. He told a friend, the Virginia professor David Boyd, "This country will be drenched in blood, and God only knows how it will end. It is all folly, madness, a crime against civilization. . . . You are rushing into war with one of the most powerful, ingeniously mechanical, and determined people on Earth. . . . You are bound to fail." When Louisiana joined the Confederacy, he resigned his post, telling the governor, "On no earthly account will I do any act or think any thought hostile . . . to the . . . United States," and moved to Missouri.

Sherman visited Washington, where his brother, the Republican senator from Ohio John Sherman, introduced him to Lincoln. Sherman remembered being terribly disappointed that Lincoln did not share his alarm concerning the lack of preparation in the North for the coming war. Few men were as exposed to the folly and to the lack of appreciation for the consequences of this war, on both sides, as Cump Sherman.

As the war began, Sherman's brother obtained a commission for him in the Regular Army as a colonel. After distinguishing himself at the First Battle of Bull Run, where he was grazed twice, he was promoted to brigadier general and given command of the Department of the Cumberland in Kentucky. Rather than being satisfied at his rapid progress, he was furious. He didn't want the responsibilities of command; he drew unwanted attention to himself by complaining about a lack of support and the shortcomings of his own troops, and he greatly overestimated the number of enemy soldiers in his region. Eventually, at his own insistence, he was relieved of his command. He suffered through a difficult period, admitting to contemplating suicide. His wife, Ellen, called Nellie, requested help from Senator Sherman, referring to "that melancholy insanity to which your family is subject." The *Cincinnati Commercial* added to his public humiliation when it reported he had gone insane.

His career was saved several months later by General Henry Halleck, who assigned him to Grant's command. He displayed his courage at Shiloh, where he was wounded twice and had three horses killed under him. He and Grant became fast friends, especially after Sherman convinced him not to resign. It was beyond improbable that these two misfits would have found each other and provided the emotional support that made such a difference to the army and the nation. As Sherman once explained, "General Grant is a great general, I know him well. He stood by me when I was crazy and I stood by him when he was drunk; and now, sir, we stand by each other always."

After being put in command of the Union army, Grant gave the Military Division of the Mississippi, the army west of the Appalachians, to "Uncle Billy," as his men called him. As Sherman wrote in his memoir, when the two commanders set out with their great armies in May 1864 to attack Richmond and Atlanta, he sent Grant a note outlining his strategy for ending the war. "If you can whip Lee and I can march to the Atlantic I think ol' Uncle Abe will give us twenty days leave to see the young folks."

By September, Sherman had done his part—he had captured Atlanta. And he then began his legendary march to the Atlantic. Sherman's five-week campaign is unmatched in American military history for its daring, its success, and its brutality. With Confederate general Nathan Forrest continuing to peck at his communication and supply lines, Sherman decided on an extraordinary strategy: he would cut loose completely. He determined to take his sixty-two thousand troops through Georgia to the sea without supplies or communications with Washington. It was as risky as it was bold, and Lincoln was skeptical. Grant convinced the president that let loose of his constraints, Sherman could deliver on his promise to "make Georgia howl." Lincoln finally agreed, asking only that the campaign be delayed until after the election.

General Hood's Confederate army had abandoned Georgia and gone west, into Tennessee and Alabama, daring Sherman to pursue him. Sherman resisted that temptation, sending General Thomas to Nashville to hold Hood there, thus leaving the entire state of Georgia open to him. With the exception of some cavalry and state militia, there were no rebels to prevent Sherman from "smashing Georgia."

Improbably, with his army staggered and his people starving, Jefferson Davis continued to insist that the war might still be won. In a late-September speech in Macon he compared

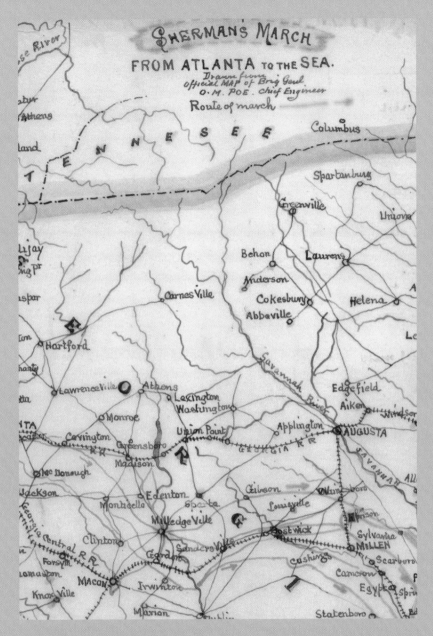

On November 15, 1864, Sherman left Atlanta with 62,204 men, twenty-five hundred wagons, and five thousand head of cattle. His march, illustrated here on Sneden's map, was hampered as much by "General Weather" as by rebel troops. Rain and snowstorms turned roads into mud and slowed them for much of the 285-mile march. Along the way, Sherman wrote, slaves were "simply frantic with joy," but any man incapable of fighting was discouraged from joining the march. When Savannah surrendered on December 21, Sherman suffered only an estimated three thousand casualties.

Sherman to Napoleon, claiming, bizarrely, that "the fate that befell the army of the French Empire and its retreat from Moscow will be reacted. Our cavalry and our people will harass and destroy his army as did the Cossacks that of Napoleon. . . . When the war is over and our independence won, (and we will establish our independence,) who will be our aristocracy? I hope the limping soldier. . . . Let us with one arm and one effort endeavor to crush Sherman."

Throughout September and October Sherman made meticulous plans for this march to the sea. The army was to be entirely dependent on its own resources. There could be no reinforcements, no supplies, no orders from Washington given or received. Relying on census records, he mapped a route that would provide sufficient food and forage for his troops and their animals. His troops would travel as light as possible, living off the land. Each regiment would have a single supply wagon and a single ambulance. All noncombatants, the wounded, and the sick were sent to the rear. Every wagon was filled with as much ammunition and stores as it could carry. Following Lincoln's landslide victory on November 8, he prepared his army to depart. But as they readied, Sherman gave one final order: burn Atlanta.

The images of Atlanta burning created for the film version of *Gone with the Wind* are seared into American memory. The impression held by most is that Sherman set fire to the city to punish the South for starting the war, and while there certainly was some truth to that, in fact his motives were more complex. He intended to make life as harsh as possible for Southerners, believing that destroying their morale was necessary to drive Jeff Davis to the peace table. But he was also determined that Atlanta would never again be capable of supplying tools to the Confederate army. For that reason he did not set fire to the residential areas of the city but rather its industrial district, which consisted of the railroad station, factories and machine shops, tool sheds, and other buildings that might be of value to the military.

Although history blames Sherman for the destruction of Atlanta, the city had already been decimated by the relentless shelling and then the fires that began when Hood blew up his munitions. Sherman simply added to the carnage. As the army marched out of the city on November 16, proudly singing "John Brown's Body," one officer took a last look back and later remembered, "Nothing was left of Atlanta except its churches, the City Hall and private dwellings. You could hardly find a vestige of the splendid railroad depots, warehouses, etc. It was melancholy, but it was war prosecuted in deadly earnest."

And then Sherman's army seemingly disappeared. "I will not attempt to send carriers back," he had telegraphed Grant before cutting those wires, "but trust to the Richmond papers to keep you well advised." For the next five weeks, no one in Washington or, it appears, Richmond, knew precisely where the Union army was heading.

Sherman divided his army into two wings of roughly equal size, marching generally in parallel but remaining twenty to forty miles apart. One wing seemed to be going toward Macon, the other in the direction of Augusta. But they marched through the South like locusts, taking whatever they needed, burning what was left, and leaving behind rubble, fear, and bitterness. As *Harper's Weekly* reported in December, apparently based on stories from Southern newspapers, "destroying as he goes, he carries a line of fire straight across the surface of the rebel section, cutting a terrible swath to the sea. General Sherman does not play at war."

Every farm animal was taken; the plantation fields were stripped bare and stored crops were seized. Sherman's orders against pillaging were often disobeyed as soldiers ransacked homes and took whatever they wanted, sometimes leaving "Sherman sentinels," as the forlorn chimneys of burnt-out homes became known. There were occasional skirmishes with rebel cavalry and militia, but they didn't even slow the march—nothing slowed it. Sherman's "scorched earth" policy horrified the Confederacy; it was beyond the accepted rules of warfare.

This 1868 engraving depicts the burning of buildings, the destruction of railroad tracks and telegraph lines, the taking of supplies, and the freeing of slaves that were daily occurrences during the march.

Sherman paid no attention, if he even heard the cries. He had set out to cut the Confederacy in half and destroy the Southern will to fight and nothing—except those sentinels—would be left standing in his wake.

Many Georgians buried or hid their provisions and valuables, sometimes disguising them as fresh graves. But often their newly freed slaves would lead the troops to these caches. As the army burned its way to the sea, a smaller force, consisting of several thousand contraband, joined and followed Sherman's trail, praising him as a prophet who was leading them to freedom. The army hired many of these men and women as teamsters, cooks, and servants, providing the labor necessary to clear obstacles and lay roads. Others provided a more valuable service, infiltrating Confederate camps and gathering intelligence. But most of these contrabands became a burden, and caring for them eventually became a significant problem. These people refused all suggestions that they return—temporarily—to their plantations, fearing that they would be put back in chains, beaten, or killed for betraying their owners.

In one especially tragic event in early December, the ironically named Union general Jefferson Davis ordered his troops to construct a pontoon bridge across the wide and deep Ebenezer Creek. But after his fourteen thousand men had crossed, he had the bridge removed, marooning the freed slaves on the other side. As Joe Wheeler's rebel cavalry approached, many of those people panicked and tried to ford the river. Colonel Charles Kerr witnessed a scene "I pray my eyes may never see again. . . . [Amid] cries of anguish and despair, men, women, and children rushed by the hundreds into the turbid stream, and many were drowned before our eyes. From what we learned afterwards of those who remained on land, their fate at the hands of Wheeler's troops was scarcely to be preferred." According to reports, many Union soldiers tried to help, lashing together downed trees for makeshift rafts or wading into the water themselves, but hundreds drowned in the icy waters of the creek.

Within hours, Wheeler's cavalry got to the creek, and the mostly women, children, and elderly who had not reached the other bank were gathered up and returned to slavery.

Like only a few great military leaders, Sherman had the unshakable ability to put aside his humanity to fulfill his mission. He accepted without question that the cost of saving the most lives was the sacrifice of other lives. The freed slaves were not the only people who suffered because of this. The Confederates had established several prisoner-of-war camps. Among them was the infamous prison built in early 1864 in Andersonville, Georgia, that officially was known as Camp Sumter. Built to house ten thousand men, within months it contained more than forty thousand prisoners, effectively making it the fifth-largest city in the Confederacy. With the South already suffering shortages because of the Union naval

The dead line Andersonville Prison. Georgia.
Shot by the guard while taking a part of The dead line for firewood.

When Union soldier Robert Kellogg walked into Andersonville prison he was stunned. "Before us were forms that had once been active and erect;—stalwart men, now nothing but mere walking skeletons." Among the horrors of the 26.5-acre prison was the "dead line," a small fence inside the prison wall that indicated the no-man's-land between the fence and the walls. As seen in this sketch, anyone crossing or touching the dead line would be shot.

blockade, the camp lacked food, shelter, sanitation facilities, medical supplies, and even clean water. Sweetwater Creek ran through the camp and was used for the disposal of trash and human and animal waste, for bathing, and, finally, as the sole source of drinking water. Malnutrition, scurvy, dysentery, and diarrhea plagued the camp, and eventually in excess of one hundred prisoners were dying there every day, more than twice as many as were dying in battle. In many cases bodies lay bloating in the sun for days. As one prisoner wrote forlornly, "Since the day I was born, I never saw such misery."

Sherman was made aware of the deplorable conditions inside Andersonville during his Atlanta campaign. Rather than diverting his army, in July he dispatched cavalry general George Stoneman with twenty-two hundred men to attack Hood's rail lines—agreeing that if Stoneman was successful he could attempt to liberate the prisoners at Andersonville. Stoneman encountered heavy resistance and was captured by the Confederates. Sherman did not make a second attempt.

Some historians believe that Sherman had little interest in saving those prisoners' lives. If he had been successful, he would have been burdened with many thousands of sick and emaciated troops who could not survive on their own, forcing him either to care for them—without sufficient food or medical supplies—or continue his offensive. Splitting his army to protect them or transport them to safety at that time might have proved to be a terrible mistake.

And so the prisoners continued dying. After Sherman occupied Atlanta, which put his troops only a fair cavalry ride away from Andersonville, Confederates transferred the healthiest prisoners to other camps. Among them was Camp Lawton in Millen, a massive prison that held more than ten thousand men. It was operational for less than three months, and was then abandoned and its prisoners moved only four days before Sherman's troops arrived. All they found there was a mass grave marked with a small wooden sign reading 650 BURIED HERE.

It is probable that this harsh treatment infuriated Sherman and his men, which provided an easy rationale for their own brutality. By the end of the war, nearly thirteen thousand Union soldiers had died at Andersonville. When poet Walt Whitman learned about this, he wrote, "There are deeds, crimes that may be forgiven, but this is not among them." Eventually the commandant of the camp, Captain Henry Wirz, was hanged in Washington, making him the only Confederate executed for war crimes.

Sherman's army remained out of communications with Washington for four weeks. He reached the outskirts of Savannah in early December. It was only a matter of time and casualties until he took that city. Confederate general William Hardee flooded the rice fields

When Confederate general William Hardee realized he could no longer defend Savannah, he ordered a complete withdrawal in the night in an attempt to save his army. A long line of wagons crossed the Savannah River on a floating bridge, carrying as much war matériel as possible. His men followed, leaving the city open to Sherman.

Hardee directed that nothing be blown up that might alert the enemy to his plan. This withdrawal was successful and may have saved the city from destruction.

surrounding the city to limit access to a few defensible causeways. But he was a realist and understood that his ten thousand men could hold out only so long. After refusing Sherman's demand that he surrender, his army abandoned the city on December 20 rather than subjecting the city to the hardships and destruction of Atlanta. Two days later a jubilant Sherman sent a telegram to Lincoln declaring, "I beg to present you, as a Christmas gift, the city of Savannah, with 150 heavy guns and plenty of ammunition, and also about 25,000 bales of cotton."

The capture of Atlanta had turned the election in Lincoln's favor; now the president hoped to put this gift to political use to help him convince Congress to pass the Thirteenth Amendment. It was a simple proposition. "Neither slavery nor involuntary servitude, except as a punishment for crime whereof the party shall have been duly convicted, shall exist within the United States." But it was fraught with political consequences. A war, which was not yet done, had been fought over this idea. More than six hundred thousand men had died, and millions more had been injured over it. And yet the Union Congress had refused to pass it. The amendment had been introduced in Washington a year earlier. The Senate had passed the proposed amendment quickly, but in June 1864, House Democrats favoring states' rights had formed a coalition with Republicans anxious about reelection. Lincoln persisted; for him passing the amendment banning slavery forever was the "fitting, and necessary conclusion" to the war.

It was a difficult fight. Some congressmen believed that passing it would actually prolong the war, making the Confederacy less likely to surrender. Others believed that even after the fighting ended, it would make reunification more challenging. Still others believed that it might be unconstitutional, that it was a decision that should be left to the states. And certainly there were racists who simply did not want black Americans to enjoy equal rights. Lincoln needed to secure about thirty additional votes. While his reputation as a statesman resonates throughout our history, when necessary he also could be a tough politician. He knew how to play the political game to achieve his objectives. As brilliantly portrayed in Steven Spielberg's *Lincoln*, he and Secretary of State Seward began horse trading with reluctant Democrats, offering all kinds of bribes and promises in return for votes or, for those who couldn't vote for it, abstention. No one really knows the extent of this deal making. They supposedly twisted arms, offered government jobs, and threatened to withhold federal support for local projects. One lame-duck congressman became the ambassador to Denmark. An appointment to an open seat on the federal court in Missouri was used to lure votes.

On January 31, 1865, the House passed the Thirteenth Amendment by two votes—with eight members abstaining. Key to passage were the sixteen Democrats who joined all of the Republicans in voting for it, fourteen of whom were lame ducks. "A great moral victory," Lincoln called it, but morals had a lot less to do with it than rewards. When the war ended, the Confederate states were forced to ratify the amendment as a condition to rejoining the Union. Fittingly, it became the law of the land in December 1865, when Georgia approved it.

While Lincoln was busy fighting for the Thirteenth Amendment and eventual freedom for all slaves, the problem General Sherman faced was right in front of him. Thousands of former slaves who had attached themselves to his army, either employed or straggling behind, had followed him to Savannah. He was preparing to march north, since there was still fighting to be done, and he wanted his army to be free of this responsibility. Lincoln sent Edwin Stanton to Georgia to help Sherman work out a solution.

In mid-January, after meeting with freed blacks in Savannah, and with the president's approval, Sherman issued Special Field Order No. 15. It was an extraordinary document. It declared that the military was confiscating from slaveholders four hundred thousand acres, about thirty miles of plantation fields and islands along the coast, and awarding no more than forty acres of land—and an army mule—between Charleston and Jacksonville to freed slaves. While the precise number of people who actually received this Sherman land is not known, estimates are as high as forty thousand people. This order also urged freed blacks to join the Union army.

This promise of "forty acres and a mule" was never fully met. After Lincoln's assassination, President Andrew Johnson revoked the order and returned the land to its previous owners.

But this order did serve to settle thousands of freed blacks, many of whom joined the Union army and helped establish a quasi-military presence there. Sherman wasn't done inflicting damage on the Confederacy, though. In February, his army left Savannah and turned north, marching into the Carolinas. The war had begun there four years earlier, and so it was right, they were convinced, that it end there. "I almost tremble at her fate," Sherman wrote as his campaign continued, "but feel that she deserves all that seems in store for her."

Sherman's army grew in size as other units joined him, eventually numbering almost ninety thousand troops. Against that Joe Johnston could barely muster twenty thousand men. There was little the rebels could do to stop or even slow the Yankee invasion. In February, Lincoln agreed to meet a delegation for a peace conference at Hampton Roads. The two sides

George Healy's 1868 oil painting *The Peacemakers* shows Lincoln and his military leaders at their 1865 meeting aboard the steamboat *River Queen*. It was here that Grant, Sherman, Rear Admiral David Dixon Porter, and the president discussed strategies for ending the war.

were brought together by the influential power broker Francis Preston Blair. The meeting lasted less than five hours; Lincoln found no need to offer any compromise. The only path to peace was reunification on Union terms, the first condition being the abolition of slavery. As the conference ended, Sherman's army continued "marching on."

There were several small battles fought along the way, at Aiken, Monroe's Cross Roads, and Bentonville, but there was little the rebels could do to stop Sherman. His army cut a wide swath through the state, leaving wreckage behind, until it reached the beautiful city of Columbia, the capital of South Carolina. Inside the city Confederate general Wade Hampton had ordered cotton bales to be collected, intending to move them to the outskirts and burn them to prevent them from falling into Union hands. Hampton knew he could not hold out

No one will ever know who set fire to Columbia, South Carolina. Whether it was flames from cotton bales set afire by retreating rebels spread by high winds, as the North claimed, or fires set intentionally by Union troops in revenge, or even whether it was started accidentally, the result was the same: about half the city was totally destroyed and Sherman was blamed for it.

against Sherman's vastly superior army. But those bales were still stacked in the middle of the main street when he evacuated the city on February 16.

The next day Sherman marched into Columbia. His men began a raucous celebration. There was considerable pillaging. A great amount of liquor was confiscated and consumed. And by nightfall the entire city was on fire.

It has never been determined who was responsible for setting those fires—although Sherman has long been blamed for it. He always claimed that those cotton bales were burning when he entered the city and were spread by gale-force winds that night. "Without hesitation," he wrote in his official report, "I charge General Wade Hampton with having burned his own city . . . not with a malicious intent, or as the manifestation of a silly 'Roman stoicism,' but from folly and want of sense, in filling it with lint, cotton, and tinder." He did admit that other fires might have been set by men "who had long been imprisoned there, rescued by us [who] may have indulged in unconcealed joy to see the ruin of the capital of South Carolina."

The fires raged throughout the night. People ran down the streets desperate to escape the flames. No one knows how many people died in the night.

There is evidence that Union troops tried desperately to maintain order within the city, protect its citizens, and prevent those fires from spreading. But as General Slocum pointed out, a drunken soldier with a match on a windy night is "not a pleasant visitor." That first night 370 soldiers were arrested, 2 were killed, and 30 more were wounded. Supposedly Sherman ordered a drunken soldier arrested and, when he resisted, had him shot.

The fires of Columbia burned out of control. "The morning dawned upon the scene of ruin," Abbott reported. "Nearly three thousand buildings were in ashes. Little remained but a wilderness of tall, bare chimneys, blasted trees, heaps of rubbish, and smoldering ruins, to show where once had been the most beautiful, refined, and aristocratic city of South Carolina."

Sherman left the city a smoking ruin two days later. When questioned about the fire, he confessed his real feelings. "Though I never ordered it and never wished it, I have never shed any tears over the event, because I believe that it hastened what we all fought for, the end of the War."

Sherman's Carolina campaign was running out of Confederates to fight. His army had traveled 425 miles in only fifty days, leaving behind similar desolation in every place they went. The war was rapidly coming to the inevitable conclusion. Outside Richmond, Grant knew it was time to force the issue.

After ten months, the rebels remained safely inside their fortifications, but their stay there was becoming increasingly difficult. Lee's troops were worn down and his supplies were running out. He realized he had few options. He could ask Grant for terms of surrender, but he refused to consider that option without specific instructions from President Davis. Or he could leave Petersburg and join forces with Joe Johnston—together they might sustain the fight for at least another year. But doing that meant abandoning Richmond, and although that would allow him to move without restraint, it would be a devastating blow to the Confederacy and Davis would never allow it. That left only one choice: stand and fight.

To finally force Lee to come out and fight, Grant dispatched General Philip Sheridan on a sweeping maneuver below the city to cut off Lee's remaining supply line, the South Side Railroad. As Sheridan's cavalry rode toward the junction at Five Forks, Lee sent General George Pickett to meet him, ordering that the vital crossroads be held "at all hazards."

The siege of Petersburg ended at Five Forks on the first of April 1865. The daylong battle

General Philip Sheridan's twenty-seven thousand troops crushed rebel general George Pickett's attempt to break the siege of Petersburg. About half of the Confederates' ten thousand men were killed, wounded, or captured. By the end of the fighting, Lee's last supply line into Petersburg was severed and the war was racing to an end.

ended with the Union taking control of the South Side Railroad, closing Lee's last supply route. Lincoln happened to be at City Point, using Grant's headquarters, the sidewheel steamer *River Queen* docked there, as his temporary White House. When captured battle flags were presented to Lincoln that night, he said with satisfaction, "This means victory—this is victory." Supposedly the president's sleep that night was interrupted by a terrible nightmare—in which he was lying in state in the White House, the victim of an assassin's bullet.

Grant attacked the next morning, believing that he might finally destroy Lee's army. In the early morning confusion, Lee's friend and adviser, A. P. Hill, was killed. "He is at rest now," the distraught Lee said, "and we who are left are the ones to suffer." He had no time to mourn if his army was going to survive to fight again. He had to lead the rebels out of the closing trap.

Jefferson Davis was in St. Paul's Episcopal Church in Richmond that Sunday morning. He was handed a telegram from Lee reading, "I advise that all preparation be made for leaving Richmond tonight." Richmond had remained relatively calm throughout the siege, its citizens supremely confident that Bobby Lee would protect them. By midafternoon, as it became clear that Lee's men were crossing the Appomattox River and abandoning Petersburg, the panic began. Government officials began burning documents. In carts and in carriages, on horseback and on foot, on boats and on barges, carrying whatever possessions they could manage, members of the government and residents abandoned the city. At eleven o'clock that night, Davis boarded a train and departed.

By that time, Richmond was burning. Earlier that day, in an effort to prevent the same type of drunken behavior that had led to the destruction of Columbia, Richmond's city council ordered all the liquor in the city destroyed. Hundreds of barrels were poured into the streets and countless bottles were smashed. According to the *Richmond Daily Dispatch*, "The gutters ran with a liquor freshet, and the fumes filled and impregnated the air . . . straggling Confederate soldiers, retreating through the city, managed to get hold of a quantity of liquor. From that moment law and order ceased to exist; chaos came, and a Pandemonium reigned."

Deserters broke into stores and set fires. Looters followed. The business district was leveled. The boatyard, food warehouses, two railroad stations, and the largest flour mill on the continent were reduced to rubble. The banks, hotels, and saloons ceased to exist. More than a half mile of buildings were burned into hollow shells. Anything of military value—the armory and its munitions, ironclads in the river, and several bridges—was destroyed. The munitions exploded with such force that tombstones in the cemetery nearly a mile away were knocked over. The *New York Times* reported that as many as fifty-four blocks and eight hundred homes were destroyed and at least forty civilians died.

On what became known as Evacuation Sunday, President Davis and his cabinet abandoned Richmond. As shown in this Currier and Ives lithograph, the fires set by retreating Confederates to deny spoils to Grant spread quickly, and ironically this time Union soldiers put them out and saved the city. Among Davis's last acts was to name Danville, Virginia, the acting Confederate capital. A day after the city was occupied, Lincoln made a visit, an event, wrote a reporter, "too awful to remember, if it were possible to be erased, but that cannot be."

Union soldiers occupied the city and, ironically, saved it. Fire brigades were organized and by the time Lincoln arrived a day later, most of the fires had been put out. The president walked with only a small escort through the streets, surrounded by cheering, dancing, and singing freed slaves, who fought to shake his hand, touch his clothing, or kiss his boots. The crush became dangerous. Finally, Union sailors fixed their bayonets and cleared a path for him to the Confederate White House, where he sat down behind Jefferson Davis's desk.

Lee was on the run. But this time Grant had hold of him and wouldn't let go. His plan was to surround the fleeing rebel army and force Lee to surrender rather than annihilating them. Down to fewer than thirty-five thousand exhausted soldiers and being pursued by a hundred thousand or more well-supplied Yankees, Lee could do little to prevent this from happening. In a series of small battles, he tried to fight his way west, toward Danville or Lynchburg, Virginia, where he might find supplies, but Grant deftly blocked him. And when Lee stopped to fight, he was thrashed: Confederate generals Richard Ewell, Custis Lee, Montgomery Corse, and Joseph Kershaw were captured at Sailor's Creek.

The last remnant of Robert E. Lee's once great army was struggling for survival. The troops were running out of food and ammunition. Many of them had realized that the war was over, dropped their weapons, and deserted. On the night of April 7, Grant sent Lee a note suggesting it was time to surrender. "Not yet," Lee replied, but he did ask what terms Grant would accept.

By the ninth, Generals Sheridan and George A. Custer had cut off Lee's escape route at Appomattox Court House. Lee had one last fight in him. That morning he tried to break through the Union lines. His troops fought their way through two lines of Union cavalry, but when a thick fog lifted they were stunned to see thousands of Union infantrymen waiting for them. Lee finally accepted that he was beaten, admitting, "Then there is nothing left for me to do but go and see General Grant, and I would rather die a thousand deaths."

Grant and Lee agreed to meet early in the afternoon of April 9, 1865, at the home of Wilmer McLean. Four years earlier McLean had lived in Manassas, close enough to Bull Run to watch the fighting from his front lawn. Sickened by the combat, he had sold that house and moved somewhere safe—near Appomattox, and the war had followed him to his front parlor.

Grant and Lee actually had met for a few moments once before, during the Mexican-American War. Grant remembered being impressed by Lee's perfectly groomed appearance; Lee remembered the meeting but could not picture the usually disheveled Grant. They arrived at this conference true to those memories, Lee in a sparkling new uniform, carrying his sword in a jewel-studded hilt; Grant in an ordinary private's sackcoat bearing the epaulets of his rank, his boots and pants muddied. They exchanged pleasantries; then Lee asked the terms of surrender.

This print, probably published in 1866, shows Grant and Lee meeting on a road at Appomattox to discuss the terms of surrender. The fact that this never took place did not stop competing publishers from issuing lithographs to commemorate it. In fact, Lee had proposed meeting Grant on the old stage road to end the war. Grant did not reply, but Lee rode to the point. He was joined there by a Union officer who delivered a note from Grant, explaining that the general had no authority to talk about peace—he could only accept a surrender. Lee hesitated, considered the consequences, then agreed.

Unconditional Surrender Grant, as he was so well known, in fact offered extraordinarily lenient conditions. The fighting would end; the officers and men would go home and the Confederate army would cease to exist. The officers would be permitted to keep "their private horses or baggage." Lee pointed out that rebel troops owned their horses and mules and requested that they be allowed to keep them as they would be needed on their farms. Grant agreed. Lee nodded his acceptance and said, "This will have a very happy effect on my army."

Grant's compassion was evident. As copies of the agreement were being drafted, he ordered twenty-five thousand rations sent immediately to the rebel troops, who had not eaten

Lee's surrender at the McLean house in the village of Appomattox Court House remains one of the most celebrated events in American history. This historically accurate oil painting by Tom Lovell was commissioned by *National Geographic* magazine in 1965 to honor the centennial of the end of the war. A footnote: On the far right Lovell depicted General George Custer, who was not actually in the room at the time of the surrender.

in several days. Later he admitted, "My own feelings . . . were sad and depressed . . . at the downfall of a foe who had fought so long and valiantly, and had suffered so much for a cause, though the cause was, I believe, one of the worst for which a people ever fought."

An embittered Jefferson Davis accepted the necessity of Lee's surrender of the Army of Northern Virginia, although it would be weeks before all the combatants finally left the battlefields. General Johnston officially surrendered the feeble Army of Tennessee and many smaller garrisons to Sherman on April 26; the last fighting took place on Palmito Ranch in Texas on May 11 and 12, and the last rebels to lay down their arms were the Cherokee, Creek, Seminole, and Osage Battalion on June 23.

The final toll was staggering. While the precise number of Union and Confederate soldiers who died from all causes in the war has never been accurately determined, it may be as high as 850,000 men, with at least twice that many wounded.

The heroes who led the Union to victory were amply rewarded in the next decades and helped shape the future of America in ways that still resonate. Among them, Grant would become the eighteenth president of the United States. Sherman probably could have secured the Republican nomination if he had wanted it, but he did not. Instead, he is remembered in political history for his declaration, "I will not accept if nominated and will not serve if elected."

A ceremonial laying down of arms and flags took place on April 12, exactly four years after the first shots were fired at Fort Sumter, South Carolina, at Appomattox Court House. By this time Lee was on his way back to Richmond and Grant to his headquarters at City Point, so General Joshua L. Chamberlain, the hero of Gettysburg, was assigned to receive the formal surrender. As the Confederate soldiers marched before the victors to lay down their weapons and unit flags, Chamberlain ordered his men to "shoulder arms," a battlefield salute. It was considered a noble gesture of respect.

There were great shows of emotion. On several occasions rebel soldiers broke ranks, walked over to the growing pile of unit flags, "and pressed them to their lips with burning tears," wrote Chamberlain. And then, he continued, "every token of armed hostility having been laid aside, and the men having given their words of honor that they would never serve again against the flag, they were free to go . . . and by nightfall we were left there at Appomattox Courthouse lonesome and alone."

Wilmer McLean, the owner of the house in which the surrender was signed, had been a successful merchant and sugar smuggler during the war, but with the end of the war his Confederate money was worthless. He defaulted on loans secured by the property, which was auctioned off and sold for $1,250 in 1872.

**THE CAPTURE OF AN UNPROTECTED FEMALE, OR THE CLOSE OF THE REBELLION.**

On April 10, Washington was awakened to an extraordinary five-hundred-gun salute celebrating Lee's surrender. But by that time Jefferson Davis had escaped. Rumors were that he hoped to reach safety in Texas, or a foreign nation, and form a government in exile. He remained on the run for six weeks. After Lincoln's assassination, he was believed to have participated in that plot, and large rewards were offered for his capture. He finally was captured in rural Georgia. As apparently he was wearing his wife's overcoat and his head was covered with a black shawl, the story spread quickly that he was caught disguised as a woman. He was widely ridiculed (above). Numerous prints were published showing him in skirts and a bonnet. Songs were written and sung, giving birth to a legend that never died.

Davis was imprisoned at Fort Monroe, in Hampton, Virginia, for more than two years, before he was released without a trial. He eventually regained love and respect in the South, but in the North he would always be remembered as the leader of the bloody war, who was finally captured wearing a hoop skirt.

# ELEVEN

# THE LAST SHOTS
## Are Fired
### The War Ends and Lincoln Is Assassinated

O Captain! my Captain! our fearful trip is done,
The ship has weather'd every rack, the prize we sought is won,
The port is near, the bells I hear, the people all exulting,
While follow eyes the steady keel, the vessel grim and daring . . .

*Walt Whitman*

On March 4, 1865, while Grant was stirring at the gates of Petersburg and Sherman had left the embers of Columbia behind to march north, President Abraham Lincoln delivered his second inaugural address. Promising conciliation when the fighting ended, he concluded, "With malice toward none, with charity for all, with firmness in the right as God gives us to see the right, let us strive on to finish the work we are in, to bind up the nation's wounds, to care for him who shall have borne the battle and for

🖙 To satisfy an overwhelming public demand, Currier and Ives quickly produced this print, *The Assassination of President Lincoln.* While usually hand-colored, many of these were sold in black and white to be colored at home.

Lincoln was inaugurated to begin his second term on March 4, 1865. Among the marchers in the parade were black soldiers and Lincoln's empty carriage—although the crowd cheered the carriage, the president was waiting in the Capitol.

his widow and his orphan, to do all which may achieve and cherish a just and lasting peace among ourselves and with all nations."

But, according to legend, among the tens of thousands of celebrants, a crowd described by the *Philadelphia Inquirer* as "sufficient to have struck terror into the heart of Lee's army (had the umbrellas been muskets)," were several men who watched with hatred: David Herold, George Atzerodt, Lewis Paine, John Surratt, Edmund Spangler, and John Wilkes Booth.

For these Confederate loyalists the war was to have another chapter. Even at that moment their plan was being formulated: they were plotting to kidnap President Lincoln and eventually trade him for the release of all the rebel prisoners. That was not as improbable as it seems; at that time the president was only lightly protected. The Secret Service did not officially begin protecting presidents until 1902, following William McKinley's assassination. Lincoln certainly was vulnerable: he was known to attend church or the theater without any security, and some nights he would walk by himself the quarter mile between the War Department and the White House. Lincoln simply refused to live fearfully, explaining, "If I am killed I can die but once, but to live in constant dread is to die over and over again."

Unknown to his fellow conspirators, John Wilkes Booth was contemplating a very different plan.

John Wilkes Booth was a noted American actor. He was the ninth of famed British thespian Junius Booth's ten children and was raised on a Bel Air, Maryland, farm worked by the family slaves. Junius Booth was a theatrical star who traveled from town to town performing lead roles supported by a local cast. He also was considered quite eccentric; he preached that all life was sacred, even that of the housefly, and once held a funeral for pigeons.

His son John Wilkes apparently inherited some of that eccentricity. He was, his older brother Edwin wrote, "a rattle-pated fellow, filled with Quixotic notions. . . . We regarded him as a good-hearted, harmless, though wild-brained boy."

Supposedly, when he was twelve years old, a gypsy fortune-teller saw doom in his palm, predicting he would have a brief but celebrated life and would die badly. Booth wrote down her prediction and carried that folded sheet of paper with him almost to the day he died. He left school at seventeen to join his older brothers, Edwin and Junius Junior, on the stage. By that time Edwin had eclipsed his father and was considered one of the foremost stars of the American stage. His younger brother John was welcomed by theater managers as a less-expensive Booth.

Edwin Booth (left) and his twenty-six-year-old brother John Wilkes Booth.
J. W. Booth was considered one of the most handsome men in Washington,
and his photograph was sold by gallery owners and photographers.

But John Booth was no mere stand-in; he brought great looks, talent, and bravura to the stage. He was a handsome man, a dark and moody charmer who instantly became quite popular with the young ladies. He became one of the first "matinee idols," and often "unruly" women would wait at the stage door until they were shooed away by the theater manager.

Within a few years John Booth was earning as much as $20,000 annually, a fortune at that time. But as the debate over slavery became increasingly contentious, he became more and more politically active. That fit his character—his sister Asia described him as a slow learner with great powers of retention, but "from early boyhood he was argumentative and fervid in debate."

Clearly, he had inherited his father's flamboyance, his talent, and his intensity, whether applying those qualities to his politics or his craft. In 1854, he became active in the anti-immigrant Know-Nothing Party and he was a strong supporter of slavery. That position may have been hardened when he was thirteen and a good friend's father, a landowner named Edward Gorsuch, was killed when he tried to reclaim runaway slaves in Christiana, Pennsylvania. In 1859, his political passions were stirred by the actions of abolitionist John Brown. When Brown was captured at Harpers Ferry and sentenced to hang, Booth impulsively joined the Richmond Grays, a militia company charged with providing security for Brown's execution. Booth was standing in front of the gallows when Brown was hanged. "He was a brave man," he admitted to his sister. By the time the war began in 1861, he was passionately committed to the Southern cause.

John Booth's acting career continued to progress nicely; his notices suggested that his stardom might even eclipse those of his brother and his father. In October 1861, the *Providence Journal* wrote, "He possesses talent and genius of a high order." But even then there was something troubling about him; as a reviewer in the *Buffalo Daily Courier* noted at about that same time, "[Booth has] the strange power and effect [of his father and brother] . . . yet with more of grotesqueness . . . he has extraordinary physiognomical power, almost electric feeling and weird and startling elocutionary effects." Standing-room-only crowds greeted him when he made his New York debut in *Richard III* in March 1862. "In the last act he created a veritable sensation," the *New York Herald* reported. But even then, as he established himself as one of America's great actors, an anger inside him was fighting to break free. During the final dueling scene in *Richard III*, for example, he seemed to lose control and literally knocked his fellow actor over the footlights and into the orchestra pit, injuring him.

As his fame grew, so did his bitterness and fury at Lincoln, at the Union army, and at the abolitionists. In a letter handed to his a fellow actor, John Matthews, that was opened after he had committed his heinous crime, he wrote:

This country was formed for the white, not the black man. And looking upon African slavery . . . I for one, have ever considered it one of the greatest blessings (both for themselves and us,) that God ever bestowed upon a favored nation. . . . I thought then, as now, that the Abolitionists were the only traitors in the land, and that the entire party deserved the same fate of poor old BROWN. . . . Day by day has [the American flag] been dragged deeper and deeper into cruelty and oppression, till now (in my eyes) her once bright red stripes look like bloody gashes on the face of Heaven.

Booth's strongly voiced support of secession caused a rift with his brother Edwin, who not only was a supporter of Abraham Lincoln and the abolitionist movement, but had actually saved the life of the president's son. In one of history's bizarre coincidences, sometime in 1864 Edwin Booth was on a very crowded train platform in Jersey City as a train arrived. Robert Todd Lincoln, a twenty-year-old Harvard student traveling to Washington, had disembarked and was leaning back against a train until the crowd thinned when suddenly, as the young Lincoln remembered:

There was of course a narrow space between the platform and the car body. There was some crowding, and I happened to be pressed by it against the car body. . . . In this situation the train began to move, and by the motion I was twisted off my feet, and had dropped somewhat, with feet downward, into the open space, and was personally helpless, when my coat collar was vigorously seized and I was quickly pulled up and out to a secure footing on the platform. Upon turning to thank my rescuer I saw it was Edwin Booth, whose face was of course well known to me.

It would be several months before Booth learned the young man he had saved was the president's son.

According to Edwin Booth, it was Lincoln's reelection in November 1864 that finally set his brother on his mission. Because of their age difference, the brothers were not close and rarely saw each other. When they did, usually at their mother's house, they often argued about their political positions. As Edwin Booth remembered years later, "[We] used to laugh at his patriotic froth. . . . That he was insane on that one point, no one who knew him well can doubt. When I told him I had voted for Lincoln's re-election he expressed deep regret,

The role Dr. Samuel Mudd in the assassination remains the subject of debate. Although there is considerable evidence that Mudd met with Booth at least three times before the assassination and that he changed his own story several times, a revisionist history put forth by his descendants has made it appear he might have been an innocent victim of circumstances.

and declared his belief that Lincoln would be made king of America; and this, I believe, drove him beyond the limits of reason."

It isn't known when he turned his hatred into action, or even with certainty if it was his concept. While the commonly held belief is simply that John Wilkes Booth assassinated President Lincoln, in fact Booth was part of a large group with connections to Confederate agents who attempted to carry out multiple attacks. The unanswered question is: who initiated this plot? Taking place almost exactly one hundred years before the Kennedy assassination, it raised the same type of speculation and the facts have never really been settled. Some historians believe that the plot actually was initiated by a Canadian-based Confederate spy ring; and in fact, among the personal papers found in Booth's hotel room were a code cipher and encoded words identical to Confederate codes then in use. And in October 1864, Booth spent ten days in Montreal, at that time a popular and safe meeting place for Confederate agents. What is known with certainty is who pulled the trigger that night.

Among the first people to join the conspiracy was twenty-one-year-old Lewis Thornton Powell. "Lewis the Terrible" Powell was a large, strong man, taller than Lincoln, and it would be his job to physically restrain the president during the kidnapping. Powell was a brute, a Civil War veteran who had fought at Antietam, Chancellorsville, and Gettysburg, where he was wounded and captured. He escaped and joined a guerrilla band, conducting raids behind Union lines. It isn't known with certainty how Powell and Booth met, but it is generally accepted that they had been introduced by another conspirator, John Surratt Jr.

The role played by Dr. Samuel Mudd has always been murky, and historians cannot agree on the extent of his knowledge or even about his willing participation in the plot. It is known that Booth met Mudd in November 1864, ostensibly to discuss buying Mudd's Maryland farm. Like

Clockwise from upper left: conspirators John Surratt, Lewis Payne (also known as Lewis Powell), who attacked Secretary Seward, David Herold, and George Atzerodt, who was assigned to kill Vice President Johnson but backed out at the last minute. Payne/Powell, Herold, and Atzerodt were hanged.

Booth, Mudd was a Confederate sympathizer. He may have experienced financial problems when Maryland abolished slavery in 1864, forcing him to put his farm up for sale. But historians agree that Mudd introduced Booth to John Surratt Jr., who became a key player in the planning.

John Surratt was a veteran Confederate spy and courier who was known to have carried information about Union troop movements across the Potomac; he met Booth in a room at the National Hotel in Washington in late December and immediately joined the cabal. If Booth wanted to contact the Confederate Secret Service, then Surratt clearly was the ideal go-between. Surratt was employed as the postmaster of Surrattsville, the small Maryland town settled by his family. During the planning of the kidnapping he became Booth's closest confidant. On the night they met, Surratt recalled, he asked Booth what precisely he was proposing. Before responding, Booth searched the room high and low, then confided, "It is to kidnap President Lincoln, and carry him off to Richmond!"

Among those people Mudd and Surratt recruited were David Herold, a pharmacist's assistant at the Washington Navy Yard, whom Surratt had met several years earlier at the Charlotte Hall Military Academy, a man who had access to materials that might prove useful, such as sleep-inducing chloroform; and George "Dirty Andy" Atzerodt, a Prussian immigrant and heavy drinker from Port Tobacco, Maryland, whose knowledge of the backroads and hidden waterways of Maryland would be vital in getting the kidnapped president to Richmond.

While these were the four men convicted of carrying out the plot, several other people were involved. The plans were made at a tavern frequented by Confederate agents. The tavern was owned by Surratt's mother, Mary, and their guns were hidden there. Booth's childhood friend, Michael O'Laughlen, was one of the original plotters in the kidnapping, although he claimed later to have dropped out.

As incredible as it seems, this was hardly the only plan put in motion to spread terror in the North. As the outcome of the war had become increasingly clear, Confederate patriots were desperate to find ways to punish the Yankees. Jefferson Davis supposedly allocated a substantial amount of money to fund these efforts. An expert on yellow fever, Dr. Luke Pryor Blackburn, living in Halifax, collected nine large trunkfuls of contaminated clothing from people who had died of the disease during an epidemic in Bermuda and planned to distribute them in New York, Washington, and other Northern cities—with one trunk being sent directly to Lincoln. On November 25, 1864, a gang of eight rebel sympathizers in New York attempted to set fire to numerous hotels, theaters, and museums along Broadway—and perhaps even blow up the Croton Reservoir, the city's primary water supply. Ironically, that night John Wilkes Booth and his two brothers were costarring in a special production of *Julius Caesar* at the Winter Garden Theatre, a charity appearance to raise funds for a planned statue of Shakespeare. It was the only time the three brothers ever performed together—and the show was interrupted when a fire erupted in a hotel next door.

The Confederate Torpedo Bureau, a unit tasked with creating and producing explosive devices of all types, slipped several men into Washington who planned to kill Lincoln by blowing up a wing of the White House, but their plot was prevented when the key explosives expert was captured in early April. At least three separate abduction plots approved by Confederate officials between 1862 and 1864 had already failed.

Another attempt on Lincoln's life had come within whiskers of succeeding. On a dark

August night in 1864, Lincoln had been riding by himself from the executive mansion to the Soldiers' Home outside the city, where his family stayed to avoid the summer heat. Just as he reached the entrance, a single rifle shot was fired from a distance he estimated at about fifty yards, knocking off his silk hat. In the morning that hat was found on the ground with a bullet hole through it. Lincoln dismissed the event as an accident, telling his friend, Ward Hill Lamon, "Personally, I can't bring myself to believe that any one has shot or will deliberately shoot at me with the purpose of killing me . . . I have about concluded that the shot was the result of accident." Lincoln kept the incident quiet and no one was ever arrested or identified.

Booth's attempt to kidnap the president took place on March 17, 1865, two weeks after he had attended Lincoln's second inauguration with several of his coconspirators and his secret fiancée, Lucy Hale, the daughter of a strongly abolitionist senator. When he learned that Lincoln planned to attend a performance of the play *Still Waters Run Deep* at Campbell Hospital near the Soldiers' Home, Booth alerted his men. They lay hidden in the bushes along a lonely stretch of road, waiting anxiously. But it turned out that the president had changed his plans and instead of the play elected to attend a reception at the National Hotel in the city.

Two nights later Booth appeared onstage for the final time. "The Eminent young American tragedian," as he was billed, starred in front of a full house in the Irish play *The Apostate*. Fittingly, he played the villain, Duke Pescara, in a benefit performance at Ford's Theatre.

A playbill for Booth's final performance, in which he, "having kindly volunteered his services, will render his great character of Pescara!"

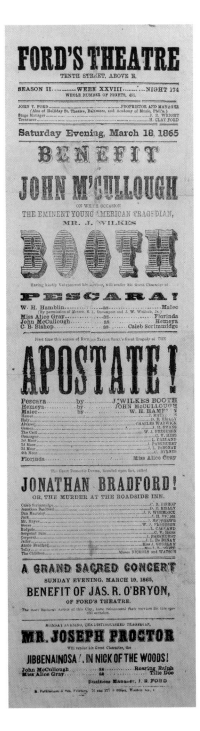

The anger that had been inside him so long finally reached the breaking point when it was announced that Robert E. Lee had surrendered. Washington erupted in spontaneous celebration, "The like was never seen before in the National Capital." Gas jets on the roof of the patent office spelled out "Union" and "Victory"; nearby letters of flame honored the heroes "Lincoln" and "Grant." Men and women paraded through the streets singing patriotic songs like "The Battle Cry of Freedom," "The Battle Hymn of the Republic," and, of course, "John Brown's Body." On the night of April 11, hundreds of people gathered in front of the White House as Lincoln stood on the North Portico balcony and, by the light of a single candle, read his prepared speech. "We meet this evening, not in sorrow, but in gladness of heart," he began. Much of his speech was about the challenge of bringing the nation together to provide equal rights to black and white alike.

Standing in that crowd were John Wilkes Booth and David Herold. The furious Booth told Herold, "That means n——— citizenship! Now, by God, I'll put him through. That is the last speech he will ever make."

Historians believe it was at that moment that Booth's plans changed from abduction to assassination. Midmorning on Good Friday, April 14, he learned that Lincoln and his wife, Mary, were going to join General and Mrs. Grant that night for a performance of the popular play *Our American Cousin* at Ford's Theatre. Booth was well known in that theater; owner John Ford was a trusted friend of his family, and he could move around easily without arousing suspicion. He would strike his blow there.

More than that, he was going to destroy the government that had made war on slavery. He intended to kill the president and the next two men in line to take his place, throwing the federal government into disarray. He gathered his conspirators and revealed his plan to them: There was a line in the play that always drew loud laughter; he estimated it would be spoken at about ten fifteen. That laughter would cover the sound of his gunshot. At that same moment, he explained, Lewis Powell and David Herold were to attack and kill Secretary of State Seward in his home, where he was recovering from a carriage accident in which he had broken several bones, and George Atzerodt was to kill Vice President Andrew Johnson in his residence in Kirkwood House. In the ensuing panic they would meet at the Navy Yard Bridge and make good their escape.

The only person who may have been troubled by this change of plans from a kidnapping to an assassination was Atzerodt, but he was convinced it was too late to back out. That day, Atzerodt rented the room directly above Vice President Johnson's in Kirkwood House, then at some point went into the bar and started drinking.

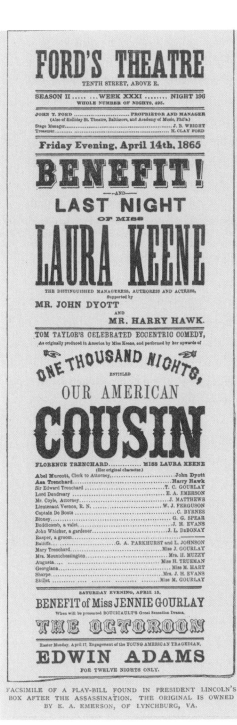

Booth apparently learned that Lincoln would be attending that night's performance of *Our American Cousin* at Ford's Theatre when he stopped by the theater to pick up mail left there for him. The building originally had been a Baptist church but had been renovated into a twenty-four-hundred-seat theater in 1861. After the assassination, the government purchased the theater for $88,000 and turned it into an office. In 1893, during an excavation of the building's basement, a forty-foot section of three floors collapsed, killing twenty-two clerks and injuring sixty-five. It was designated a National Historic Site in 1932 and rededicated in 1968.

Lincoln had arisen at seven o'clock that morning and began working. At breakfast an hour later Mrs. Lincoln told him they had tickets for the performance of *Aladdin* at Grover's Theatre that evening but she decided she would prefer to see *Our American Cousin* at Ford's. She suggested that General and Mrs. Grant might join them. He agreed to make the arrangements. The president then spent the morning meeting with his cabinet to discuss reconstruction. Among the questions to be answered was how the leaders of the rebellion would be treated. While no decision was reached, the president pointed out that "enough lives have been sacrificed."

At some point during the day, General Grant informed the president that he and Mrs. Grant would not be attending the theater that night; instead they would be taking the evening train out of the city to visit their children. As with every small decision made that day, had Grant decided differently, history might have been altered.

In the afternoon, Lincoln signed a pardon for a deserter who had been sentenced to death, telling his secretary, "I think the boy can do us more good above ground than underground." Then he met with a former slave whose husband was missing some army paychecks; he promised to look into the matter. As he and Mary Lincoln left the White House for an afternoon carriage ride, a soldier who had lost an arm yelled to him, "I would almost give my other hand if I could shake that of Abraham Lincoln." Lincoln walked over to him and shook his hand, telling him, "You shall do that and it shall cost you nothing."

At three o'clock, he and Mrs. Lincoln rode to the Navy Yard to tour the ironclad USS *Montauk*. After years of stress, after reading the endless lists of casualties, this was a beautiful day.

Booth's conspirators continued their preparations. In the afternoon, Mary Surratt took a package containing binoculars given to her by Booth to the family tavern and told her tenant to get "those shooting irons," two Spencer carbines that had been left there.

Booth stopped at Ford's Theatre at about six o'clock, purportedly to ask stagehand Edmund Spangler to find a halter for his horse, which was kept in the stables behind the theater. Spangler was busy making preparations for the presidential visit, removing a partition between the presidential box and an adjoining box.

At seven o'clock, Booth met with Powell, Azerodt, and Herold and gave them their final instructions. Powell and Herold then went to Seward's house and stood outside, waiting for the appointed hour.

Booth already knew that the president would be sitting in the state box, which was about eleven feet above the stage. A year and a half earlier the president had sat there watching Booth in the Ford Theatre's production of *The Marble Heart*. Booth had once again played the villain, and twice while uttering threats he had approached the president and practically waved his finger in Lincoln's face. He repeated that gesture a third time, and a member of the president's party, Mary Clay, later claimed she had said, "Mr. Lincoln, he looks as if he meant that for you." To this the president purportedly replied, "Well, he does look pretty sharp at me, doesn't he?"

The president and Mrs. Lincoln left the White House after dinner, and en route to the theater they picked up a young couple, Major Henry Rathbone and his fiancée, Clara Harris, who were joining them for the evening. The play had already begun when they arrived at the theater, but it was paused and the theater orchestra played "Hail to the Chief" as the party entered the box.

A Washington police officer named John F. Parker had been assigned to guard the president that night. He was supposed to be sitting in a chair outside the box during the performance. But for reasons never satisfactorily explained, he was not there. It is known that during intermission he went to the nearby Taltavull's Star Saloon for a drink.

Booth got to the theater after nine o'clock, but rather than going inside he went to Taltavull's Saloon to have a drink.

At about ten p.m., the conspirators went into action. As Herold waited outside with their horses, Powell knocked on Secretary Seward's front door, telling the servant who responded that he had brought a prescription for Seward. The servant, suspicious, offered to take it himself, but Powell pushed past him and started for the staircase. When Frederick Seward, the secretary's son, attempted to stop him, Powell pulled a revolver and tried to shoot him at point-blank range. When that gun jammed, Powell began clubbing Frederick Seward with it, fracturing his skull and putting him into a coma that lasted two months. As Frederick Seward collapsed, Powell barged into William Seward's third-floor bedroom. Now a second son, Augustus Seward, tried to stop him, and Powell stabbed him with his twelve-inch-long bowie knife. Inside the bedroom the hulking Powell, intent on committing murder, slashed Seward's bodyguard, George Robinson, a male nurse, and shoved Seward's daughter, Fanny, out of the way.

Supposedly screaming, "I'm mad! I'm mad!" he stabbed William Seward in the neck and breast. It was bedlam in that bedroom. Robinson and the nurse were desperately trying to claw Powell off Seward. Another son, Augustus Seward, was stabbed as he raced into the room. Powell finally fled—stabbing a State Department messenger in the back as he escaped. But when he got outside he was stunned to discover that Herold had gone, apparently panicked by the screaming from inside the house. Powell jumped on his horse but quickly got lost in the confusing streets. Eventually he spent the night hiding under a tree in the congressional cemetery.

All of Powell's victims survived. A splint Secretary Seward was wearing to immobilize his broken jaw had deflected Powell's knife and probably saved his life.

George Atzerodt insisted later that he did not know anything about a murder plot until the fateful day. And then, for his own reasons, he refused to carry out his mission. He spent

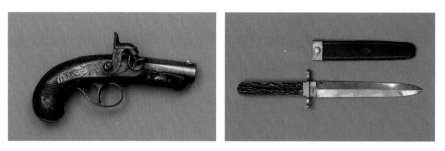

Booth knew he would have only one shot: his weapon was a .44-caliber derringer that held a single bullet. If he missed, he would have no opportunity to reload. He always carried a horn-handled Rio Grande camp knife, which he used to stab Major Henry Rathbone, with the inscriptions "Land of the Free / Home of the Brave" and "Liberty / Independence" etched into the blade.

the day and evening in the bar, getting drunk. There is some question of whether he ever even went to Vice President Johnson's room. When he learned that Lincoln had been shot, he began walking the streets, clearly considering his options.

Booth walked into Ford's Theatre slightly after ten o'clock, armed with a derringer and a knife. The third act of the play had just begun. He waited for the punch line, and when he heard actor Harry Hawk say, "Don't know the manners of good society, eh? Well, I guess I know enough to turn you inside out, old gal—you sockdologizing old mantrap," he opened the door to Lincoln's box, lifted his derringer, and from less than four feet away fired one bullet into the president's skull. The bullet entered slightly above Lincoln's left ear and penetrated about seven inches. The president collapsed and never regained consciousness.

The details of the next few moments have been discussed and debated since the night of the slaying. After shooting Lincoln, Booth stepped onto the balustrade and jumped down to the stage, shouting, *"Sic semper tyrannis!,"* a Latin phrase meaning "Thus always to tyrants." But there are people who heard him shout other phrases, among them "The South is avenged." Major Rathbone thought he heard "Freedom."

Booth ran or hobbled across the stage. Edmund Spangler held a rear door open for him. Behind the theater another young hand, Joseph Burroughs, was holding his horse. Booth mounted and rode fast out of the city. As he left, Spangler supposedly warned Burroughs, "Don't say which way he went."

During his escape Booth broke the fibula in his left leg. It is generally accepted that as he

The photo above is the view of the stage from Lincoln's box on the night of his death. The photo at right, in which a single soldier stands guard at an empty Ford's Theatre, was taken the day after the assassination.

To fill the international demand for anything connected to the assassination, the title of this lithograph, *Assassination of President Abraham Lincoln*, was printed on its face in three languages: English, French, and German. Note that in this illustration, Booth's foot has been caught in a banner, which caused him to break his leg.

jumped, his foot caught in the ceremonial bunting decorating the box, causing him to crash onto the stage and break his leg, but Booth would claim that his leg was broken later that night when his horse fell on him.

While he made good his escape, there was great confusion inside the theater. Very few people actually heard the shot over the laughter, and at first many members of the audience believed the leaping man to be part of the show. Then someone shouted that the president had been shot, and the screaming began.

The fatally wounded president was carried across the street to a boardinghouse owned by William Petersen. At 7:22 the following morning, he was pronounced dead. Upon being informed of Lincoln's death, Secretary of War Edwin M. Stanton supposedly uttered his famous words, "Now he belongs to the ages."

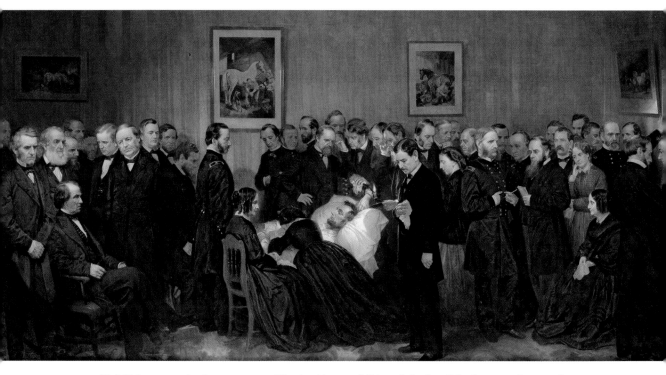

Publishers rushed numerous illustrations of Lincoln's deathbed onto the market within weeks of the president's death, all of them based loosely on a photograph of the room taken hours after Lincoln died. *Harper's Weekly* published a wood engraving of the empty room, which quickly was filled by the imagination of artists.

Slightly more than two hours later, Andrew Johnson was sworn in as president. The plot to create total chaos in the government had failed.

Booth and David Herold met at the Navy Yard Bridge. They rode directly to Mary Surratt's tavern, where they picked up the binoculars and carbines left there earlier. They then departed. Booth was in terrible pain, so they went to Dr. Samuel Mudd's farm, arriving there at about four in the morning. Mudd would later claim that he did not know Booth and certainly could not have been aware of the assassination, but he simply treated a stranger with a broken leg who showed up at his door in the middle of the night. While Mudd dressed his wound, Booth shaved off his well-known mustache. A carpenter living nearby quickly fashioned crutches for Booth, and Booth and Herold left Mudd's farm, moving south as quickly as possible. Booth's hope was that the contacts he had developed to help smuggle the

Three hours after Lincoln died, eleven men gathered in Andrew Johnson's room at Kirkwood House, where Chief Justice Chase administered the oath of office. It was rumored that Johnson had visited the president as he lay dying and that Mary Lincoln had demanded he leave instantly.

president to Richmond after his kidnapping would now help him evade capture.

When John Surratt learned of the assassination, he fled to Canada, where he hid from authorities in a small village outside Montreal until he sailed to England under an assumed name the following September. His mother, Mary Surratt, immediately became a suspect. On April 17, authorities searched her home and found incriminating evidence, including pictures of John Wilkes Booth and Jefferson Davis hidden behind another picture. While they were searching her rooms, Lewis Powell arrived, carrying a pickax. When questioned, he told investigators he had been hired to dig a gutter. Mary Surratt, trying to sever any link between them, claimed, "Before God, sir, I do not know this man, and have never seen him." Both of them were taken into custody.

When detectives searched George Atzerodt's abandoned room in Kirkwood House they found a revolver, a bowie knife, and a bankbook belonging to John Wilkes Booth. Atzerodt was arrested at his cousin's house on April 20.

Following the evidence, investigators arrested everyone conceivably connected to the conspiracy, among them Dr. Mudd and Edmund Spangler, the stagehand at Ford's Theatre. But the largest manhunt in American history failed to turn up John Wilkes Booth and David Herold.

While Booth was still on the run, massive crowds in Washington paid tribute to the president. More than forty thousand people, among them the all-black 22nd US Colored Infantry, marched behind his casket as it was carried from the White House to the Capitol where the president's body would lie in state. Countless more lined the streets as his body was

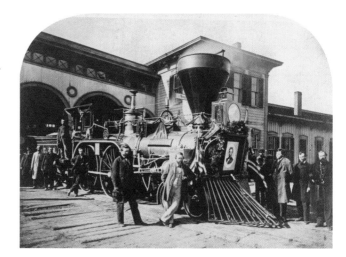

Lincoln's funeral train steamed slowly through 180 cities, stopping in several ranging in size from Philadelphia to Herkimer, New York. At each stop the president's coffin was removed and put on view. People waited five hours or more to pay their respects.

taken to the train station for his final trip home. That funeral train passed through 180 cities, 444 communities, and 7 states on the way to Springfield, Illinois. In every village and city, thousands of people, including numerous soldiers, stood silently in respect as the train sped by.

In the South the reaction, understandably, was quite different. While in public many people professed sympathy, in private many more people celebrated the "tyrant's" assassination. In several instances Union soldiers arrested people who taunted them about the murder, and

In the North, the euphoria over the end of the war was replaced almost immediately by deep sorrow at the president's death; in the South those emotions were reversed. The nation mourned for the three weeks it took for the president's coffin to arrive in Springfield, Illinois, to end his journey. After a White House funeral on April 18, massive crowds lined the streets and bells tolled as Lincoln's coffin was carried the mile and a half down Pennsylvania Avenue to the Capitol.

there were unconfirmed reports of others being tarred and feathered and forced out of town and isolated stories of furious troops shooting and killing people.

Edwin Stanton took charge of the search for the killers. A $50,000 reward was posted for information leading to Booth's capture, and $25,000 was offered for both John Surratt and David Herold. But Booth and Herold seemed to have disappeared into the countryside. After leaving Dr. Mudd's house, they took refuge in a pine thicket and stayed there for almost a week. Booth was greatly disappointed that the outpouring of Southern support, which he believed would be forthcoming, never materialized. In fact, it was precisely the opposite; he was shunned. The cost of aiding him in any way was simply too high. Booth and Herold approached several contacts but were quickly turned away. So while thousands of Union troops searched for them, they hid in those woods, hungry and cold, with Booth's broken leg causing him great pain.

In a diary entry written while hiding out, Booth claimed to be stunned that he was being condemned rather than lauded for his action. He wrote:

> I struck boldly, and not as the papers say. . . . I shouted Sic semper before I fired. In jumping broke my leg. . . . I can never repent it, though we hated to kill. Our country owed all her troubles to him. . . .
>
> For striking down a greater tyrant than they ever knew, am looked upon as a common cutthroat.

In this diary Booth mused about returning to Washington "and in a measure clear my name." But he remained adamant that he had struck a blow for freedom.

Finally, eight days after the assassination, Booth and Herold successfully crossed the Potomac into Virginia. A sympathizer arranged for the two men to spend the night in the ramshackle cabin of a freed black man named William Lewis. The racist Booth refused to sleep there with a black man, and his threats forced Lewis and his family to sleep outside. A day later, after crossing the Rappahannock River, assisted by three Confederate soldiers on their way home, the two fugitives were advised to hole up at the farm of a man named Richard H. Garrett.

Garrett was told that Booth and Herold were rebel soldiers looking to rest up for a few days as they made their way home. And so he welcomed them. His two sons had just gotten home from the war and he was a grateful man. But that Southern hospitality disappeared when Garrett learned that the two men had lied, that they were not veterans. He sent them to sleep in the tobacco barn.

Search parties were crisscrossing vast areas of Maryland and Virginia. A twenty-six-man detachment from the 16th New York Cavalry, led by federal detective and professional man-hunter Luther Baker and Everton Conger, finally picked up the scent. Baker tracked down one of the rebel soldiers who had helped Booth and Herold cross the Rappahannock; Baker's threats convinced him to reveal the fugitives' hiding place.

The search party got to Garrett's farm at about two a.m. The two men had "gone to the woods," Garrett told them. But when the investigators threatened to hang the old man for lying, one of his sons admitted that the assassins were hiding in the barn.

Like so much of history, the details of this event differ depending on who is telling the story. But it is known that the barn was surrounded and Booth and Herold were ordered to come out or the barn would be burned down with them inside. As a soldier began piling up hay and pinecones against the barn, Booth threatened, "If you come back here I will put a bullet through you."

Soldiers looking through knotholes could see the two men. As Booth began to accept

*Seisure and Death of the Murderer Wilkie Booth* was one of the many prints illustrating the scene inside Richard Garrett's barn, although it isn't clear why the mortally wounded Booth is still holding a rifle. There remains speculation that rather than being shot, Booth committed suicide.

his fate he yelled to them, "Well, my brave boys, prepare a stretcher for me, and place another stain on our glorious banner."

Herold was less willing to die there. When smoke from the burning brush began seeping into the barn, he decided to surrender. As he came out, Sergeant Boston Corbett fired a single shot, striking Booth in the neck. Corbett claimed later that Booth was raising his carbine to shoot at Herold or the soldiers. At the sound of the gunshot, Lieutenant Edward Doherty rushed into the barn and, as he testified, "as he [Booth] was falling caught him under the arms and pulled him out of the barn. The burning building becoming too hot, I had him carried to the veranda of Garrett's house . . . at seven o'clock Booth breathed his last. He had on his person a diary, a large bowie knife, two pistols, a compass and a draft on Canada for 60 pounds."

On a brutally hot day, July 7, 1865, four members of the assassination plot were hanged in front of about a thousand people at the Old Arsenal Penitentiary (now part of Fort Lesley J. McNair). According to a guard, Lewis Powell shouted from the ten-foot gallows, "Mrs. Surratt is innocent. She doesn't deserve to die with the rest of us!"

Dozens of people were rounded up in the days following the assassination, and suspects were held on the navy ironclad ships **USS** *Montauk* and *Saugus* while being questioned. How deeply Edmund Spangler (left) was involved was never determined, although he spent four years in prison before being pardoned in 1869 and returning to work in a theater. Samuel Arnold (right) confessed to being part of the plot to kidnap Lincoln, but he had dropped out and played no known role in the assassination. He was tried and sentenced to life but also was pardoned.

The surviving conspirators were tried by a military commission and four of them—Powell, Atzerodt, Herold, and Mary Surratt—were sentenced to hang. While awaiting trial, the men were shackled with balls and chains, their heads covered with canvas sacks. A total of 371 witnesses testified during the seven-week-long trial. There were some questions raised about Mary Surratt's complicity. In fact, the majority of the commission recommended to President Johnson that rather than being hanged, she spend the rest of her life in prison. Johnson refused, describing Surratt as the person who "kept the nest that hatched the egg."

On July 7, 1865, Lewis Powell, David Herold, George Atzerodt, and Mary Surratt were hanged at the Old Arsenal Building in Washington. Surratt became the first woman in American history to be executed for a federal crime. Her son, John Surratt, read about the trial and hanging from his hiding place in Canada but did nothing to intercede.

Dr. Samuel Mudd, Michael O'Laughlen, and Samuel Arnold, an early supporter of the plan who dropped out before it went into action, were sentenced to "hard labor for life." Edmund Spangler was given a six-year prison term. O'Laughlen died in prison, but in 1869 the three remaining conspirators were pardoned by President Johnson. John Surratt was captured in Alexandria, Egypt, in 1867, and extradited. He was tried in civil court because the statute of limitations had run out on all except one charge—and he was released after a mistrial. An attempt to charge him with treason also failed.

One can only imagine how differently Reconstruction might have proceeded if Lincoln had lived, but certainly Johnson acted far more harshly than Lincoln had proposed. There is little doubt that the South—and the newly freed slaves—would have fared better if John Wilkes Booth had failed.

While the fighting in the Civil War ended in 1865, the repercussions have echoed through the decades. As much as this country was formed by the founding fathers, so it was shaped by this war. While the fundamental changes in rights for all Americans that resulted from the Union victory have made this a stronger, better country, in some ways we still feel the scars.

And are left to wonder, what if . . .

My Captain does not answer, his lips are pale and still,
My father does not feel my arm, he has no pulse nor will,
The ship is anchor'd safe and sound, its voyage closed and done,
From fearful trip the victor ship comes in with object won;
Exult O shores, and ring O bells!
But I with mournful tread,
Walk the deck my Captain lies,
Fallen cold and dead.

# HARPER'S WEEKLY.

## A JOURNAL OF CIVILIZATION.

VOL. IX.—No. 445.] NEW YORK, SATURDAY, JULY 8, 1865. [SINGLE COPIES TEN CENTS.
$4.00 PER YEAR IN ADVANCE.

Entered according to Act of Congress, in the Year 1865, by Harper & Brothers, in the Clerk's Office of the District Court for the Southern District of New York.

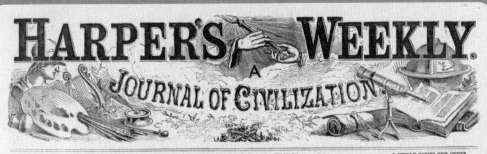

PEACE—FOURTH OF JULY, 1865.

# ACKNOWLEDGMENTS

A project of this size, with all of the potential complications, requires a smart and strong editor, and we were fortunate to have that person in Gillian Blake, who holds it all together and always with a smile. She is ably assisted in that by Eleanor Embry, who so easily moves all the pieces. It was a pleasure to work once again with Nancy Singer and Liz Seramur, who understand how to use illustrations to tell a story and so successfully turned their vision into the striking book you are holding in your hands.

This book is based on the TV series created and hosted by Bill O'Reilly and I am grateful to him for the opportunity to turn that material into this book, which I hope adds to your pleasure. The series was produced by an amazingly talented group of people at Warm Springs Productions in Missoula, Montana, who also go out of their way to make my job easier. I truly appreciate the work and the assistance of Bridger Pierce, Jason Broome, Sam Dolan, Ajax Broome, Gardner Linn, and the crew.

For me, each of these books is an amazing learning experience. My guide through this period in our history, my expert adviser, was Dr. Allen C. Guelzo, Henry R. Luce Professor of the Civil War Era and director of the Civil War Era Studies Program at Gettysburg College. We have endeavored to produce a historically accurate telling of this story, and if we have failed, that is my due.

I was invited to participate in this series by the legendary TV Hall of Fame members Carole Cooper and Richard Leibner, who made N.S. Bienstock the greatly respected name that it is, and whom I am proud to call my friends.

My agent on this project was Paul Fedorko. Simply, nothing happens without him, and I am grateful for his personal and professional friendship.

During an intense period a writer relies on friends to remind him that real life is going on all around, and in that I am so lucky to have my friends Rich Soll, John Lindsey, Jerry Stern and his in-box, Frank Biondo, and Joe Maresca.

And last but never least, my family: my sons, Taylor and Beau Stevens, and my wife, Laura. It would be impossible to have a more loving or supportive partner in all that I do than Laura Marie Russo Stevens Fisher. I would be remiss for not also including Willow Bay (Willie) the wonder dog, a small pile of love.

# SOURCES

I relied on numerous sources in the writing of this book. Certain publications and websites proved valuable throughout the entire process. These include:

Abbott, John S. C. *The History of the Civil War in America*. Springfield, MA: Gurdon Bill Publisher, 1866.

Catton, Bruce. *The Civil War*. Boston: Houghton Mifflin Company, 1960.

Garrison, Webb B. *Civil War Curiosities*. Nashville, TN: Rutledge Hill Press, 1994.

———. *Civil War Trivia and Fact Book*. Nashville, TN: Rutledge Hill Press, 1992.

Rhodes, James Ford. *History of the Civil War, 1861–1865*. Edited and with an introduction by E. B. Long. New York: Ungar, 1961.

I also found myself returning often to these websites:

*Harper's Weekly* magazine (1861–1866), SonOfTheSouth.net

EyewitnessToHistory.com

CivilWar.org/education/history/weblinks.html

NPS.gov/CivilWar/index.htm

HistoryNet.com

Books.Google.com

For each chapter I relied on a variety of sources, which include:

## CHAPTER 1

"The Conspirators Biographies." http://www2.iath.virginia.edu/jbrown/men.html.

"Dramatic Newspaper Coverage of the Battle of Fort Sumter: The Attack That Began the Civil War." NewsInHistory.com. www.newsinhistory.com/feature/dramatic-newspaper-coverage-battle-fort-sumter-attack-began-civil-war.

"The Election of 1860." USHistory.org. http://www.ushistory.org/us/32d.asp.

Goodheart, Adam. *1861: The Civil War Awakening*. New York: Alfred A. Knopf, 2011.

"John Brown's Raid, 1859." EyeWitnessToHistory.com. http://www.eyewitnesstohistory.com/john-brown.htm.

Linder, Douglas O. "The Trial of John Brown: A Commentary." http://law2.umkc.edu/faculty/projects/ftrials/johnbrown/brownaccount.html.

"Raid on Harpers Ferry." HistoryNet.com. http://www.historynet.com/raid-on-harpers-ferry.

*Slave Trade: Africans in America*, part 3, WGBH/NPR. http://www.pbs.org/wgbh/aia/part3/3narr6.html.

"10 Facts About Abraham Lincoln." CivilWar.org. http://www.civilwar.org/education/history/lincoln-hub/lincoln-ten-facts/10-facts-lincoln.html.

Whitman, Karen. "Re-evaluating John Brown's Raid at Harpers Ferry." *West Virginia Archives and History* 34, no. 1 (October 1972): 46–84. http://www.wvculture.org/history/journal_wvh/wvh34-1.html.


## CHAPTER 2

"Clara Barton." HistoryNet.com. http://www.historynet.com/clara-barton.

"First Battle of Bull Run." History.com, 2011. http://www.history.com/topics/american-civil-war/first-battle-of-bull-run.

Goodheart, Adam. "How Slavery Really Ended in America." *New York Times Magazine*, April 2, 2011. http://www.nytimes.com/2011/04/03/magazine/mag-03CivilWar-t.html?_r=0.

Hattaway, Herman, and Archer Jones. *How the North Won: A Military History of the Civil War*. Urbana: University of Illinois Press, 1983.

"The Official 'Rebel Rose' O'Neal Web Site." ONealWebsite.com. http://www.onealwebsite.com/RebelRose/default.htm.

Toomey, Daniel Carroll. "Where the Civil War Began." *Baltimore Magazine*, April 2011. http://baltimoremagazine.net/2011/4/4/where-the-civil-war-began.


## CHAPTER 3

Abbot, Willis John. *The Story of Our Army from Colonial Days to the Present* Time, vol. 2. New York: Dodd, Meade and Company, 1916; Forgotten Books, 2016.

"The Civil War Part 1: The Opening Years." SageAmericanHistory.net. http://sageamericanhistory.net/civilwar/topics/civilwar1860_62.html.

"The Generals and Admirals: John Pope (1823–1892)." MrLincolnsWhiteHouse.org. http://www.mrlincolnswhitehouse.org/residents-visitors/the-generals-and-admirals/generals-admirals-john-pope-1823-1892/.

Smith, David M. "They Were Made for Each Other: John Pope and George McClellan at Second Manassas." Cincinnati Civil War Round Table, September 19, 1991. http://www.cincinnaticwrt.org/data/ccwrt_history/talks_text/smith_pope_mcclellan.html.

"U.S.-Mexican War: Biographies." PBS.org. http://www.pbs.org/kera/usmexicanwar/biographies.

Wert, Jeffry D. *General James Longstreet: The Confederacy's Most Controversial Soldier*. New York: Simon & Schuster, 1993.

## CHAPTER 4

"African Americans and Emancipation." The Gilder Lehrman Institute of American History. http://www.gilderlehrman.org/history-by-era/african-americans-and-emancipation/essays/african-americans-and-emancipation.

Brasher, Glenn David. *Peninsula Campaign and the Necessity of Emancipation: African Americans and the Fight for Freedom*. Chapel Hill: University of North Carolina Press, 2012.

CivilWar.Org.

Douglass, Frederick. *The Frederick Douglass Papers: Autobiographical Writings*, vol. 3. Boston: DeWolfe & Fiske, 1892.

Dunn, James. "Clara Barton at Antietam." National Park Service. https://www.nps.gov/anti/learn/historyculture/clarabarton.htm.

Hinman, Allison. "William H. Seward and the Emancipation Proclamation." CivilWar.org. http://www.civilwar.org/education/history/emancipation-150/william-h-seward-and-the.html.

"Jefferson Davis Reaction to Emancipation Proclamation." SonOfTheSouth.net. http://www.sonofthesouth.net/leefoundation/civil-war/1863/january/southern-reaction-emancipation-proclamation.htm.

Williams, David. *I Freed Myself: African American Self-Emancipation in the Civil War Era*. New York: Cambridge University Press, 2014.

## CHAPTER 5

"Abraham Lincoln and George B. McClellan." Abraham Lincoln's Classroom. http://www.abrahamlincolnsclassroom.org/abraham-lincolns-contemporaries/abraham-lincoln-and-george-b-mcclellan/.

"An Account of Jackson's Death and Funeral—Part One." May 8, 2008. Headquarters: Army of Northern Virginia. http://headquartersanv.blogspot.com/2008/05/account-of-jacksons-death-and-funeral.html.

Frye, Dennis E. "Stonewall Jackson's Triumph at Harpers Ferry." *Hallowed Ground Magazine*. http://www.civilwar.org/battlefields/harpersferry/harpers-ferry-history-articles/harpersferrytriumphfrye.html.

Harper's Weekly Original Civil War Newspapers. http://www.sonofthesouth.net/leefoundation/the-civil-war.htm.

Jackson, Mary Anna. *Life and Letters of General Thomas J. Jackson (Stonewall Jackson)*. New York: Harper and Brothers, 1892.

Riley, Elihu Samuel. *"Stonewall Jackson": A Thesaurus of Anecdotes of and Incidents in the Life of Lieut.-General Thomas Jonathan Jackson*. Riley's Historic Series, Annapolis, Maryland, 1920.

Wharton, Henry Marvin, ed. *War Songs and Poems of the Southern Confederacy, 1861–1865*. Philadelphia: John C. Winston Co., 1904.

## CHAPTER 6

"The American Civil War: The Battle of Gettysburg." BrothersWar.com. http://www.brotherswar.com/Gettysburg-2e.htm.

Brann, James R. "Defense of Little Round Top." *America's Civil War Magazine*. HistoryNet.com. http://www.civilwar.org/battlefields/gettysburg/gettysburg-history-articles/defense-of-little-round-top.html.

"Gettysburg Battle Description." SonOfTheSouth.net. http://www.sonofthesouth.net/leefoundation/civil-war/1863/july/gettysburg-battle-description.htm.

## CHAPTER 7

"Grant on Slavery." In John Russell Young, *Around the World with General Grant*, part 7. New York: The American News Company, 1879. http://www.granthomepage.com/grantslavery.htm.

White, Ronald C., Jr., and Ronald C. White. *American Ulysses: A Life of Ulysses S. Grant*. New York: Random House, 2016.

## CHAPTER 8

Abraham Lincoln: Military Order of the Loyal Legion of the United States ... by Military Order of the Loyal Legion of the United States. Pennsylvania Commandery, Henry Cochrane.

"Abraham Lincoln in the Black Hawk War." *San Francisco Call* 105, no. 69 (February 7, 1909).   http://cdnc.ucr.edu/cgi-bin/cdnc?a=d&d=SFC19090207.2.199.8.1.

Fesler, J. W. "Lincoln's Gettysburg Address." *Indiana Magazine of History* 40, no. 3 (September 1944): 209–26. https://scholarworks.iu.edu/journals/index.php/imh/article/view/7490/8693.

Kelly, James R., Jr. "Newton Knight and the Legend of the Free State of Jones." Mississippi History Now. http://mshistorynow.mdah.state.ms.us/articles/309/newton-knight-and-the-legend-of-the-free-state-of-jones.

Schreiner, Lilian Stair. "Lincoln in the Black Hawk War." *Farm Journal* 37 (January 1913). https://books.google.com/books?id=CtxGAAAAYAAJ&pg=PA47&dq=Lincoln+took+oath+of+allegiance+to+US+from+jefferson+Davis+Black+Hawk+War&hl=en&sa=X&ved=0ahUKEwiHr-42V1oXQAhWn1IMKHU3FAv4Q6AEIKjAC#v=onepage&q=Lincoln%20took%20oath%20of%20allegiance%20to%20US%20from%20jefferson%20Davis%20Black%20Hawk%20War&f=false.

## CHAPTER 9

Klein, Christopher. "Lincoln's Battlefield Brush with Death, 150 Years Later." History.com, July 10, 2014. http://www.history.com/news/lincolns-battlefield-brush-with-death-150-years-ago.

Lewis, Lloyd. *Sherman: Fighting Prophet*. Lincoln: University of Nebraska Press, 1993.

Lewis, Thomas A. "When Washington, D.C. Came Close to Being Conquered by the Confederacy." Smithsonian.com, July 1988. http://www.smithsonianmag.com/history/when-washington-dc-came-close-to-being-conquered-by-the-confederacy-180951994/.

Long, David E. "Battle of Cold Harbor." *Civil War Times* magazine, June 1997. HistoryNet.com. http://www.civilwar.org/battlefields/coldharbor/cold-harbor-history-articles/battle-of-cold-harbor.html.

Schultz, Duane P. *The Dahlgren Affair: Terror and Conspiracy in the Civil War*. New York: W. W. Norton, 1998.

## CHAPTER 10

Chamberlain, J. L. "The Last Salute of the Army of Northern Virginia." *Boston Journal*, May 1901. Source: *Southern Historical Society Papers* 32, Richmond, VA, January–December 1904. http://www.civilwar.org/education/history/primarysources/the-last-salute-of-the-army.html.

Leigh, Phil. "Who Burned Atlanta?" *New York Times*, November 13, 2014. http://opinionator.blogs.nytimes.com/2014/11/13/who-burned-atlanta/?_r=0.

Scott, Robert Nicholson, George Breckenridge Davis, Frederick Caryton Ainsworth, and Joseph William Kirkley. *The War of the Rebellion*, vol. 46, part 1. Washington, DC: Government Printing Office, 1890.

Staub, Jerry. "Sherman's Inability to Liberate the South's Most Notorious Prison." eHistory.osu.edu. https://ehistory.osu.edu/articles/shermans-inability-liberate-souths-most-notorious-prison.

## CHAPTER 11

Clarke, Asia Booth. *John Wilkes Booth: A Sister's Memoir*. Edited and with an introduction by Terry Alford. Jackson: University Press of Mississippi, 1999.

Hyslop, Steve. *Eyewitness to the Civil War*. Edited by Neil Kagan. Washington, DC: National Geographic, 2006, p. 330.

Levins, Hoag. "The Gang That Killed Abraham Lincoln," Camden County, NJ, Civil War Connections. http://historiccamdencounty.com/ccnews142.shtml.

Loux, Arthur F. *John Wilkes Booth: Day by Day*. Jefferson, NC: McFarland & Company, 2014.

Morrow, Kevin, "The Lincolns and the Booths," *New York Times*, December 30, 2013. http://opinionator.blogs.nytimes.com/2013/12/30/the-lincolns-and-the-booths/?_r=0.

Schein, Michael. *John Surratt: The Lincoln Assassin Who Got Away*. Palisades, NY: History Publishing Co., 2015.

Schein, Michael. "This Meeting 150 Years Ago This Week Led to Lincoln's Assassination." History News Network, December 21, 2014. http://historynewsnetwork.org/article/157887#sthash.YVPsdXJ2.dpuf.

# INDEX

# CREDITS

Page 6: © Boston Athenaeum/Bridgeman Images Page 9: Courtesy of the Library of Congress, LC-USZ62-7816 Page 11: Courtesy of the Library of Congress, LC-DIG-pga-08982 Page 12: "Universal History Archive/UIG / Bridgeman Images" Page 14: Courtesy of the Library of Congress, LC-DIG-cwpbh-00788 Page 15: Granger, NYC — All rights reserved. Page 16: J. T. Vintage / Bridgeman Images Page 18-19: Library of Virginia Page 20: © Look and Learn / Bridgeman Images Page 21: Bridgeman Images Page 22: Courtesy of the Library of Congress, LC-DIG-ppmsca-38003 Page 26: National Portrait Gallery, Smithsonian Institution / Art Resource, NY Page 28: Courtesy of the Library of Congress, LC-USZ62-15324 Page 31: Courtesy of the Library of Congress, LC-DIG-ppmsca-19305 Page 31: Courtesy of the Library of Congress, LC-USZ62-1092 Page 33: "Courtesy of the Library of Congress, LC-USZ62-104990" Page 34: American Antiquarian Society / Bridgeman Images Page 36: Courtesy of the Library of Congress, LC-DIG-cwpb-05636 Page 38-39: "Atlanta Historical Society / Photo © Civil War Archive / Bridgeman Images" Page 38-39: Confederate Memorial Hall, New Orleans / Photo © Civil War Archive / Bridgeman Images Page 38-39: Chicago History Museum / Bridgeman Images Page 38-39: Courtesy of the Library of Congress, LC-USZC2-3767 Page 38-39: "Gilder Lehrman Collection / Bridgeman Images" Page 38-39: Courtesy of the Library of Congress, LC-DIG-ppmsca-31703 Page 38-39: "Photo © Don Troiani / Bridgeman Images" Page 38-39: Courtesy of the Library of Congress, LC-DIG-ppmsca-40623 Page 40: Peter Newark Military Pictures / Bridgeman Images Page 42: "Bridgeman Images" Page 43: Courtesy of the Library of Congress, LC-USZ62-36161 Page 44: Courtesy of the Library of Congress, LC-DIG-ppmsca-39361 Page 47: H244 Courtesy of the Maryland Historical Society Page 47: Courtesy of the Library of Congress, LC-USZ62-89738 Page 50: Courtesy of the Library of Congress, LC-USZ62-5795 Page 52: Granger, NYC — All rights reserved. Page 55: 'Detail' from Rose O'Neal Greenhow and daughter by Matthew Brady, National Portrait Gallery, Smithsonian Institution / Art Resource, NY Page 56: © Collection of the New-York Historical Society / Bridgeman Images Page 59: Courtesy of the Library of Congress, LC-DIG-ppmsca-19388 Page 61: Library of Congress, Geography and Map Division, vhs00061 Page 62-63: Courtesy of the Library of Congress, LC-DIG-ppmsca-34117 Page 65: American Antiquarian Society / Bridgeman Images Page 67: Newberry Library / Bridgeman Images Page 68: Courtesy of the Library of Congress, LC-DIG-pga-03975 Page 69: Courtesy of the Library of Congress, LC-DIG-cwpb-07433 Page 70-71: Courtesy of the Library of Congress, LC-DIG-pga-08199 Page 70-71: Universal History Archive/UIG / Bridgeman Images Page 78: Boston Athenaeum / Bridgeman Images Page 78: Civil War Sheet Music, Library of Congress, Music Division Page 78: Civil War Sheet Music, Library of Congress, Music Division Page 78: Granger, NYC — All rights reserved Page 80-81: Courtesy of the Library of Congress, LC-USZC4-6209 Page 83: Courtesy of the Library of Congress, LC-DIG-pga-00385 Page 85: Library of Congress, Geography and Map Division, vhs00215 Page 87: Courtesy of the Library of Congress, LC-USZC4-12604 Page 89: Sarin Images / Granger, NYC — All rights reserved. Page 90: Library of Congress, Geography and Map Division, cw0299000 Page 90: DEA PICTURE LIBRARY / Granger, NYC — All rights reserved. Page 92: Courtesy of the Library of Congress, LC-DIG-cwpb-06342 Page 93: Courtesy of the Library of Congress, LC-DIG-ppmsca-34124 Page 94-95: © Boston Athenaeum / Bridgeman Images Page 97: Library of Congress, Geography and Map Division, vhs00215 Page 98: Courtesy of the Library of Congress, LC-DIG-ppmsca-20562 Page 101: Courtesy of the Library of Congress, LC-DIG-ppmsca-08368 Page 105: Courtesy of the Library of Congress, LC-DIG-ppmsca-07770 Page 105: Newell Convers Wyeth, "Barbara Frietchie," 1922, oil on canvas, Permanent Collection of The Hill School, Pottstown, PA Page 106-107: Courtesy of the Library of Congress, LC-DIG-pga-05058 Page 110-111: ©Ann Ronan Picture Library / Heritage-Images / The Image Works Page 110-111: © Newagen Archive / The Image Works Page 110-111: Peter Newark Military Pictures / Bridgeman Images Page 110-111: Ivy Close Images / Agefoto Page 110-111: ©Charles Phelps Cushing / ClassicStock / The Image Works Page 110-111: Ullstein bild / Granger, NYC — All rights reserved Page 115: Newberry Library / Bridgeman Images Page 119: Historical Society / Bridgeman Images Page 121: Courtesy of the Library of Congress, scsm000950 Page 122-123: Antietam Battlefield Park, Maryland, USA / Photo © Civil War Archive / Bridgeman Images Page 124: The Stapleton Collection / Bridgeman Images Page 125: Courtesy of the Library of Congress, LC-USZ62-108564 Page 127: Courtesy of the Library of Congress, LC-DIG-ppmsca-33171 Page 129: Library of Congress, Washington D.C., USA / Bridgeman Images Page 131: Courtesy of the Library of Congress, LC-DIG-pga-02040 Page 133: Universal History Archive/UIG / Bridgeman Images Page 134: © Massachusetts Historical Society / Bridgeman Images Page 136: Corcoran Gallery Of Art / De Agostini Picture Library / Bridgeman Images Page 138-139: The Stapleton Collection / Bridgeman Images Page 141: Courtesy of the Library of Congress, LC-DIG-ds-00288 Page 143: Courtesy of the Library of Congress, LC-DIG-ppmsca-20629 Page 145: Courtesy of the Library of Congress, LC-DIG-stereo-1s02842 Page 149: Courtesy of the Library of Congress, LC-DIG-ppmsca-23719 Page 150: Courtesy of the Library of Congress, LC-DIG-ppmsca-19393 Page 151: Peter Newark Military Pictures / Bridgeman Images Page 152: Universal History Archive/UIG / Bridgeman Images Page 155: Courtesy of the Library of Congress, LC-DIG-cwpb-06979 Page 157: Courtesy Everett Collection Page 158: Courtesy of the Library of Congress, LC-DIG-ppmsca-19394 Page 160: Courtesy of the Library of Congress, LC-DIG-cwpb-07033 Page 163: Courtesy of the Library of Congress, LC-DIG-pga-01844 Page 165: Courtesy of the Library of Congress, LC-DIG-ppmsca-41821 Page 166: Courtesy of the Library of Congress, LC-USZ62-88802 Page 168: Courtesy of the Library of Congress, LC-DIG-ppmsca-34751 Page 168: Courtesy of the Library of Congress, 3g02725u Page 170: akg-images Page 172: Courtesy of the Library of Congress, LC-BH83- 616 Page 173: Courtesy of the Library of Congress, LC-USZ62-73618 Page 174: Courtesy of the Library of Congress, LC-B813- 6785 A Page 174: Courtesy of the Library of Congress, LC-B813- 1467 A Page 176: Courtesy of the Library of Congress, LC-B811-2402 Page 177: Library of Congress, Geography and Map Division, cw0350000 Page 178-179: Courtesy of the Library of Congress, LC-DIG-ppmsca-35051 Page 181: Courtesy of the Library of Congress, LC-USZ62-100659 Page 182: Courtesy of the Library of Congress, LC-BH831-934 Page 183: Courtesy of the Library of Congress, LC-DIG-stereo-1s03751 Page 185: Courtesy of the Library of Congress, LC-BH83- 3754 Page 186-187: Granger, NYC — All rights reserved. Page 189: Courtesy of the Library of Congress, LC-DIG-cwpb-00907 Page 190-191:

DAKOTA
TERR.

MINNESOTA

WISCONSIN

*Mississippi River*

CANADA

Lake Huron

Lake Ontario

Lake Michigan

MICHIGAN

NEW YORK

Detroit •

Lake Erie

PENNSYLVANIA

Philadelphia

NEBRASKA
TERR.

IOWA

ILLINOIS

Chicago •

INDIANA

OHIO

Ohio River

MARYLAND

Area of detail

KANSAS
(1861)

*Missouri River*

St. Louis •

Springfield •

Indianapolis •

Cincinnati •

WEST
VIRGINIA
(1863)

Washington, D.C. ★

*Mississippi River*

MISSOURI

Ohio River

Louisville •

VIRGINIA

Richmond ★

KENTUCKY

*February 16, 1862:*
Union captures Ft. Donelson

INDIAN
TERR.

ARKANSAS

*February 6, 1862:*
Union captures Ft. Henry

TENNESSEE

*November 23–25, 1863:*
Battle of Chattanooga

NORTH CAROLINA

Raleigh •

Memphis •

Charlotte •

Little Rock •

*April 6–7, 1862:*
The Battle of Shiloh
(Pittsburg Landing),
the first major
battle in Tennessee

*September 19–20, 1863:*
The Battle of Chickamauga

*May 7, 1864:*
Beginning of the Atlanta,
Georgia, Campaign

Columbia •

*January 1865:*
Sherman advances north
from Savannah, Georgia,
through the Carolinas

*May 19–July 4, 1863:*
Siege of Vicksburg

Atlanta •

*September 1–2, 1864:*
Sherman takes Atlanta

SOUTH
CAROLINA

Charleston •

TEXAS

LOUISIANA

ALABAMA

GEORGIA

*April 12, 1861:*
Southern forces fire upon
Fort Sumter. The Civil War
has formally begun.

MISSISSIPPI

*February 27, 1864:*
Andersonville Prison

*November 15–
December 21, 1864:*
Sherman's march
through Georgia

Savannah •

◄ *1846:*
The Mexican-American War

*Mississippi River*

Mobile •

• Tallahassee

New Orleans •

FLORIDA

Gulf of Mexico

## Key

- ● Abraham Lincoln
- ● Ulysses S. Grant
- ○ William. T. Sherman

- ● Jefferson Davis
- ● Robert E. Lee
- ○ Thomas "Stonewall" Jackson
- ○ John Wilkes Booth

| Union States | Confederate States | Border States |